RACISM
A WORLD ISSUE

By
Edmund Davison Soper

NEGRO UNIVERSITIES PRESS
NEW YORK

Reprinted 1969 by
Negro Universities Press
A DIVISION OF GREENWOOD PRESS, INC.
NEW YORK

SBN 8371-2788-2

PRINTED IN UNITED STATES OF AMERICA

RACISM: A WORLD ISSUE

TO MY SONS

ROBERT and HERBERT

PREFACE

This book can scarcely be understood without knowing something of the process of its preparation. The task was begun with no thought that a book would be the outcome. A seminar on "Race" was conducted in Chicago during the autumn and winter of 1942-43. This was in preparation for a conference on "Christian Bases of World Order" to be held in Delaware, Ohio, March 8-12, 1943. There a report based on papers prepared by members of the Chicago seminar was presented. In the autumn and winter of 1943-44 ten seminars on the theme "Racism and World Order" were held with topics, leaders, and locations as follows:

Urban Minorities in the United States	Lynn J. Radcliffe	Oak Park, Illinois
Rural Minorities in the United States	Merrill R. Abbey	Milwaukee, Wisconsin
The Far East	Russell W. Lambert	Rockford, Illinois
India	Paul Burt	Urbana, Illinois
The Southwest Pacific	Lowell B. Hazzard	Bloomington, Illinois
South Africa	Otto Scott Steele	W. Lafayette, Indiana
Russia	Oscar M. Adam	Madison, Wisconsin
Germany	E. Burns Martin	South Bend, Indiana
Brazil	William W. Sweet	Chicago, Illinois
Spanish-speaking Latin America	Charles S. Braden	Evanston, Illinois

The reports from these seminars furnished the basis for the discussions at a conference on "Racism and World Order" held at Garrett Biblical Institute, Evanston, Illinois, March 16-20, 1944.

Having conducted the original Chicago seminar and having been responsible, with my wife, for the general direction of the seminars in the Chicago area, I was given the task of using the mass of material produced by the seminars and the material gathered in my own study to prepare a book for general use. This volume is the outcome. During the writing of the first draft of the manuscript I conducted a seminar on "Race" four hours a week for one quarter in Garrett Biblical Institute and profited by this contact with the student mind.

The original draft was written during the first six months of 1945. This was revised, and sent out in mimeographed form to a hundred experts in various parts of the country. In October, 1945, I spent a week in New York meeting seven small groups of these experts who had read the relevant chapters or the whole of the manuscript. The composition of these groups was as follows:

Negroes in America

> George E. Haynes, executive secretary, Department of Race Relations, Federal Council of Churches of Christ in America
>
> William Stuart Nelson, professor in Howard University, Washington, D. C.
>
> Leslie Pinckney Hill, president, Cheyney Training School for Teachers, Cheyney, Pa.

China

> Timothy T. Lew, educator and author
>
> B. A. Liu, Chinese News Service, New York

Africa

> Jackson Davis, associate director, General Education Board
>
> Emory Ross, Africa Committee, Foreign Missions Conference of North America
>
> Thomas S. Donohugh, associate secretary, Central and Southern Africa Division of the Board of Missions of the Methodist Church

Latin America

> Alberto Rembao, director, *La Nueva Democracia*
>
> Huberto Rhoden, Brazilian author
>
> B. H. Hunnicutt, president, McKenzie College, Brazil

India

> Eddy Asirvatham, professor, Madras University
>
> B. N. Gupta, Indian importer, New York

Germany

Paul J. Tillich, professor, Union Theological Seminary, New York

Frederick J. Forell, refugee pastor from Germany, now in New York

Entire Manuscript

L. S. Allbright, International Missionary Council

John C. Bennett, professor, Union Theological Seminary, New York

J. W. Decker, International Missionary Council

Wynn C. Fairfield, Foreign Missions Conference of North America

Daniel J. Fleming, professor (retired), Union Theological Seminary, New York

Charles T. Iglehart, professor, Union Theological Seminary, New York, returned from thirty-five years in Japan

E. C. Lobenstine, former secretary, National Christian Council of China

R. E. Diffendorfer, executive secretary, Foreign Division, Board of Missions of the Methodist Church

Not only did I have the advantage of these penetrating and unhurried conferences, but many whom I was unable to consult face to face communicated with me by letter. I cannot enumerate all of these but feel that I must list the names of a number who sent me their careful criticisms both favorable and unfavorable. In this group are the following:

Will W. Alexander, director for race relations, Julius Rosenwald Fund, Chicago

Albert E. Barnett, professor, Garrett Biblical Institute, Evanston, Illinois

Martin H. Bickham, chairman, Illinois Interracial Commission

Ina Corinne Brown, professor, Scarritt College, Nashville, Tennessee

Paul Burt, director, Wesley Foundation, Urbana, Illinois

H. T. Chu, Chinese News Service, New York

Clarence Tucker Craig, professor, Oberlin Graduate School of Theology

Earl Cranston, professor, Dartmouth College, Hanover, New Hampshire

R. B. Eleazer, General Board of Education, The Methodist Church

Jay C. Field, Kennedy School of Missions, Hartford, Connecticut

Lewis O. Hartman, bishop, Boston area, The Methodist Church

Eugene B. Hawk, dean, Perkins School of Theology, Dallas, Texas

Edward H. Hume, secretary, Christian Medical Council for Overseas Work, New York

Paul Hutchinson, managing editor, *The Christian Century*
Carol Jacobson, The American Russian Institute, New York
Corlis Lamont, The American Russian Institute, New York
Kenneth Scott Latourette, professor, Yale Divinity School, New Haven, Connecticut
Murray H. Leiffer, professor, Garrett Biblical Institute, Evanston, Illinois
Leroy Loemker, professor, Emory University, Atlanta, Georgia
Alice Rigby Moore, Woman's Division, Methodist Board of Missions
T. Otto Nall, managing editor, *The Christian Advocate*
Malcom Pitt, dean, Kennedy School of Missions, Hartford, Connecticut
Robert Redfield, dean, division of the social sciences, University of Chicago
Thelma Stevens, Woman's Division, Methodist Board of Missions
Ernest E. Tuck, superintendent of the Philippines, Methodist Board of Missions

These men and women are mentioned because in a peculiar sense their contribution entered into the process of making this book. I hereby convey to them my deep appreciation of the time and energy they have put into this task. The book could never have been what it is had it not been for their criticisms and suggestions. I think I may be permitted to say that they did not agree at all points. That was inevitable, but at a number of important points it placed upon me the burden of deciding on which side of the fence I would come down.

The guiding genius of the entire project from beginning to end was Dr. Ralph E. Diffendorfer. It was he who caught the vision of the Delaware conference on "Christian Bases of World Order" and who planned the holding of the seminars in the Chicago area and the conference on "Racism and World Order" at Garrett Biblical Institute. He invited me to share in the carrying out of these seminars and conferences, incited me to prepare this volume, and has stood by with counsel, sympathy, and financial backing to pay necessary expenses. Without him the book would never have been written. And may I say that, once having started me on the task, he has kept hands off, so that, for weal or woe, the hundreds of decisions which had to be made are mine?

I wish also to express gratitude to my wife, who typed the difficult first draft, and President Horace Greeley Smith, of Garrett Biblical Institute, for unfailing encouragement and the courtesy of providing for the third typing of the manuscript.

So I send this frail boat out on the waters. Far more than in other books I have written I have in the nature of the case been dependent on the expert opinion of others. All that I can say is that, so far as time and strength and the press of other duties permitted, I have tried to present a correct picture of racism as a world issue, knowing full well that in a world changing as rapidly as the one in which we live it is impossible to be sure that new facts might not change the picture almost overnight. I have had the experience of realizing that this manuscript would not stay revised even in the very process of revision.

Only one other item is necessary. I have deliberately quoted from unpublished seminar papers and have felt justified in doing so in view of the high quality of many of these papers, based as they are on recognized authorities. Copies of these papers are now available in the Missionary Research Library, New York, and the library of Garrett Biblical Institute, Evanston, Illinois.

E. D. S.

Garrett Biblical Institute
Evanston, Illinois

CONTENTS

13

Chapter I

Races of the World

According to the latest trustworthy figures the population of the world is approximately 2,169,868,000.[1] This population is unevenly distributed over the five continents and in all the greater and many of the lesser islands of the seven seas. The inhabitants of the earth are divided into many differing groups, for which for the first time in the year 1749 the term "race" was employed. The French scientist Buffon, in his work on natural history, made use of the term to differentiate the six groups into which he more or less artificially divided mankind.[2] It is very difficult to define the word "race" and even more difficult to group humanity into racial divisions which are significant in the attempt to differentiate and evaluate the various peoples and nations of the world. But with all the criticisms which the term has received it may still be used as a convenient designation of the groupings of mankind found scattered over the earth.

Scientists are agreed that all the races have a common origin. In generations gone by, a conflict was waged between the "monogenists" and the "polygenists," those who believed that mankind came from one human stock and those who held that each race had a different origin. Some went so far as to claim that the different races were really different species and not differentiations of one species. This conflict has long since died down among scientific investigators, the only persons holding the theory of

[1] *League of Nations Statistical Year Book, 1940-1941,* which contains data as of Dec. 31, 1939, as quoted in *The World Almanac 1945,* p. 284. The statement is added that "in many cases the exact population of countries is not known and the population figures are more or less uncertain and even hypothetical."
[2] M. F. Ashley Montagu, *Man's Most Dangerous Myth: The Fallacy of Race* (2d ed., rev. and enl.), p. 18.

15

separate and distinct origin being the vociferous propagandists of the racial superiority of the white race, special pleaders who on political and national grounds find it necessary to make so extreme a claim. It was the theory held by Hitler and the Nazi leaders in Germany. To them it was an essential dogma of the Nazi creed. But in the world of science the conviction is strong that all the races came from one stock and that the differences have come about through long ages of dispersion and isolation in different parts of the earth.

At this point modern science and the biblical and Christian viewpoints coincide. The early chapters of Genesis present mankind as being called into existence in a single creative word by the voice of God, all the later families and tribes and peoples being descended from the first single pair, Adam and Eve. In the New Testament, to use only one passage, the words of Paul in Athens carry the same thought: God "hath made of one blood all nations of men" (A.V.). The word "blood" is not to be found in a number of the ancient Greek manuscripts, so we have the rendering in the Revised Standard Version, "And he made from one every nation of men." Moffatt's translation uses different words to the same effect, "All nations he has created from a common origin." What they indicate is that all human beings are descended from the same basic stock.[8]

Many attempts have been made to classify mankind and place human beings in different racial groups. At best these attempts have not been conspicuously successful. That is, no investigator seems able to make a classification which satisfies his fellow workers in the field. The bases of classification are so indefinite and insecure that confusion cannot be avoided no matter what conclusions are reached. One of the sources of difficulty lies in the various meanings which the word "race" has been made to carry. At times it has been made identical with nationality—then there are as many races as there are nations. This use however would

[8] Ruth Benedict and Gene Weltfish, *The Races of Mankind*, pp. 3-5; now also included as an Appendix in Ruth Benedict, *Race: Science and Politics* (rev. ed.).

16

make the word "race" meaningless and unnecessary. More frequently races have been identified with linguistic groups. The Indo-European peoples, who are to be found from India and Persia to the western bounds of the European continent, are referred to as a "race." The truth is that these people are bound together by linguistic ties rather than by biological interrelatedness. The same may be said of the Semitic peoples. The peoples comprising this group may or may not be biologically related; the significant fact is that they speak one or another of the Semitic languages. The confusion in terminology becomes even greater when the word "race" is applied to lesser groups within a single nation as contrasted with others from whom they may differ in some noticeable way.

The only way in which the term "race" may justifiably be used is to designate divisions of mankind which transcend national barriers and include peoples who in a broad way resemble each other in a number of physical traits and can thus be classified as belonging to a group fairly distinct from other large groups. Even with this understanding the task is a difficult one. There is always the problem as to where to place this group or that in the classification. Professor Clyde Kluckhohn makes the striking statement:

> With some qualifications and exceptions, one may almost say that, if all living humans are ranged in a single sequence according to degree of resemblance, there would be no sharp breaks in the line but rather a continuum where each specimen differed from the next by almost imperceptible variations.[4]

It will be useful to give a brief survey of the different features or traits which have been taken as bases of classification. What strikes anyone who travels and sees men and women of different races is the difference in the color of the skin. It is so evident that it cannot be escaped. There are white people and yellow people and black people. But one has not proceeded far before he begins to realize that color and color alone does not furnish a sufficient basis of

[4] *Religion and Our Racial Tensions* ("Religion in the Post-War World," Vol. III), pp. 16 f.

classification. Yes, there are white and yellow and black people, but there are so many intermediary shades of color between a flaxen-haired blond Swede and a black-as-midnight Senegambian that, if color were the only criterion, one would be put to it to make a satisfactory classification. And yet men do differ from one another in color, and this must be one of the items to be taken into consideration. In general three main colors separate great groups of people despite the grading off into intermediary shades which is found everywhere. The difference between black people and white is of course more pronounced than that between yellow people and white. Professor Franz Boas came to the conclusion that the peoples of the world belonged to only two main groups, the yellow and the black, the white people being a variation of the yellow with no significant color difference between them.

Eye color and form are also sufficiently evident to attract immediate attention. But eye color is a poor basis of identification as between groups, nations, and races. Different-colored eyes are to be found in almost every group. Blue eyes may not be found among the Bantu in Africa, but black eyes and brown eyes and gray eyes all exist side by side with blue eyes in northern Europe. In a broad way the color of the eye will assist, but it never can be determinative of race. A word only needs to be said with respect to eye form. Among yellow Asiatics "slanting" eyes are at times found. This peculiar feature is caused by a fold of skin, called the epicanthic or corner fold, toward the inner corner of each eye, which gives the eyes the appearance of slanting downward toward the nose. But by no means is this characteristic of all the people of eastern Asia. At a breakfast table in Tientsin, China, old-timers in the country called my attention to the slant eyes of the Chinese servant who was waiting on the table as being exceptional!

Three kinds of hair are clearly distinguished: straight lank hair, wavy hair, and kinky hair. In general straight hair is found among the Mongoloid peoples of eastern Asia and the Eskimo; wavy hair among the peoples of Europe, India, and Australia; and kinky hair among the Negroes and some of the peoples of the Pacific Islands.

18

Under the microscope these kinds of hair are found to differ in cross section. Straight hair is round, kinky hair is oval, while wavy hair lies between these two extremes in varying degrees. So important is this difference supposed to be that some anthropologists have used it as the most important basis of racial classification. But again there is difficulty; differences in hair form do not coincide with other differences in bodily traits which are quite as significant. There are black men with wavy hair as well as with kinky hair, and white men have straight hair as well as wavy hair.

The further one goes in the attempt to classify different groups of men, the more he is baffled by the confusing character of the evidence. No wonder the conviction grows that any classification must be looked upon only as a convenient basis of identification and not as a means of determining completely exclusive traits.

Still other differences are to be noted. The shape of the face, particularly of the nose, is a very noticeable feature. The jaw in some people protrudes, and in some it is recessive. We find men with very high cheek bones and others with very high foreheads or low receding brows. But none of these facial features has received the attention of comparative anatomists as has the shape of the nose. The chief difference is that between the narrow nostrils of Europeans, Eskimos, and Arabs, and the flat broad nostrils which are characteristic of the Negro. It is well known that narrow nostrils are better adapted to breathing cool air and wide nostrils to breathing in hot countries—a good illustration of adaptation to climatic environment. But again flat noses are not confined to hot countries nor narrow noses to cold. No hotter country can be found than Arabia, but the Arab who has made his home there from time immemorial has a high narrow nose. Among the Japanese most of the people have low noses, sometimes without any bridge at all, but there are some Japanese with high noses. These latter are fewer in number and are considered more handsome than their more numerous fellow citizens, but they are all Japanese.

A word in passing may be given to physical stature. There are tribes noted for their height, and there are pygmy tribes as well, but in general every nation and group has tall men and short men. This variation is so common that little can be expected from comparative stature in classifying mankind.

We have a much more important basis of determination in the shape of the head. Head form has been made the object of widespread and very exact measurement. The results are given in scientific treatises in a percentage ratio of the breadth and length of the head as seen from the top. This "cephalic index" is reached "by dividing the maximum breadth of the cranium by its maximum length and multiplying by 100" (Webster). The dolichocephalic, or narrow long-headed people, have an index under 75; the brachycephalic, or broad short-headed people, have an index over 80; between the two are the mesocephalic, or medium-headed people. Extreme cases of broad- or long-headedness can easily be detected by anyone looking for such differences, but it requires careful measurement to determine the cephalic index in most cases. An enormous amount of such measurement has been done on people in every part of the world. The differences that have been discovered are real but inconclusive in disclosing significant differences between races and nations. The man of northern Europe and the Negro both have long narrow skulls, while the people of the Alpine race of Central Europe and the Mongols in central Asia have broad round skulls.

These are the major physical characteristics which distinguish the peoples of the world. We must have come to the conclusion, already more than once stated or hinted at, that the classification of races is difficult and, when made, is more or less uncertain and indefinite. It is a description of physical traits which at best helps as a basis of identification, conveniently breaking the various peoples into groups which differ from one another and which can thus be made the object of study and comparison.

It would not be profitable even to list the many attempts at classification which have been made in modern times. One investigator, J. Deniker,[5] recognized twenty-eight racial groups; at the other extreme was Franz Boas, who, as already stated, recognized only two. These classifications have been based on the color of the skin, the nature of the hair, the cephalic index, and other physical features alone or in combination. As time has passed the practice has become common to distinguish the most evident primary stocks or stems and then to classify under these headings the secondary groups which are clearly derived from the primary stocks. We shall present one of these classifications, made by a competent worker in the field, the late Ales Hrdlicka, for many years connected with the United States National Museum in Washington.

According to this anthropologist there are three great racial stocks and one which is lesser and quite small: the whites, the yellow-browns, the Negroids, and finally the small stem, "a remnant of an ancient stock, the Australian."[6] This writer makes the explanation: "The term 'Whites' as those of the 'Yellow-Browns' and 'Negroids' must be taken in a broad sense and as including the physical characteristics in general"; that is, there is no single trait, color of skin, form and color of hair, etc., which alone can be used to distinguish them. All of these items taken in combination in a broad way distinguish one group from another. Special reference must be made to the Australian or Australo-Tasmanian. This small group, now found entirely in Australia, is a "remnant of a once much larger stock of old." Even this remnant is probably mixed with other peoples so that it is difficult to determine what it would have been like had it remained in isolation.

Of the white race the statement is made that there are five main divisions and a number of lesser subsidiary divisions. These five are the Semitic, Mediterranean, Nordic, Alpine (or Celtic), and Hamitic. And then of course there are subdivisions under each of these heads too numerous to mention. To say that two

[5] Ales Hrdlicka, "The Races of Man," *Scientific Aspects of the Race Problem*, p. 175.
[6] This and other references in this section are to the article "The Races of Man" in *Scientific Aspects of the Race Problem*, pp. 177-86.

peoples belong to one branch or subdivision of a race does not mean that cultural affinity or friendly relations exist between them. On the contrary, national lines are drawn so tightly and have been for so many centuries that antagonisms of the most serious nature have at times become habitual. Examples are the rivalry between the Germans and the French and the agelong feud between the Arabs and the Jews. Ibn-Saud, the king of Saudi Arabia, the most conservative and reactionary of Moslems, made the ominous pronouncement that he would declare jihad or holy war against the Jews if a Jewish Palestinian state were created at the coming peace conference. Even the individual peoples of Europe are in no case of one strain. The English, for example, are Celtic-Nordic-Slav-Baltic.

The people of the yellow-brown race are just as difficult to herd into one corral, and even when fairly satisfactory boundaries have been constructed, the various groups are found to merge extensively into each other. All of these groups seem to spring from the so-called "Old Asiatics," the oldest stem of these peoples before they began to separate into divergent groups. From this basal stock branched off certain peoples now looked on as remnants, such as the Igorottes in the Philippines, ancient tribes in Tibet and Formosa, and scattered fragments in Manchuria, Mongolia, and Siberia. To another branch of the yellow-brown race belong the American Indians, who are now generally believed to have crossed over to the American continent in the region of Bering Strait. They probably emigrated from Asia in little groups entirely separated from each other and gradually made their way down the west coast of the two Americas until in the course of many centuries they were scattered quite generally over the land area of the western continents. Distinct from the Indians but coming from the same parent stem were the Aleuts of Alaska and the Eskimo, who spread widely over the northern part of the continental area and the islands north of the Arctic Circle. All of these are accounted for as deriving from the Old Asiatics. They had a common origin with, but are now quite different from, the peoples who are grouped together as the Neo-Asiatics, the Mongols, Chinese, Manchus, the Neo-Siberians or Koreans, and the Japanese. Far removed from the peoples of the central and more northern parts of the Asiatic continent are the many tribes of Malaya—the "brown race" as they have often been called—who came originally from the same major stem as the Mongols and the Chinese. This is the classification of one investigator. Many agree with him, while others do not. But let us remember that with all the uncertainty involved we must attempt to classify if we are to deal with the peoples of the world in more or less manageable groups.

And finally there is the Negroid stock. Coming out of the mists of pre-history, this major race separated into distinguishable groups. The most important subdivisions are "the Negrito (with the Negrillo), the Bushman-Hottentot, and the Negro proper," all finding their homes in the African continent. The Negro proper of north central Africa and the Atlantic coastlands is distinguished from the Bantu of central and south Africa chiefly by linguistic differences. We shall also find people of this stock in North and South America and far east in the island world of the Pacific.

But any classification inevitably fails to include peoples who do not fit into any of the groups, broad as they are in this threefold arrangement. "They are either intermediary between or an old blend of two or more stems or races," says Hrdlicka. They include the semi-white, semi-Mongoloid peoples of eastern Europe and northern Asia, the old Finno-Ugrians, the older Turkish people, and the Tatars. And then there are the Ainu, the aborigines of Japan, "apparently an older blend of the Yellow-Browns and Whites or Near-White" people, who fit into no pigeonhole of classification. There are others such as the Polynesians out in the broad reaches of the Pacific Ocean and the Melanesians somewhat farther to the west and nearer the mainland of Asia. And finally we are faced with the startling fact that the people of India cannot be fitted into any system of classification. They include "the blood of the

Dravidian, Aryan, and Mediterranean and Semitic Whites, of the Negrito, and the Mongol, and the Malay."

In the end Hrdlicka takes account of the people of the United States, who incorporate "practically all the races aside from the Australian." Everywhere changes are taking place before our eyes by mixture of the most diverse stocks. "Man is still plastic. . . . In twenty-thirty thousand years, in consequence, there will be racially, as well as otherwise a new human world, with bare traces or remnants of the present." In fact we shall not have to wait until then to find very definite differences in racial types. Hrdlicka predicts that "in another two thousand years mankind will have assumed racial physiognomy considerably different from the present." The mills of God grind slowly, but they are grinding continuously and never more rapidly and evidently than in the world in which we live, and nowhere more strikingly than on the American side of the Atlantic.

We have created a problem for ourselves by a number of the claims which have been made. On one hand mankind is basically one; on the other a survey, even as sketchy as that just given, discloses a situation which is confusing in its multiplicity. We have not been able to give a very satisfactory classification of the peoples of the world, but at the same time we cannot but realize that men differ from each other in a hundred ways. They can be distinguished not only by physical traits but by customs and habits which differ even more widely than fundamental body features. The problem is, How are these differences to be accounted for and explained? If men are basically the same, if they hark back to the same physical origin and have ultimately the same human heritage, how did they change and develop into the diverse peoples to be found in the world, even those not distantly separated from each other geographically? If one proceeds no farther than the development of human speech, he is filled with amazement at the infinite diversity of languages and dialects. But, besides, there are differences in methods of travel and transportation, in clothing and adornment, in housing and architecture, in methods of securing a

24

livelihood, in ways of defending themselves and attacking their enemies, in religion and ethics, and in social and family customs— all these and other differences in addition to the biological distinctions such as color of skin, form of hair and face, and cephalic index already noted. All that can be attempted here is to describe certain clues, which might be developed at length, by which the anthropologist feels he is able to give some sure insights into the way these differences took form and worked themselves out into what we find today.

One fact must ever be kept in mind—that of time. We would be hard put to it were we to follow Archbishop Ussher's chronological scheme according to which the creation of man was placed exactly 4004 years before Christ, that is, not quite 6000 years ago. Many Bibles in the King James or Authorized Version still carry dates based on this chronology, and there are those who think they are a part of the Bible itself. We would have a hopeless task if these were the limits within which the entire development of the peoples of the world were to be placed. Very long reaches of time, going into hundreds of thousands of years, are necessary to account for changes as profound as those which human groups have experienced. Manifestly it is impossible to make any satisfactory estimate, but eminent geologists and anthropologists working together make the estimate that 300,000 [7] years have elapsed since our species, *homo sapiens,* began its life on our planet. Others would place the beginnings in a more distant past.

A factor of the greatest importance is that man has been a wanderer from the beginning. He began to migrate from his place of origin—somewhere in central Asia some would say—very early and has never given it up. These migrations must be taken into account to explain all that follows. Early man carried out his migrations so persistently that at the earliest period of which we can find any evidence he had already penetrated to the most distant lands and made his home in as widely scattered sections of

[7] Sir James Jeans, *The Universe Around Us,* p. 13, as quoted in Arnold J. Toynbee, *A Study of History,* I, 148 n.

the earth as he occupies today. This in itself was a marvelous feat, for illiterate, crude men, with little or no equipment and organization, facing the most stupendous obstacles and still forging ahead despite sickness, loss, and death, making homes for themselves in the most inhospitable climes where everything in nature was seemingly against them. We may surely call this *wanderlust* a human impulse of the most fundamental kind, so inalienable that man continues to have the instincts of a migrant to the present day. No more conspicuous illustration could be cited than the grand trek of peoples from Europe into the western continent, especially into the United States, during the last four hundred years.

In the early days of human prehistory men must have started off in little groups in all directions never to return to the ancestral home. And as they wandered they changed. The influence of environment, climatic and geographical, registered itself at every stage. This is the first clue to the differences which began to appear. But another factor must be mentioned, without which migration alone might explain change but not differences between various groups. That new factor was isolation. The earth seemed very large in those days, with only a few people occupying it, and it was not only easy but inevitable that one group should be separated from others for long periods of time. Whether they were always on the march, living the life of nomads, or, after traveling shorter or longer distances, settled down into a permanent habitat made comparatively little difference. They were isolated in either case, and that was the significant point. Even though some remained nomads during the ages, the areas of their periodic migrations were restricted, and it could be said of them as truly as of those who had a more permanent habitation that they were localized. This is important, for localization provides for what have been called "areas of characterization," in which during the centuries were developed those peculiar individual traits which have marked off the groups and differentiated them from one another. Of course there were many of these areas, in which the groups occupying them gradually took on definite form, and their characteristic

26

traits became more or less fixed. Then perchance they fell in with other peoples who had developed their traits in the same manner and the agelong mixing of races began.

The explanation which has just been given is doubtless correct, but it is an external, formal explanation and no more. It provides the framework in which changes and development must have taken place, but it does not penetrate beneath the surface and help us to see what was happening inside the lives of the men and women who were in the process itself. It is at this point that recourse must be had to the biologist and eugenist. The whole problem of heredity is immediately involved, and we must seek the best guidance we can get. Heredity is a thorny subject and most difficult. A little knowledge is a dangerous thing, and many fallacies are being exposed which once passed as accepted truth. Besides, the study has not yet been carried to the point where positive results can be affirmed in all areas. So much, however, has been learned that it is possible to speak with confidence on the main issues, particularly on the vital questions with which we are concerned.

We may start with the ascertained fact of the variability of the vital factors or materials with which each individual of the human race is endowed as he begins his life. Mutation or change soon begins to take place in one or more of these original life factors which are the heritage of every human being. Every life begins as a single cell in which are present all the possibilities of change and development. This cell is microscopic in size but extremely complex. It has a nucleus which contains all the materials determining the direction that growth and development shall take. This nucleus is made up of structures known as chromosomes, and each chromosome is a string or chain of genes. Now the genes determine the traits of the individual person. Their pervasive significance can be realized in the statement of a leading authority, "Thus every cell of the body—at least until a late stage of development if not in all stages—contains the full set of chromosomal materials that were present at the beginning of development." [8] Every individual person inherits two sets of chromosomes, one from each parent. No two sets are exactly alike; so when they are united to form a new individual, a new combination comes into existence, thus accounting for variations. Were it not so, each succeeding generation would continue to be exactly like its predecessors, and human life would remain fixed.

This is putting the matter rather strongly and from one side only, for not only heredity but environment plays its part in human development. But the point should be made clear that environment must act on that which is given, and if that does not change, human development would be so greatly restricted that it would be like attempting to make music on a set of strings that cannot be tuned.

But changes do take place, and men grow up in groups in which every individual is somewhat different from his fellows or either of his parents. This possibility of change and development and the direction they take, let it be said again, are determined by the chromosomes and their genes. Each man is born with a definite set of genes and becomes physically what his genes call for and nothing else. The color of his skin, the form of his skull, the shape of his nose—all these are determined by the particular genes which he possesses and which are commissioned to perform that duty. Thus through the centuries mankind has been slowly changing, so that we have today the varied groups composing the human race. No one can say just how much is caused by the environment and how much is due to hereditary endowment. Both must have played their parts at each stage of development, but it is impossible to disentangle the roles. A man may be born with a white skin, but he may live in a sunburned country or deliberately expose his body to the sun's rays. As a result his skin becomes as brown as that of a Negro. But if he has children, provided his wife is also

[8] H. S. Jennings, "The Laws of Heredity and Our Present Knowledge of Human Genetics on the Material Side," *Scientific Aspects of the Race Problem*, p. 14; see also H. S. Jennings, *The Biological Basis of Human Nature, passim.*

white, they will be born with white skins. How long must a group be exposed to the burning rays of the sun so that not only will the individuals who are exposed develop dark skins but their children will be born with dark skins? Environment must play its part, but environment cannot make a change which will be transmitted through the generations unless a change takes place in the relation of the genes which control the color of the skin—and so on with other physical changes in human beings.

Heredity evidently accomplishes much, but it has its limitations. We receive our genes from our parents but not their skills, their beliefs, their knowledge, their likes, or their dislikes. These are acquired by each one for himself. A man inherits his bodily traits, but his mental life and achievements are determined by his post-natal environment. So far-reaching is this fact that, if two children of the same family are separated at birth and are reared in entirely different surroundings, they will not change essentially in their physical traits but will grow up with an entirely different mental outlook. This is a matter of the highest importance when studied in relation to races. The physical traits are transmitted from one generation to another but not the attitudes toward life and all things which make up the social and mental life. These attitudes are the result of education, taken in its widest definition—all that environment and training and example bring into human life. This can be discovered very conclusively in the Japanese-Americans of the second and third generation in the United States. They are Japanese in their physical traits, but that is all. In other respects they are Americans with as enthusiastic and sincere an American patriotism as any so-called Old American of many generations who is proud of his European extraction. In the words of Ruth Benedict, "Heredity takes no notice of the glories of civilization, whether they are in science or in technology or in art; these can be perpetuated in any group, not by nature but by nurture." [9]

Mankind differs from the lower animal at this significant point. To use an illustration:

[9] *Op. cit.,* p. 63.

A diving bird brought up in complete isolation from other birds of its species will nevertheless dive like its ancestors when released near a body of water. But a Chinese boy brought up in an English-speaking American household will speak English and be as awkward at using chopsticks as any other American. A boy of American parentage, brought up in China by Chinese foster parents, will not only speak Chinese but will also have motor habits and a facial expression that strikes his blood cousins as completely alien.[10]

We can but learn from facts such as these that there is a vast difference between *physical heredity,* which human beings share with the animals, and *social inheritance,* which depends entirely upon the environment in which a human being is brought up and nurtured and which differentiates him entirely from all other living creatures. So when we are considering the human groupings called "races," we are dealing with two things which must always be kept distinct. We are what we are physically because our forebears were what they were—plus, of course, the unexplained mutation in the genes and changes in physical environment which work slowly through the years—but we are what we are in every other respect, in all our mental traits and in our manners and customs, because of the social environment in which we have lived, which molds us into a member of that social group.

The trite adage, "Blood will tell," is both true and untrue. Blood tells in the Oriental born in the United States in that he cannot change his Oriental face nor grow a luxuriant beard like a Russian, but it does not tell in determining his language, his religion, his ethical standards, or his patriotism. These come to him, not from physical heredity, but from the society in which he is brought up and from his own free choice.

Applying all these considerations to the problem we are discussing, we realize again that the word "race" must be used with caution. We may use the term to call attention to groups of people who are more or less alike among themselves and more or less different from others, but just as soon as we proceed a step further

[10] Clyde Kluckhohn, *op. cit.,* p. 10.

and make "race" mean differences in mental characteristics and moral quality we have gone beyond the facts and have entered the region of unjustified theories and assumptions. It is these theories and assumptions that are producing the race problem in the world today; and because they exist with so much virulence and are creating such serious tensions in our human family, we must deal with them with great care. There are those who fortunately are able to accept the verdict of science and of biblical religion and believe that all men are brothers and act accordingly, but this is not the case with great numbers of people among us who still hold tenaciously to the belief that differences in race necessarily involve differences in mental and moral quality. So long as persons hold such an opinion—as falacious as it is—and act in accordance with their conviction—as dangerous as it is to the peace of the world—it is necessary to consider the sources and meaning of their conviction and meet it with verifiable facts which must come to control the thinking of serious-minded men if catastrophe is to be avoided. So we turn to a discussion of "racism," which goes far beyond the ascertained facts we have thus far considered and originates in preconceived ideas and unfounded but ancient animosities and antagonisms. Professor Robert Redfield makes the significant statement: "In the troubled affairs of men race is of consequence because of what men think and feel about it and not because of anything that race is of itself. That is the cardinal fact." [11]

[11] Robert Redfield, "Race and Human Nature: An Anthropologist's View," *The Challenge of Race*, p. 3.

31

Chapter II

Racism: Fact and Problem

Racism, according to Webster, is the "assumption of inherent racial superiority . . . of certain races, and consequent discrimination against other races; also, any doctrine or program of racial domination and discrimination based on such an assumption." The word "inherent" in this definition is very important. In racism we are dealing with an issue very different from that of race as a fact among the peoples of the world. The words of Ruth Benedict are pertinent: "Race, then, is not the modern superstition. But Racism is. Racism is the dogma that one ethnic group is condemned by Nature to hereditary inferiority and another group is destined to hereditary superiority." [1]

The antagonisms between peoples in the early western world, in Greece and Rome, were "not racial but cultural." [2] Aristotle, who was an ardent advocate of slavery, did not "argue that Greek blood must be kept pure." [3] The Romans, who conquered many peoples, held no doctrine of superiority of one race over others. Slavery has existed from the earliest periods of which we have historical records, but the dogma of inherent racial superiority and inferiority was not held. Certain people were "barbarians or outsiders," and therefore should be made to serve those who were more cultivated—no other justification was necessary.

But all this is changed in the modern world. The new attitude of racial superiority came to full growth in the age of discovery in the fifteenth century and later, with the opening up of the new

[1] *Race: Science and Politics* (rev. ed.), p. 98.
[2] *Ibid.*, p. 101.
[3] *Ibid.*, p. 102.

world and the exploitation of the natives of the Americas and Africa. In the words of Professor W. W. Sweet:

> The roots of race prejudice go back at least as far as the Crusades, when Europeans first came in contact with non-Christian colored races. The invasion of the Iberian peninsula by the Moslems in the eighth century; their conquest of all the southern part of what is now Spain and Portugal; and the long wars which lasted from the eleventh to the fifteenth centuries fixed the pattern of race prejudice for the Spanish and the Portuguese, which they were later to carry into their American colonies in the sixteenth and the seventeenth centuries and apply to the native races of America.[4]

The native peoples with whom the European colonizers came into contact were looked upon as a new welcome supply of laborers. Black men as servants and workmen began to appear in Spain and Portugal. In many cases in the early days they were well treated. They even married into the communities where they served and set up homes of their own, "but," says Professor Sweet, "as their numbers increased their treatment became less and less liberal."[5]

In America the Spainards exploited the native population. It was a regular part of the program of colonization. The Aztecs and Incas of Mexico and Peru became serfs under the system of *encomienda*. This was not exactly slavery, since the individual Indians were not bought and sold, but a system of serfdom or peonage in which they remained attached to the land when it passed from one owner to another. Let it be said to the credit of at least some of the Roman Catholic missionaries, who accompanied the conquistadors and gave themselves to the welfare of the Indians, that they stood against the abuses which they saw on every hand. The name of the famous Dominican Father Las Casas stands out as that of one who nobly defended his beloved Indians. He made several trips to Spain to protest against their

---

[4] "Historic Roots of Race Prejudice." (Unpublished.)
[5] *Ibid.*

33

cruel treatment. The one blot on his escutcheon is that in his love for the Indians, who were being exterminated on the islands of the West Indies, he suggested that Africans might be imported to take their place because they could better stand the forced labor which was carrying the Indians off by hundreds and thousands. He lived to rue the day when he gave such advice, realizing that the release of one people had only given place to the enslavement of another. But it was too late; the bars had been let down; and we soon read of the horrors of the middle passage across the Atlantic and of the slave markets in both American continents, from which the black man was sold far and wide and was made unwillingly to serve his white masters in lands utterly strange and uncongenial.

The attitude of the English colonists farther to the north was just as bad. The two attitudes are strikingly different. The Spaniards thought of the Indians as a part of their society, far down in the social scale, but as belonging to the community and having a place in it. The English did not give the Indians any place in their society. "The Spaniards with guns on their shoulders drove the Indians into the church; the English went to church with guns on their shoulders to keep the Indians out."[6] The Roman Catholics at times manifested less race discrimination than the Protestants. Protestants almost completely excluded other races from their social and political life. Two theories about the Indians have been held, the "noble-savage" theory and the so-called "dirty-dog" theory. It was the "dirty-dog" theory which came to prevail. John Wesley's experience is illuminating. He came to Georgia in 1735 not only to work among the colonists but to preach the gospel to the "noble savages," as he thought of them. His surprisingly naive words are, "They are as little children, humble, willing to learn, and eager to do the will of God, and consequently they shall know of every doctrine I preach whether it be of God."[7] Before he left Georgia less than three years later,

[6] *Ibid.*
[7] *The Journal of the Rev. John Wesley, A.M.*, ed. Nehemiah Curnock (standard ed.), Vol. VIII, Appendix XII, p. 289.

the sadly disillusioned Wesley's opinion had changed completely. He could not refrain from using the strongest language in portraying the depravity of the Indians he had come to know. They were "gluttons, drunkards, thieves, dissemblers, liars . . . implacable, unmerciful, murderers," and so on at some length in the same strain.[8] Dr. Sweet concludes with a summary statement: "Generally speaking the 'noble-savage' idea flourished among those who had only long distant knowledge of the savages."[9]

Negro slavery was justified by church leaders in North America on religious grounds. Their idea was that it was a splendid move to bring the black man into an environment where he could hear and accept Christian teaching. Not only so, but did not the curse uttered by Noah against Ham condemn all dark peoples to perpetual servitude? Noah's words, according to the Genesis account, were, "Cursed be Canaan; a servant of servants shall be unto his brethren."[10] By "Canaan" he meant the children of Ham, one of his three sons. The name "Ham" has traditionally been interpreted as "black," which is probably not its true meaning. It is evident that we are not here dealing with individual "sons" of Noah but with peoples.

Canaan is here not an individual, but the *representative of the Canaanites,* the native races of Canaan, who, if not destroyed, were ultimately subjugated by the Israelites, . . . and the intention of the passage is in reality to account for the enslaved condition of these races as the Hebrews knew them.[11]

But even if we take the words literally as referring to actual sons, Ham is just as much a blood brother of Shem as Japheth; so there is no basis for a doctrine of superiority and inferiority. Slavery as inauguarated in America was simply carrying out the principle of "obedience of the inferior to the superior . . . for the

[8] *Ibid.,* I, 407.
[9] *Op. cit.*
[10] Gen. 9:25.
[11] S. R. Driver, *The Book of Genesis* (9th ed), p. 119.

mutual benefit of both." [12] It was an easy transition from these and similar theories to full-fledged racism, the belief that the white race is inherently superior to the black. In fact the white man considered himself superior to all who belonged to other races, for the same attitude was taken by Europeans to Asiatics, the brown man in southern Asia, and the yellow man in the Far East.

Man's inhumanity to man has a long history, but what we may now definitely identify as the dogma of "racism" is of comparatively recent origin. It was just a hundred years ago (1853-57) that the classic work on racism, Count Joseph Arthur de Gobineau's *Essay on the Inequality of Human Races*,[13] appeared in France. This is the work which even to this day, despite the fact that its arguments have been overthrown time and again, is looked upon as the foundation upon which inherent racial superiority and inferiority can be demonstrated. Gobineau's "object was to fight well against the growing demands of the underprivileged" [14] who were in his eyes threatening the ascendency of the aristocracy. This proud French aristocrat came to the conviction "that everything great, noble, and fruitful in the works of man on this earth . . . belongs to one family alone, the different branches of which have reigned in all the civilized countries of the universe." [15] All these came from the Nordic race. He was defending the "role of the aristocratic remnant endangered by the bastard proletariat." [16] This is hardly the kind of book with which believers in democracy should seek to prove the rights of one race over others. This defender of aristocracy "never preached the doctrine of pure race as the basis of any civilization." What he proclaimed was the "fixity of racial type—in the individual, not in the nation." [17] He was not interested in nations

[12] Sweet, *op. cit.*
[13] Translated in part by H. Hotz, "the Alabama pro-slavery protagonist"; see Montagu, *Man's Most Dangerous Myth: The Fallacy of Race*, p. 22.
[14] Benedict, *op. cit.*, p. 115.
[15] *Ibid.*
[16] *Ibid.*, p. 116.
[17] *Ibid.*, p. 117.

and races; his dominant motive was to defend the privileges of the aristocrats who, he believed were all Nordics.[18]

The argument advanced by Gobineau that the narrow-headed Nordics and they alone had the right to prosper and dominate the world was furthered by the law of evolution by natural selection propounded by Charles Darwin at just the time Gobineau's work was being read in Europe and America. The doctrine of the survival of the fittest was splendidly illustrated by the white man's conquest of the world which was then proceeding apace. "A 'scientific' reason had been discovered which sanctified the old axiom that might makes right."[19] At a consideable later date writers like Madison Grant and Lothrop Stoddard on this side of the Atlantic took up the cause of Nordic superiority and attempted to show that the prosperity of the United States depended upon the dominance of that "race" in all the world. So they stood for restricted immigration, especially from south and southeast Europe, as well as complete exclusion of all the peoples of Asia. The very title of Lothrop Stoddard's work indicates his fear, *The Rising Tide of Color Against White World-Supremacy,* and Madison Grant dolefully writes on *The Passing of the Great Race.* Ales Hrdlicka, the eminent anthropologist, put their statements to a test, and in his volume on *Old Americans* showed the fallacy of the assumption that America had been made by the Nordics, as those who composed the constructive core of American genius and achievement. The fact is, he says, "The Nordic element in the 'Old Americans' is small."[20]

So we come to our own time, with many men and women scattered over the world holding the theory that one race is inherently superior to all others. The inferior peoples, they declare, are by nature incapable of taking their place on the same level with the white race. That race is superior by native endow-

---

[18] See L. L. Snyder, *Race, A History of Modern Ethnic Theories,* chaps. VI-VII, pp. 103-30, for an extended discussion of Count de Gobineau.

[19] Benedict, *op. cit.,* p. 119.

[20] P. 125.

RACISM: A WORLD ISSUE

ment, a superiority passed on from generation to generation and destined to continue dominant to the end of time. Like the traditional orstrich, their heads are in the sand of opinionated and ignorant prejudice from which nothing seems to be able to dislodge them. They are, however, likely to have an awakening forced by the "rising tide of color," which on every hand is daily becoming more evident and vocal and unquenchable.

A duty rests upon those who do not share the racial attitudes just outlined to study the problem and discover whether there is any factual foundation for the conviction that one race is inherently superior to others. The first facts which emerge—ones which have already been presented—are that there are many groups of people in the world; that they are different, at times very different, from each other; and that in accomplishment some groups have been far ahead of others. No progress can be made in the discussion by attempting to minimize these facts. But another statement should immediately follow—that all which has been here presented concerning "racial" differences has been in the realm of biology. Biology has to do with the bodily traits transmitted by heredity from one generation to another. It does not deal with mental states and the functioning of the mind. By failure to make this distinction endless confusion and difficulty have been encountered. Heredity has been held responsible not only for bodily features, but for the thought life, the emotions, and the will; it has been made the explanation of the cultural life of peoples, including science, art, and religion. Could this double claim for heredity be substantiated it would not be necessary to proceed further—the case would be closed. The advocates of inherent hereditary radical superiority and inferiority would have a firm basis for persisting in their claim.

But the whole weight of scientific opinion is on the opposite side. There is practical unanimity of conviction that races are not inherently superior or inferior. Racism then becomes a myth, "Man's Most Dangerous Myth," according to the title of Ashley

Montagu's recent book. In the balanced words of the late Professor Franz Boas:

> In recent times the belief in a close interrelation between mental behavior and bodily build has come to be a matter of great social importance. Positive evidence for such relation has never been given.[21]

He later came to an even more definite conclusion:

> The only safe conclusion to be drawn is that careful tests reveal a marked dependence of mental reactions upon conditions of life and that all racial differences which have been established thus far are so much subject to outer circumstances that no proof can be given of innate racial differences.[22]

And again:

> It has never been proved that form of the head, color of hair and form of nose have any intimate association with mental activities. On the other hand the study of cultural forms shows that such differences are altogether irrelevant as compared with the powerful influence of the cultural environment in which the group lives.[23]

Even more impressive are certain recent declarations of scientific bodies as they were led to state their conclusions in the face of growing and widespread racial prejudice. The American Anthropological Association (December, 1938) stated:

> Anthropology provides no scientific basis for discrimination against any people on the grounds of racial inferiority, religious affiliation, or linguistic heritage.

The American Psychological Association, in the same year, included the following sentence in its pronouncement:

> In the experiments which psychologists have made upon different peoples, no characteristic inherent psychological differences which

---

[21] "Race," *Encyclopedia of Social Sciences*, XIII, 25.
[22] *Ibid.*, p. 34.
[23] *Ibid.*

39

fundamentally distinguish so-called "races" have been discovered. . . . Certainly no individual should be treated as an inferior merely because of his membership in one human group rather than the other.

One more quotation, from the angle of the biologist, may be given. This is taken from the statement issued by the Seventh International Genetics Congress, held in Edinburgh in August, 1939:

In the first place there can be no valid basis for estimating and comparing the intrinsic worth of different individuals without economic and social conditions which provide approximately equal opportunities for all members of society instead of stratifying them from birth into classes with widely different privileges.[24]

By what processes did the scientists in the various fields arrive at their conclusions? An immense amount of study has been given to this subject in the past half century, especially since World War I. These investigations have been of two kinds—field study by anthropologists of peoples widely scattered over the face of the earth and laboratory study by psychologists and biologists dealing with the functioning of the human mind and the working of the laws of heredity in the propagation of the human species. It is on the basis of such careful investigations that the conclusions just presented have been formulated. And, in addition, these convictions have been held more and more confidently as the years have passed and new studies have made ever clearer the correctness of the findings. We may say that one of the assured results of modern science—that segment dealing with man in his inner constitution and with his relations in society—is that no innate differences which would account for present actual differences in social status and physical condition have been discovered.

As one studies the races of men, the conviction must arise that in general there has been adaptaton to environment which makes

---

[24] For these references see Benedict, *op, cit.,* pp. 195-99.

it possible for men to live under very different conditions of climate and location. There is the tendency for the color to be dark when men live in torrid lands, but that does not signify as great a difference as many believe. The pigmentation of Negro skin is not chemically different from the brown spots which frequently appear on the back of the hands of the mature white man or from the freckles on white youngsters. Thus, even so marked a difference as color is not one which marks off one race from another as a barrier which is finally fixed; it is rather one which comes out of a common human heritage but which develops to a greater degree in some groups and in some individuals than in others. It is possible to run through all the distinctive marks which characterize the so-called races and come to the same conclusion.

The claim that the possession of one kind of physical feature as contrasted with another is a sure mark of superiority or inferiority has been carried to the point that bodily form is taken as evidence that one race in particular, the Negro, is nearer the primordial ape than the white man or the yellow man. Does not the Negro have a flat nose just like the monkey and unlike the white or the yellow man? So what better proof would one want of the inferiority of the black flat-nosed race? But stop. It is about as long as it is short, for the monkey has thin lips and so have the white and the yellow man. What deduction is to be made from that? The absurdity of the whole attempt becomes apparent at once.

One does not get much further when he turns from these features to what is not so immediately evident but much more significant, namely, the blood. A great deal of nonsense has been written about the blood of Negroes as contrasted with that of whites when in fact there is no difference. There is no way of determining from what race or people blood has been taken once it has been removed from the blood donor. There are several types of blood, distinguished by the letters O, A, B, AB, and other symbols. It has been found that type O blood can be mixed with the other three but that none of the other types can be mixed with each other without the danger of "clumping," a condition which is quite serious, sometimes causing death. This is why it is essential to know the type of blood which is used in direct transfusions. But the most important fact which has been discovered about blood is that all the races of men have all these blood types. There is no way of determining beforehand what type of blood any individual may have. When blood plasma is prepared for later use, the same is true; no differences can be discovered between the blood of black or white man. The most powerful microscope is unable to determine from what race any specimen is taken. Science reiterates with increasing conviction Paul's declaration that God "hath made of one blood all nations of men for to dwell on all the face of the earth." We inherit our bodily traits from our ancestors, but all of us have many ancestors who were very different in physical traits from each other. This means that in height, color of skin and hair and eyes, and shape of the head and nose no one can predict before we are born exactly what any of us will be like. This is just as true of the type of blood as of any other of our bodily traits.

The scientists have gone still further. Mental tests have come into vogue in almost every phase of education and in industry; the "I. Q." (Intelligence Quotient) has become a part of our educational vocabulary. What do these tests show with respect to racial differences? The final results up to the present time indicate that no conclusions as to racial superiority or inferiority can be reached by these methods. On the contrary, the further these tests have been carried, the deeper grows the conviction that the various races are so nearly alike in mental capacity and ability that racial differences should not play any part in our judgment of individual men and women and what they may accomplish.

This conclusion is so important that it is well to tell as briefly as possible the story of the development of mental tests as applied to individuals and groups representing various races. At first, when the tests were applied, they showed significant differences between races, which were taken as furnishing sure confirmation of innate differences between these ethnic groups. In a number of cases Orientals in the United States and Negroes in the South made low scores as compared with white Americans in the same localities. There might be bright, intelligent single members of these nonwhite groups but that proved nothing; the race as a race showed inferiority. Did not these tests prove it? So the word went out, confirming the opinion of those who, on other grounds, had long been convinced that they as white people were inherently superior to men and women of color.

But the last word had not been spoken. It was discovered that colored people made a very different showing under changed conditions. The results were strikingly different when the tests were applied to Negroes in the North as contrasted with Negroes in the South. Not only so, but comparisons were instituted between the scores made by Negroes in the North and white people in the South. The following table is most illuminating.[25]

Median Scores on A. E. F. Intelligence Tests

Southern Whites:	Mississippi	41.25
	Kentucky	41.50
	Arkansas	41.55
Northern Negroes:	New York	45.02
	Illinois	47.35
	Ohio	49.50

What the results indicate is not inherent superiority and inferiority as between whites and Negroes but the effect on any group, white or black, of a change in environment. To quote again: *"The differences did not arise because people were from the North or the South, or because they were white or black, but because of differences in income, education, cultural advantages, and other opportunities."* [26]

[25] Benedict and Wetltfish, *The Races of Mankind,* p. 18.
[26] *Ibid.* (Italics are in the original.)

43

Analysis and evaluation of mental tests and their variability have been made by Professor Otto Klineberg of Columbia University in various publications, one of which, "Mental Testing of Racial and National Groups," is to be found in *Scientific Aspects of the Race Problem*. His general conclusion is as follows:

We have the right to say that the results obtained by the use of intelligence tests have not proved the existence of racial and national differences in innate mental capacity, and also that as the social and economic environments of the two ethnic groups become more alike, so do their test scores tend to approximate each other.[27]

In his discussion Professor Klineberg—and he is not alone in his conclusions—has discovered that a number of factors entered into the successful application of the tests and that results could not be depended upon unless these were allowed their full influence. He speaks of the following factors: motivation (a difference was found between those who were anxious to do well and those who were indifferent as to the results obtained); rapport (the relationship between the one giving the test and the person who is being tested; in other words, is there sympathy or an attitude of suspicion on the part of the subject?); language (at times there is failure on the part of the one being tested to understand what the one conducting the test means); socioeconomic status ("Investigations have been reported from various parts of the world, and with a large variety of tests, all establishing the fact that children and adults in the higher economic groups obtain better scores than those in the lower brackets."[28]); and schooling (the results are strikingly different according to the amount and kind of schooling the subject has had).

One must immediately recognize that the attempt to take a further step and measure personality traits, having to do with honesty and other moral factors, is far more difficult and open to criticism. But again even here, so far as these studies have

[27] Pp. 283 f.
[28] *Ibid.*, p. 164.

been carried, there is no demonstrable difference between ethnic groups. Some of the tentative results which have been obtained are not flattering to white Americans. Klineberg tells of a study made by Murdock in which he gave an honesty test to Japanese and white American children. Here "the results showed that 99% of the Japanese children surpassed the average Anglo-Saxon in honesty."[29] Further study is needed to make such conclusions finally authoritative, but we can take as a fair statement the words with which Professor Klineberg closes his article, "For personality tests, as for tests of intelligence, there can be only one safe conclusion—that innate racial or ethnic differences have not been demonstrated."[30]

Results have been reached by some—to their own satisfaction— on the basis of the size of the brain in the different races of men, that the larger the brain, the greater the possibility of mental achievement. The fact however, is "that the size of the brain has nothing to do with intelligence. Some of the most brilliant men in he world have had very small brains. On the other hand the world's largest brain belongs to an imbecile."[31] As between the races the differences in brain size are very small, while between individuals in the same race the differences are very great.

Very eminent Europeans have had brains that were unusually small. The real point is how the brain functions. . . . Anatomists have studied cross sections of the brain under the microscope, but no anatomist with the finest microscope can tell to what race that brain belongs.[32]

The most telling argument against the theory that the races, or some of them, are so different that they constitute different species is that any race can intermarry with any other and produce healthy offspring. This is one of the surest signs of common racial origin and of the homogeneity of the whole human

[29] *Ibid.*, p. 289.
[30] *Ibid.*, p. 291.
[31] Benedict and Weltfish, *op. cit.*, p. 8.
[32] Benedict, *op cit.*, p. 68.

45

family. Members of any two human groups can produce offspring with the hereditary qualities of the two races from which they come, but they are all human beings belonging to one family. When two races thus mingle, a real mixture takes place and "all the king's horses and all the king's men" can never unscramble the mixture. And whenever men of different races meet and live in close contact, such mixtures occur; historically, intermixing is one of the inevitable results of geographical propinquity. There seems to be no alternative to ultimate amalgamation of peoples living in close proximity no matter how greatly they differ from each other in hereditary traits—unless of course a majority group is willing and able to exterminate a differing minority people. This, as we shall see, is what Hitler and his Nazis actually attempted to do with the Jews. Mingling may not occur within the recognized bonds of marriage, but it occurs nevertheless. And always a new stock is produced, not just like either of the parent stocks but inheriting the bodily characteristics of both according to the laws of heredity.

The doctrine was taught even by scientists of a very recent generation that when such racial mixtures occurred, the worst traits of both races were conveyed to the new offspring and not the best. Scientists do not make that claim today. The same laws of heredity obtain when two races mingle as when members of the same race intermarry. Again we must remind ourselves that only bodily traits are subject to the laws of heredity. No child inherits the moral character of his parents; that is a matter of education, of environment, of nurture. We cannot overemphasize the deepening conviction of scientists that social and moral characteristics acquired by one's forebears are not transmitted to their offspring. Every generation starts out anew and must, by industry and nurture, by application and earnest purpose, acquire for itself its moral character, religious life, artistic attainment and skill, and all those features which make men what they are. This does not mean that individuals do not differ, but these differences are not a racial inheritance. When we find, as is so often the case, that people of mixed races—those whose parents belong to groups very different in culture and economic status—are unhappy in their frustrations, the explanation lies in the heavy handicap which bears down on these persons. They are looked upon as mongrels; they are often not welcomed into either group to which their parents belonged; they develop the usual inferiority complex which can be expected of people under such conditions of frustration and repression. These attitudes become intensified when frequently, in addition, these persons are, branded as illegitimate and go through life with that stigma attached to them.

But the most important statement is yet to be made. Instead of being an unfortunate circumstance, racial mixture has proved in human history to be quite the opposite. The idea that nothing good can be expected when races mingle is erroneous. There are no pure races today; all the known ethnic groups are the product of the mingling of different peoples and are stronger and more able to meet the conditions of human life because of the intermixture. This does not mean that we should recommend the intermarriage of men and women of different races. The reason, however, is not biological but entirely social and cultural. As conditions are found in many communities in the world at the present time, such marriages result in unhappiness and frustration in the children to such an extent that no man in his senses would willingly plunge his own children into such an unnatural situation.

But when all has been said about the undesirability of intermarriage between members of groups which are far apart culturally and socially, we must face the overwhelming fact that all the races of the present day are mixtures of diverse strains. A "pure race" is an undiluted myth. Even the aboriginal "black fellows" in Austrailia are considered by many anthropologists to show signs of an intermingling of different strains. When it comes to the peoples of Europe, no nation can point the finger of scorn at others as if its record did not reveal mixtures and intermixtures of diverse stocks. Clyde Kluckhohn makes the uncomplimentary declaration:

47

Virtually all human beings are mongrels. For countless millennia human beings, as lone individuals or in small bands or large hordes, have been wandering over the surface of the globe, mating with whomever opportunity afforded or fancey dictated. . . . Throughout the bulk of Europe, the Americas, Africa, and Asia, constant formation of new and largely unstable blends has been the keynote of the past thousand years. This means that the diversity of genetic strains in even a superficially similar population is very great.[33]

Many times in the studies which follow attention will be called to this feature, so widespread and characteristic that it must be looked on as one of the cardinal facts in the life and history of mankind.

There is little need to elaborate the argument further or to produce more evidence against the view that one race may look down upon another race as inherently inferior. Those who desire to pursue these more general studies have open to them a large and ever-growing list of books and pamphlets on every phase of the question,[34] some of which have been indicated in the footnotes. The main purpose of this volume is quite different. It is to present racism as a world problem, not confined to any one nation, or even to two or three, but a problem making itself felt in every continent and among all major ethnic groups. The plan is to make a survey of the world, picking out the places where the racial conflict is most keenly felt, discovering if possible the peculiar nature of the tension in each locality, and determining the seriousness of the issues and what is being done to relieve the condition. This of course can be done only in outline, but the study is being attempted because of the conviction that too few men and women recognize the

[33] *Op. cit.,* pp. 11, 13.
[34] See L. L. Snyder, *op. cit.,* for a full discussion of various theories and extended bibliography. His own summary (pp. 315 f) is as follows:

1. All mankind consists of but one species: *homo sapiens.*
2. There are no pure races.
3. There are no inferior peoples; within every people there are inferior individuals.
4. The differences between various peoples, both physical and psychological, are by no means as great as those between individuals of the same so-called "races."

wide range of the conflict and the seriousness of the issues involved. It may be that by the time this study has been carried to the end it will be realized that the race problem is one of the world's most important and serious issues—one that in one way or another involves all others—and that without its solution there is no assurance that peace among the nations or harmony within nations will prevail.

Chapter III

The Nazi Dogma of the Master Race

The first country to be surveyed is Germany. The Nazi regime under Adolf Hitler has come to an end. What the future has in store no one can say. It is impossible to believe that Nazism, with its relentless cruelty, has died in the hearts of men who only a few months ago were ardent supporters and participants in unbridled rage against the Jews. But the story we have to tell is that of a historical episode which had a beginning and an end. We may study it as a completed event.

Nowhere in the world was the doctrine that one race is superior to all others proclaimed more confidently and more relentlessly than in Nazi Germany under Alolf Hitler—and nowhere with less justification. Traditionally a "German" is a tall creature with long narrow head, blond hair, and blue eyes. He has been called a Nordic, a Teuton, a Cymric, and an Aryan. Roman writers, notably Tacitus, first painted the picture. In addition to the physical characteristics just mentioned, the Romans thought of the Germans as fierce fighters and hard drinkers, who on the other hand had respect for their women and, in contrast to corrupt Romans, were pure in their sex relationships. There is strong suspicion that Tacitus was glad to show up the accepted Roman morality in contrast with a people who were looked down on as barabarians but who at least in this respect were superior. Be that as it may, this picture of the Germans has come down through the years, and the Nazis were very glad to make use of it to promote their claim to superiority.

This claim on the part of the Nazis and this description of the typical German make necessary an inquiry into the facts. Do the Germans match the stereotype? If not, what is the racial background of the people who consider themselves in the unity of the German commonwealth? Many years ago, in the days of Kaiser Wilhelm II, long before the Nazis and their theories were dreamed of, "a Commission was appointed to undertake a vast anthropological investigation throughout the German Empire."[1] Very few reports from this investigation were ever published. Professor Eugene Pittard intimates that there were suspicions that the kaiser was unwilling that the facts which emerged should be broadcast, for to his surprise it was shown that the German people were not racially homogeneous. But the failure to make public the results of this study did not prevent the facts from being made known—facts well established through the work of other investigators in many parts of Germany.

The stereotype of the tall, blond, blue-eyed man does not falsify the facts in certain parts of Germany. In the north, particularly the northwest, the bulk of the people conform more or less to this type, but even there some are quite different in their physical features. In south Germany the people are of a very different type. They are shorter, with wide skulls and brown eyes, and are very evidently members of the Alpine (Celtic) peoples of south central Europe. While this division into those of the south and of the north may be accepted as a general rule, there are so many exceptions that no hard and fast division can be made. Professor Pittard speaks of Berlin as "an anthropological microcosm of the whole Reich."[2] He makes clear that the Germans can make claim to racial purity no more than other European states—all are of mixed extraction.

But even this rough division into north and south must be supplemented. There is east Germany, the last part of the country to be incorporated into the nation. This great section was originally populated by Slavic peoples, Poles, and other subdivisions of that group. They were partly driven out during the Middle Ages and replaced by German colonists. This accounts for the presence

[1] Eugene Pittard, *Race and History*, p. 155.
[2] *Ibid.*, p. 158.

farther east in Esthonia, Latvia, and Lithuania—now incorporated in Russia—of Germanic peoples, Lutheran and Roman Catholic in religion, and in no sense Russian in outlook. But with this partial displacement of populations another movement was in progress, that of amalgamation. Germans and Slavs mingled their blood, but even more important, great numbers of Slavs remained in Germany with no intermixture and became completely incorporated into the German state. We find then strong Nordic, Alpine, and Slavic strains which together have made up the people we call German.

This survey of ethnic groups in Germany is essential in any attempt to understand the attitudes of the Nazis. Whatever their origins, Nazified Germans were most strenuous in their claim to racial superiority. Adolf Hitler made this a major theme in his ill-conceived volume, *Mein Kampf,* often styled the "Nazi Bible." Even though his spleen was vented especially against the Jews, Hitler was more inclusive in his vituperations. All races which were not "Aryan" were inferior and should be subjugated and held in bondage by this chosen race of heroes and strong men. When it came to other groups such as Negroes, he held them in utter contempt and believed they should not be educated or given any advantages. He was not careful to state just who the Aryans were and on what basis they might claim to be separate and distinct. Hitler took it for granted that the Aryans were superior, and that was sufficient for him.

The pages of the voluminous and inchoate *Mein Kampf* give ample evidence of Hitler's obsession with the importance of race. Page after page is filled with disdainful remarks about other peoples, especially the Jews. He could see nothing good in them. Jews were dirty; they had never done anything constructive in the world; they had destroyed everything they had touched. They delighted in mingling with other groups and spoiling what might have been a worthy and beautiful product. To intermarry with this race was a cardinal sin—a sin the more awful because it was irretrievable. Once a mixed progeny had been produced, the evil had been done once and for all. Keeping the Aryan race pure was then a sacred duty above all others. To use his own words, "The man who misjudges and disdains the laws of race actually forfeits the happiness that seems destined to be his. He prevents the victorious march of the best race and with it also the presumption for all human progress." [3]

According to Hitler the Aryan race was superior and should dominate all others, a right unequivocally based on race and race alone.[4] "All that is not race in this world is trash," [5] is the Führer's own way of dashing it off in a reckless, petulant, but deeply revealing explosion. Belonging to the Aryan race gave his Germans the right to lord it over all others. In fact an essential ingredient of Hitler's theory was the subservience of all other peoples in order that the dominant Aryan might be able to carry out a program of world conquest and dominion. He made this stand out very clearly; "without this possibility of utilizing inferior men, the Aryan would never have been able to take the first steps towards his later culture." [6]

There are no Negroes in Germany, but there are many in the former German Africa, so Negroes came within the scope of Hitler's contempt. Here are his words:

From time to time it is demonstrated to the German petty *bourgeois* . . . that . . . a negro has become a lawyer, teacher, even clergyman, or even a leading opera tenor or something of the kind. While the stupid *bourgeoisie,* marveling, takes cognizance of this miraculous training, filled with respect for this fabulous result of our present educative skill, the Jew knows very slyly how to construe from this a new proof of the correctness of his theory of the equality of men which he means to instill into the nations. It does not dawn upon this depraved

[3] Adolf Hitler, *Mein Kampf* (unexpurgated ed.; New York: Reynal and Hitchcock, 1939), p. 397.

[4] *Ibid.,* pp. 389-455.

[5] *Ibid.,* p. 406.

[6] *Ibid.,* p. 404.

bourgeois world that here one has actually to do with a sin against all reason; that it is a criminal absurdity to train a born half-ape until one believes a lawyer has been made of him. . . .[7]

These quotations—and many more are scattered through *Mein Kampf*—indicate the fundamental direction of Hitler's thinking. He runs counter, either through ignorance or sheer perversity, to the findings of all modern scientific investigators.

But this attitude is reprehensible on a more severe count. Suppose it were true that races were inherently superior and inferior; the attitude of those who consider themselves superior need not be Hitler's. It would not be necessary for them to despise and hate and maltreat those who cannot help being inferior—but this was essential to Hitler's program. Force, coercion, crushing out in all others any sense of worth and dignity, were to be the undeviating role of the conquering Aryans until in the end, when all resistance had been made impossible and inferior peoples had humbly taken their places as obsequious servants and slaves of the dominant race, there might be peace. But what a peace—the unruffled calm of crushed peoples who no longer had enough spirit to resist or even to hope that a better day might be theirs. This is the picture of the utopia of Adolf Hitler, of the Nazi party, and unfortunately of millions of Germans who were made drunk on this virulent poison.

We must turn to other writers to find a more reasoned attitude and justification of the Nazi position. Dr. Lothar G. Tirala, "a leading exponent of Nazi 'race science,'" declares that it is "a well-grounded view that it is highly probable that different human races originated independently of one another and that they evolved out of different species of ape-men. The so-called main races of mankind are not races but species."[8] It was a desperate expedient for an author thus to run counter to the verdict of scientific opinion in order to provide backing for a theory which he

[7] *Ibid.*, pp. 639 f.
[8] *Rasso, Geist und Seele,* as quoted in M. F. Ashley Montagu, *Man's Most Dangerous Myth: The Fallacy of Race* (2d ed., rev. and enl.), p. 6.

must endorse to give plausibility to Nazi arrogance. But what else could he do when the Führer made racial antagonism the basis of his whole campaign of aggression? To promote so unscientific a contention it did not make much difference whether race was exactly defined or not. By what was really a *tour de force* the Germans, or Aryans, were assumed to form a racial unity superior to all others. So if by definition such a unity could be created and could succeed in holding the German people together, what more was to be desired?

A generation ago when the famous Kaiser Wilhelm II was looking out over the world and thinking in terms of a larger Germany, world wide not only in influence but through conquest and domination, a most influential book was published. One of Gobineau's earlier disciples, Houston Stewart Chamberlain,[9] "a renegade Englishman," son-in-law of the famous German composer Richard Wagner, published in 1899 a startling literary production. Some years later, in 1911, it appeared in English dress under the title *Foundations of the Nineteenth Century*. While Chamberlain was a disciple of Gobineau, his thesis was somewhat different. Gobineau held that the aristocracy in Europe was composed of Nordics who had demonstrated their right to pre-eminence over all other classes in the course of European history; hence they should hold their advantage and not associate with the unworthy proletariat. Chamberlain was not interested in the aristocracy. The difference between the two is very important. Gobineau was an aristocrat whose sole interest was to preserve the privileges of his social caste, not only in his own nation, but in other European countries. Being a Frenchman, an Englishman, or a German made relatively little difference to him. With Chamberlain—and Hitler—the case was quite different. Their purpose was to extol the Teutons and make Germans conscious of their innate supremacy over other peoples. Oswald Spengler, in his *Decline of the West*, predicted the eclipse of the whole structure of Western civilization. He too was a Ger-

---

[9] See L. L. Snyder, *Race, a History of Modern Ethnic Theories*, chaps. VIII-IX, pp. 131-61, for an extended presentation of Chamberlain.

man, but his thesis controverted the contentions of Chamberlain, indicating that the Nazi theory was not universally accepted in his own land.

Now who were these Teutons? Here we come to a strange feat of intellectual juggling. Chamberlain performed a slight-of-hand feat, and presto Germans of all kinds were alike members of one homogeneous race. The long-headed Nordic, the wide-headed Alpine, and, stranger still, the more distant and foreign Slav— all were Teutons and members of the chosen race. They were to keep their blood pure and uncontaminated and hold themselves aloof from others as inferiors over whom they had the right to rule. Dogmatism could scarcely reach a lower depth of degradation than this. Flying in the face of facts and giving himself to a ridiculous fallacy, all at the behest of the egoistic theory that somehow these Germans were the noblest race, unique and unassailable, Chamberlain laid the foundation on which Hitler built. One can believe anything of Nazi prejudices and ambitions when he knows the fallacious assumption on which they rest.

The attempt was made by the Nazis to interpret the greatest German literary heroes, Goethe and Schiller, as favorable to their claims. Nothing could be more impossible when their real attitude is understood. Goethe was a cosmopolitan whom no nation could hold within its narrow limits. In fact, there was no united German state in his day, only a number of states, each with its own ruler and form of government, but speaking the same German language and feeling themselves to be bound together by the same cultural bonds. Goethe was a world man, with interests and sympathies which made him feel a relationship with all human beings struggling toward intellectual illumination and recognize the rights of men as members of one human family. It is well known that Schiller had a passion for human freedom. He gloried in the successful fight by the Swiss to gain their independence. How could such men be brought into the circle of the Nazi ideology?

It is quite different with Richard Wagner. In order to realize the fascination which he exercised upon Hitler we must distinguish between two sides of the work of Wagner. On the one hand he was the dramatist of tragedy. Into this realm Hitler could not enter with any true understanding. He reveled in the old tales of the Niebelungenlied, which were the sources of much of Wagner's inspiration. Here the genius of the mighty musician made Siegfried live again in the imagination of his hearers. Hitler saw the knight in shining armor, the hero conqueror, the paragon of all excellence. His soul became intoxicated with German megalomania, so much so that he was blinded to all else 'and went his way to make good in his generation the superior greatness of the Germanic race. Hitler found this in Wagner instead of the sense of tragedy, which has its appeal to the soul of man, all men, not Germans alone. But of course Wagner was German to the core, and even anti-Semitic, which also helps to explain his influence over Adolf Hitler.[10]

Since the Jews were the special object of Nazi venom, it is necessary to look at them more closely—their race, their achievements, and their position, particularly in Germany. In the first place we run into the disconcerting fact that there is no such thing as a Jewish race. Of course, originally, the Jews were Semitic and doubtless came out of Arabia, the "cradle" of the Semites. In the Bible we come upon the Jew first in the person of Abraham, the Father of the Faithful, in Ur of the Chaldees in southern Mesopotamia; then in Haran, in the upper reaches of the same valley; and after that in Palestine, which the Jews today look upon as their ancestral home. Even in a relatively early day there was mixture with other peoples. The purpose of the little book of Ruth seems to be to show that David, the ideal king, was descended from Ruth, who was not Jewish at all but a Moabite. But, as we shall see later, racial purity became a part of the creed of loyal Jews, particularly in the days after the return from the Babylonian captivity. After that there must have been little intermarriage for hundreds of years—at least during the period recounted in the

---

[10] I am indebted to Professsor Paul J. Tillich for ideas in this discussion of Wagner and Hitler.

Old Testament, the Apocrypha, and the New Testament. In later periods, however, there is another story to tell. The evidence is not definite and satisfactory, but the resulting differences among Jewish peoples leave no doubt of intermingling with other groups. In the words of Professor Pittard:

> The Jews belong to a religious and social community, to which, in every period, individuals of different races have attached themselves. These Judaized people have come from every kind of ethnic stratum, such as the Falashas of Abyssinia and the Germans of the Germanic type; or the Tamils—Black Jews—of India, and the Khazars, who are supposed to be of the Turki race.[11]

Even among the Jews of Europe there are so many types that to assign each to a definite racial or ethnic stock is well-nigh impossible. The same becomes evident when one travels in Asia. The Jews in central Asia are quite heterogenous. Instead of belonging to the long-headed people, a large proportion of these Jews have broad heads. The same divergence is found in Persia, Mesopotamia, the Caucasus, and Arabia where Jews are to be found.

The strange phenomenon which becomes increasingly apparent is that the Jews of any section show a strong tendency to have the same physical traits as the people among whom they live. This would argue for the gradual incorporation into the Jewish community of men and women of other stocks who by marriage have brought with them these alien traits. Wherever one goes, to Syria, Palestine, or North Africa, the same phenomenon is observable, not on casual acquaintance to be sure, but upon scientific investigation. A student in New York City who made three thousand measurements came to the conclusion "that there is a complete lack of unity in the Jewish race." [12] One further very significant quotation from Professor Pittard will be in place:

> And therefore we also see the poverty of the arguments at the disposal of that anti-Semitism which would set up a Jewish race in

[11] *Op. cit.,* p. 337.
[12] *Ibid.,* p. 348.

opposition to the Christian races. There is no more a Christian race than a Musulman race. And neither is there any such thing as a Jewish race.[13]

But while there is no alternative to taking these findings as correct, the Jews, wherever they are found, are separate from the rest of the community and at best have only limited and partial relations with others. They are a people set apart and looked upon as different from others. This is not entirely the fault of the Gentiles. The Jews insist on maintaining themselves as a separate people, religiously and socially. They are fundamentally opposed to intermarriage with Gentiles, even though it does take place fairly frequently in some communities. This means in many cases—though not in all by any means—a severing of the bonds of the newly formed family from Judaism. In a deep sense it is a matter of life and death for a minority group which desires to preserve its identity to lose numbers in this manner. Their firm attitude can be understood even though one may not sympathize with Jewish separatism. All this is of the highest importance in thinking of the Jewish problem in any land. At the opening of World War II the Jews in the world were said to number 16,000,-000. Of these about 600,000 were in Germany. They were a minority group but of considerable size. Be it also said that they were the only minority group in Germany which had the slightest significance. The Germans did not have Indians, Filipinos, Mexicans, Japanese, and Negroes to deal with as have the people of the United States. The entire racial problem—in so far as we can call it racial at all—was caused by the presence of this one group in their midst.

The story of the Jews in Germany has had its ups and downs. It has not been altogether unpleasant or unfavorable to the Jews. This is well to remember in a time like the present when Nazi Germany has turned so relentlessly against these people and

[13] *Ibid.*, p. 351.

treated them as badly as any people have ever been treated in history. Martin Luther's attitude is curious in its inconsistency. Early in his career he exposed the ambigous attitude of the dominant church in vigorous language:

Our fools, the popes, bishops, sophists, and monks, have hitherto conducted themselves toward the Jews in such a manner that he who was a good Christian would have preferred to be a Jew. And if I had been a Jew and had seen such blockheads and louts ruling and teaching Christianity I would have become a swine rather than be a Christian, because they have treated the Jews like dogs and not like human beings.[14]

In a pamphlet entitled *Jesus Was Born a Jew,* Luther continues in the same vein:

If we would help them, so must we exercise, not the law of the Pope, but that of Christian love—show them a friendly spirit, permit them to live and work, so that they have cause and means to be with us and amongst us, . . . and if some remain obstinate, what of it? Not every one of us is a good Christian.[15]

But as he grew older Luther changed, a change which was caused by his disappointment, surprise, and indignation because the Jews persistently refused to become Christians. He wrote a pamphlet *Concerning the Jews and Their Lies* in which he shows that he had become a bitter enemy of these people, "accusing them of poisoning wells, murdering Christian children and remaining stubborn in the face of Christian revelation. He urged the Princes to destroy the Jewish synagogues and to confiscate their wealth and to devote it to maintain those who had accepted Christianity." [16] There is more, but this is sufficient to provide a background against which it is not so difficult to account for the atrocities of our own day. We who would heal the breach and make relations

[14] A. L. Sachar, *A History of the Jews* (2d ed.), p. 203.
[15] *Ibid.,* p. 228.
[16] *Ibid.,* p. 229.

between Jews and Gentiles tolerable would do well to study the depths of intolerance and cruelty we have to overcome, the more so because in Luther's case this intolerance and hatred sprang from a breast fundamentally and deeply religious.

Luther, as we have seen, reprobated the attitude of the Roman Catholic Church toward the Jews. On what was his condemnation based? The glorious thirteenth century, one of the most wonderful from the standpoint of the power and influence of the church, was far from glorious for the Jews. In the words of Sachar, "It meant only an intensification of the torments which they had endured in the eleventh and the twelfth centuries." [17] The hand of the church was heavy upon them. It was under the control of one of the mightiest and ablest of the popes, Innocent III. Above all else he wanted the church to be all-embracing and all-dominant. Consequently he was passionately opposed to all forms of heresy and did not hesitate to give himself to unworthy persecution and heresy-hunting. Naturally he was an enemy of the Jews. We must credit him with sincerity. As Sachar puts it: "Innocent honestly believed that the Jews were an accursed people, suffering for rejecting Christ, and never to be given rest and peace." [18] In one of his letters this pope gave a summary of his policy: "The Jews, like the fraticide Cain, are doomed to wander about the earth as fugitives and vagabonds, and their faces must be covered in shame. They are under no circumstances to be protected by Christian princes, but, on the contrary, to be condemned to serfdom.[19] The Roman Catholic Church took the stand that the Jews should be segregated, kept apart from Catholics, because they had rejected Jesus Christ and would contaminate those whom they might influence. In order that the faith of many might not thus be subverted the Jews were to carry a mark on their clothing which would immediately identify them. Segregation in ghettos

---

[17] *Ibid.*, p. 192.
[18] *Ibid.*, p. 193.
[19] *Ibid.*

followed naturally from this policy and added to the dismal tale of repression and frustration.[20]

We must make the distinction between anti-Judaism and anti-Semitism. One is religious and the other racial, though often intermingled. As far back as the first century, antagonism against Judaism as a religion was to be found in the Christian ranks. The Fourth Gospel itself is in a deep sense anti-Judaistic in its opposition to those among the Jews who were opposed to Christianity, who had taken part in the antagonism against Jesus which resulted in his death on the cross, and who remained bitter enemies of the young Christian community. This form of opposition has continued through the centuries and is to be distinguished from so-called racial anti-Semitism, which may have very little Christian conviction back of it and which results in hatred, hounding, and slaying of Jews because they belong to a despised people. This form of opposition has been the significant characteristic of the clashes which have marred the past century and a half.

In mid-nineteenth century Germany, Jews were not seriously molested. During this period some Jews became Christians and in doing so were received into the Christian community with no sense of inferiorty. Several men of prominence were in their number. David Mendel, who changed his name to Johann Neander, "new man," when he became a Christian, was from 1813 to his death in 1850 professor of church history in the University of Berlin, one of the most famous of his time. A little later came Franz Delitzsch, who until his death in 1890 was the professor of Old Testament in the University of Leipzig. He became famous as a scholar, translator of the New Testament into Hebrew, and a writer of commentaries which were translated into English and became widely influential.[21] These names give a side of the story

[20] Again I am indebted to Professor Paul J. Tillich for suggestions lying back of the discussion of the relation of Roman Catholicism and the Jew.

[21] Some doubt has been cast on the Jewish origin of Franz Delitzsch, but he was thought of as a convert from Judaism and illustrates the attitude of the Christian community toward one coming from that faith.

of Jewish-Gentile relations quite different from the usual rehearsal of atrocities and indignities. But with all this the situation of the Jews was in no sense ideal. In spite of it all, however, Jews made remarkable advances and especially in the learned professions and the sciences made names for themselves second to none.

In fact that was one of the chief difficulties. Jealousy had its part to play in the increasing attitude of hostility, which grew during the years and which could be made use of by Hitler and his Nazi collaborators in fomenting bitterness and resentment toward the Jewish people. Increasingly Jewish doctors, lawyers, scientists, and professors were taking places which Gentiles believed belonged by right to them. Besides that, Jewish businessmen were prospering, and whenever that has happened in Europe it has whetted the envy and the cupidity of Gentiles, often resulting in raids on the Jews to secure their wealth. Moreover, men have always sought a scapegoat for their ills, and the Jews have played that role many times in European history. It is incredible but true that they were made responsible for the Black Death, which swept over Europe in the fourteenth century and carried off from a fourth to a half of the population in a number of countries. It was convenient and easy to lay this on the Jews and to treat them as criminals of the worst sort. There is difficulty in laying one's finger down on this or that motive and making it responsible for anti-Semitism, when probably in different degrees at different times and places a variety of motives have played their part. It was always possible, however, to fall back on the motive underlying all others, that the Jews belonged to a despicable group of people which was capable of anything unworthy—and that was enough.

With this background we must relate the sorry tale of the Nazi persecution of the Jews and try to understand what it means. The violent harassing of the Jews began as soon as Hitler was appointed German chancellor in 1933. It soon became apparent that what he was aiming to do was to eliminate the Jews completely from German life.[22] Probably most Germans had no idea at first of the lengths to which Hitler would lead them, but unfortunately it did not take many of them long to fall in with even the most extreme features of his program. From April, 1933, to September, 1935, was the period of "initial legislation," during which the Jews were made to realize that they were no longer German citizens, could not expect education for their children, and could not hold public positions as lawyers, teachers, judges, and other public officers. No bodily violence was committed during this "legal" period of persecution. That was to follow shortly, but these legal disabilities tended to harden the mind of the public against a class which had been a part of their state but was now being eliminated.

This preparatory period was followed by more stringent regulations.

Jewish matters were handed over to the Gestapo, which excluded them automatically from all legal jurisdiction and left them at the mercy of the storm troopers. Being without any rights was equal to being outlawed. More and more incidents of personal attack happened, thousands of Jews were thrown into concentration camps and subjugated to torture and confiscation of their property.[23]

This was soon followed by "wholesale confiscation." The purpose of these forms of violent persecution was "mainly to secure speedy emigration." This period lasted until 1938, when a new and more rapid program was initiated. This had as its purpose nothing less than the complete annihilation of Jewry in Germany. Stimulated by Propaganda Minister Goebbels, a so-called "spontaneous uprising of the German people" was turned against the Jews in every part of the land. The first result was that "all houses of worship were destroyed" during the night of November 9-10, 1938. This marked the beginning of the last stage of the persecution, which continued until the collapse of German military re-

---

[22] I am indebted in this part of the presentation to an unpublished paper by Stephen Sherman, "The Persecution and Attempted Annihilation of the Jews in Germany."

[23] Sherman, *op. cit.*

sistance in May, 1945. That signal event of course put an end to the atrocities.

In the last phase, just mentioned the Jews, in addition to all other indignities, were robbed of all their possessions, deprived of the right to attend public places of amusement, forbidden the right of assembly, and labeled so that their membership in the despised race might be evident on sight. All Jewish men over sixteen and women over twenty were forced to labor as slaves. But even this was not the end. Mass deportations were begun. It would seem that the Nazi plan was to deport the Jews eastward into Poland and leave them to their fate. The Nazis had conquered Poland and could do with it and the Jews as they liked. But the Nazis faced a problem. The number of Jews in Poland, natives and those driven into the country from farther west, would make the problem of disposing of the Jews in this fashion slow if not impossible. So another more horrible method was made use of at once, that of mass murder in various forms.

At places Jews were crowded into ghettos where malnutrition, disease, and death would soon combine to rid the land of this pestilential race. Concentration camps, crowded with miserable refugees, earned the title of "extermination camps," where they were done to death by neglect, brutality, and actual murder. Even before the war came to an end, Americans began to learn the terrible facts about concentration camps and mass murder by slow processes of starvation and the quicker and more merciful use of firearms.[24] Since the fall of the Third Reich, when investigators have been able to travel freely, detailed reports of the extent to which the atrocities were carried have brought to light conditions which are far more horrible than could have been imagined. It is not our purpose here to tell the story of horrors as revealed in the Buchenwald and Dachau murder camps. We can only contrast the 600,000 Jews in Germany before the war with the pitiable

---

[24] See *Information Service,* Department of Research and Education of the Federal Council of Churches of Christ in America, Vol. XXII, No. 17, Apr. 24, 1943, for authenticated details of some methods of extermination which were being practiced.

remnant of 25,000 more or less who remain. We may never know the exact number of those who were murdered, but no estimate is less than 4,000,000 killed in Germany and Poland, and some would place the number much higher. What was exposed to a horrified world was the most diabolical attempt in human history to exterminate an entire people—an attempt which was more successful than any like purpose ever formulated.

We are undertaking in this book to show that racism is a worldwide phenomenon, and in the first country chosen for consideration we make the discovery that the people who have been the object of hatred and persecution are not a distinct race at all. The Jews are persons who belong to a widely scattered group of people who practice the religion of Judaism. Biologically they have affinities with many other ethnic stocks, and yet they form a compact body of religionists as separate and distinct as if they belonged to a race entirely different from the people among whom they live. In fact the basic contention of Adolf Hitler and the Nazi party was that the Jews did belong to a different race and should be eliminated on that account. Thus the stage was set for the display of the most characteristic forms of racism, with the results which have been recounted. We shall make the same discovery again in country after country. This fact will make clear that the problem with which we are dealing is not a simple one. At times the antagonisms are based on caste distinctions rather than on clearly marked racial differences, but that does not prevent them from being as bitter and violent as if two distinct races were involved. We shall also be made to realize that economic and religious factors—one or the other or both—enter into racial conflicts in almost every case. Rarely if ever does a difference in race alone cause the conflict. But when the fact of difference in race enters, the antagonism becomes all the more bitter and greater is the danger of long-continued and determined opposition.

All of these factors played their part in Germany. What of the future? It cannot but be different for the simple reason that so few Jews remain. Even the return of a certain number to their former homes will not affect the conditions appreciably. Our concern is not so much for them as for the condition of mind and heart of the German people. Can they come to think of the Jews as fellow citizens worthy of a place with them in the new Germany which is to be? Everything depends upon the answer to that question. When it is put in this form, the problem of anti-Semitism in Germany merges into the larger problem of anti-Semitism in other countries in Europe and in North and South America, where we shall meet it again.

Chapter IV

Russia: Many Peoples, One Nation

Who are the Russians? They are more kinds of people than can be found anywhere else under a single government. In the first place there are a great many of them, numbering approximately 200,000,000. To be more exact, the estimated population in 1941 was 202,043,910.[1] This includes lands returned to Russia, such as the Baltic states, western Ukraine, and western Belorussia (taken by Poland in 1921), Bessarabia, and northern Bukhovina. Not only is the population large, but it is extremely varied. It is not necessary to enumerate the long list of different peoples, but the diverse composition of the population must be disclosed in order to demonstrate the remarkable achievement of Russia[2] in being able to unite such a multitude of peoples in one governmental unit. That is one side of the shield; but, when all the facts are known, it will be seen that the task has not been as difficult as the diversity of peoples would at first sight indicate. According to Hrdlicka, "Taking the present Soviet population as a whole, it may be estimated to be roughly eight-tenths white, about one-tenth yellow-brown, and the rest intermediate. There are no Blacks."[3] So there are many peoples, but the vast majority of the population of the entire U.S.S.R. are white people of Slavic stock living in European Russia.

The central bloc of Russians comes first. European Russia has

[1] These figures are based upon estimates made by the American Russian Institute in *The Soviet Union Today* (1945). Figures and certain important statements in this chapter come from the same source. See also Corlis Lamont, *The Peoples of the Soviet Union.*

[2] The terms "Russia" and "Russian" are used because they are well known. In place of the complete name, Union of Soviet Socialist Republics, the term "Soviet Union" will also be used.

[3] Ales Hrdlicka, *The Peoples of the Soviet Union,* p. 2. The last sentence in the quotation is not strictly correct. There are a few blacks in the Caucasus.

passed through many changes of a very profound character during its history, and these outward changes have left an indelible imprint on the racial fabric of the Russian people. It might in general be said that they are all Slavs, one of the important branches of the widespread Indo-European peoples, who more than two thousand years before our era roamed the grassy plains of eastern Europe and the hinterland of western Asia. They probably did not all belong to one racial stock; but, while widely scattered, there was sufficient contact between the different groups to result in the use of a common language and the development of common customs and ideas, cultural, religious, and mythological. No unanimity has been reached as to the original habitat of these peoples. It may never be known. One very significant bit of evidence is that the Lithuanian tongue even today shows a closer relation to the various Indo-European languages—from the ancient Sanskrit of India to the Celtic spoken in the Highlands of Scotland, Wales, and Ireland—than any other. This might indicate that the original center of the Indo-European peoples was somewhere in European Russia rather than in western Asia, as has been more frequently maintained. Be that as it may, membership of the peoples of European Russia in the Slavic ethnic group is well established.

The people to whom the Russians belonged are called "Slavs," the derivation of which term has been subject to controversy. It is likely that it came from a root meaning "to glorify." The origins of the nation cannot be traced with certainty. Tacitus seems mistakenly to have included the Slavic peoples farthest west among the Germans. The people of European Russia did not begin to develop into a group with any political unity until the ninth century of our era. Then it was that princes of a people called the Variags or Varangians, coming in from across the Baltic Sea in Scandinavia, brought about unity among the divided Slavic tribes. There were three brothers, the oldest of whom was Rurik, who is said to have united the people into one nation. The Variags may have been invited, but on the other hand they may have seized the power and made themselves rulers. The historian Shestakov is sure that they were not invited by the Slavs; they were robber bands, who looted the Slavs and sold their booty to the Greeks at Byzantium. But at any rate such unity as was achieved was the beginning of the Russian state. At about the same time the people began to be called "Rus," which is probably derived from a word meaning "fair-haired" or "blond."

After this time for several centuries their story is a troubled one, but the great event which determined the direction of subsequent Russian history and affected deeply the racial development of the Slavs was an incursion from without. This was the Tatar or Mongol invasion and occupation of a large part of southern Russia. To quote:

The southern Russians were overwhelmed and subjected to Tatar yoke, or forced to flee. The southern and southwestern parts of Russia became seriously depopulated and were occupied by the roaming Tatars of the "Golden Horde"; and Russia as a whole suffered from the effects of the invasion for 300 years.[4]

The struggle with the Mongols began with the conquests of Genghis Khan, who died in 1227, and their sway did not cease until after the middle of the fifteenth century, although for many decades the burden had become lighter and lighter because of the weakening of the Mongol rule. Attention is called to this period of Russian history because it not only affected the course of their history but resulted in a certain amount of racial infiltration whose effects can be seen in southern Russia today. This fact gives some point to the caustic and intentionally derogatory remark, "Scratch a Russian and you find a Tatar."

Out of the terrible and long-continued dislocation of populations, differences among the Russian people developed which are still significant. There are the Great Russians, numbering 114,337,428, or about 65 per cent of Slavic Russia; the Little Russians or Ukranians, with a population of 42,272,943, or about 25 per cent; and the White or Belorussians, with 10,525,511, or less than 10 per cent.

[4] George Vernadsky, *A History of Russia* (rev. ed.), p. 3.

These groups were more or less divided politically, and "it was not until the nineteenth century that the three branches of the Russian people were reunited in a single state." [5] These branches, thus brought together, form the center and dominant group in the Soviet Union.

Of the other groups of the Soviet Union, we consider first those in Europe. The Cossacks, found in the south, have played a large part in Russian military history in recent centuries, being known as superb horsemen and intrepid fighters. For the most part the Cossacks are Russian in blood but have a different history. They are Ukrainians with some mixture with other peoples whom they have met. What makes them different is that they were originally serfs from the more settled north who escaped and built up an independent political life along the banks of the Dneiper and Don rivers in the wide spaces of southern Russia. With difficulty they were brought under the rule of the czars and with greater difficulty they were very recently forced to submit to socialization and other features of the new government of the Soviets. But what Hindus call the "reconciliation" did take place, and there are no more loyal adherents of the new order. They played an important part in the recent war and show signs of being leaders in the Russia which is now taking shape.[6]

Lithuanians, Latvians, Livonians, and Estonians are found along the Baltic seacoast. "The Lithuanians are now a mixed group of people whose original racial identity is still a matter of controversy." [7] They number 3,134,070. The Latvians, or Letts, numbering 1,950,502, are closely related to the Lithuanians. The Livonians are almost extinct as a separate people. They are related closely to the Estonians, who are not Slavs but Finno-Ugrians, a primitive people from the north who in an early day covered much of central and eastern Russia. Of the Estonians there are 1,120,000. The Finns belong to the same racial group, some of them in Finland

[5] *Ibid.*, p. 11.
[6] See Maurice Hindus, *The Cossacks, passim.*
[7] Ales Hrdlicks, *op. cit.*, p. 19.

proper and some in the Russian-controlled Karelian Peninsula between the former Finland and Russia. The Karelo-Finnish Republic numbers 469,000. Among these people of the north must be noted the Lapps and Samoyeds (now called the Nenets), who are Asiatic in origin though now considerably mixed with the white population. Mention should also be made of the Moldavian Republic, close to Rumania, numbering 2,321,225.

Turning in another direction, we find a confusing racial situation in the Caucasus. To use the words of Hrdlicka, "This region has been since ancient times the eddy and refuge of remnants of nations";[8] but in spite of the mixtures which exist the Slav is the largest single group, "approximately 40 percent of the total." Among the others are the Armenians and the Georgians. Both are white, though there has been considerable intermixture with other peoples. The Armenians in Russia number 1,346,709 and the Georgians 3,722,252, both fairly large groups. Not all the Armenians are within the bounds of the Soviet Union, but it is that part of these people in whose relations we are interested here. The Georgians are a Japhetic people. They appear in history in the twelfth century B.C., and so have had a long history. They were among the earliest people to accept Christianity. They and the Armenians suffered from the invasions of Genghis Khan in the thirteenth century and Timur (Tamerlane) in the fourteenth. From the standpoint of the relation between the many people of the Soviet republics it is of significance that Josef Stalin is a Georgian, a member of a minority group, the man chosen by Lenin to work out the relationships of the various peoples in the new nation after the Bolshevik revolution in 1917. The Azerbaijanians, also of the Caucasus, a Turkic or Tureo-Tatar people, number 3,372,794.

Then there are the Jews. Before World War I they numbered approximately 4,000,000, of whom 1,300,000 were in Russian Poland and 50,000 in the Caucasus. In addition there were about 50,000 in Siberia and central Asia. We shall have occasion to deal with the Jews again, for at no point can the Russian change in

[8] *Ibid.*

attitude toward alien groups be studied more advantageously. The Jews suffered the horrors of many *pogroms* under the czarist regime, but now are enjoying the rights and privileges of Soviet rule as equals with all other races and peoples. As in a number of other lands the key to the understanding of race relations in Russia is the treatment accorded the Jews.

It is impossible to overlook the fact that another of the constituent elements in the Russian population is the German, numbering about 1,800,000 at the beginning of the World War I. They are scattered all over the country, especially in the cities. They had been a privileged class, keeping themselves separate from the surrounding Russians. They were really outposts of Germany in an alien land. One of these German groups, that on the Volga, had been one of the Soviet republics, but it was abolished in 1941, the people being removed and resettled in Siberia and central Asia. They were members of the Russian state, but had not ceased to be Germans in spirit and purpose—hence the drastic measures taken to neutralize their influence.

Of the Asiatic peoples in the Soviet Union only the leading groups can be mentioned. The Tadzhiks, numbering 1,560,540, come from non-Slavic stock. They are a mixture of Iranian and Turkmen and live in the mountain region east of the Caspian and north of Afghanistan, forming the larger part of the population of the Soviet Tadzhik Republic. The Turkmen people are of old central Asiatic stock. They are really white, though at places considerably mixed with the Tatars. From them came the Osmanli Turks, who overran what we now know as Turkey and became famous as the conquerors of Constantinople in 1453, one of the crucial dates in the history of the world. The Turkmen Republic numbers 1,317,693. In addition to these there are literally scores of other groups with all degrees of intermixture between whites and people of Mongoloid origin. Among them mention should be made of the Uzbeks in central Asia who number 6,282,446 and Kazaks who number 6,145,937. The latter have a huge territory, rich in coal and other mineral deposits, in western Asia.

73

According to Hrdlicka, "Aside from the larger ethnic units in the south, there exist in the vast stretches of Siberia, along the rivers, on the seacoasts, and in the forests, many remnants of ancient tribes and peoples."[9] They are too numerous to mention. This author lists the names of twenty-seven of these tribes and remnants of tribes in northern Asiatic Russia. When it is remembered that white Russians from Europe have been in Siberia since traders made their way across the Urals in the eleventh century, and that the vast region as a whole was made a part of Russia as early as 1580, it can be realized how arbitrary and impossible is the customary division into European and Asiatic Russia. The Urals are not really a boundary; it is one country both east and west of these rounded, low-lying ranges. Not only have Russians been living in this vast land for hundreds of years, but they have been intermarrying with the ancient inhabitants. So far has this been carried that the racial type is slowly but surely changing decade after decade in this peaceable and easy fashion. This is likely to continue indefinitely in the centuries to come until in the end there will be a completely unified people stretching from the Baltic to the Pacific.

But while this amalgamation may be predicted, at present real differences exist. One of the most marked is that of language. In all, 125 languages are spoken, including lesser tongues of the smaller groups. Again, as in the case of the population, the Russian language dominates. It may be that ultimately one language will crowd out the others, for Russian is taught over the entire Soviet Union in addition to the local language or dialect in each section, but for the time being and for many years to come there will remain the problem of securing unity in national life in spite of diversity of tongues. In addition to this difficulty there are others caused by differences in customs, habits, old prejudices, and above all religion. Russia has declared itself a nonreligious nation. Religion has been repudiated officially by the government, but in spite of such action religion continues to exist. The Russian Orthodox

[9] *Ibid.*, p. 25.

Church still maintains a strong hold on the people and will doubt-less do so more strongly in days to come, if present signs are true indications of trends which are permanent and deep. There are in addition many in Russia who cling to minor Christian sects, such as the Baptists and the Lutherans in the Baltic countries. Then there are Jews, Buddhists, and primitive animists in Siberia, also many Moslems in Siberia, the Volga basin, the Caucasus, Trans-caucasus, and especially in central Asia. Again it may be asked, How can Russia achieve the complete unity she seeks with differ-ences as marked as these? That is really the question of questions in the Soviet Union.

The Soviet Union has learned to deal with the problem of minority groups more successfully than any other nation. A great change in policy took place as a result of the Bolshevik revolution in 1917, when the old regime was completely superseded and new ways of dealing with every feature of Russian life—not only po-litical but economic, social, educational, and religious—were set up. We shall discover that changes in policy and practice did not take place at once and that there were maladjustment and suffer-ing—on the part of the Jews and Cossacks in particular—for a number of years, but the year 1917 marked the turning point and opened the door to changes which slowly came into effect. We must describe these changes, especially those which concern the relation of the racial and other groups in that vast country; but before doing so it is necessary to give a sketch of the Russia before the Revolution of 1917. That earlier period must be scanned in or-der to know not only what Russia and Russians are like, but what the background is, against which all that has taken place since that time must be studied in order to be understood at all. Russia is today what it is partly because of attitudes and experiences dur-ing the czarist regime.

The policies of the Russia of the old regime were essentially re-actionary. The Russian Orthodox Church was the state religion, and the church was subservient to the state; it was in reality an agency of the state to carry out its absolutist policies. All other religions were suppressed and oppressed. The peasants were kept in a state of ignorance and superstitious darkness. The priests were for the most part untrained, ignorant men completely subservient to their superiors. One procurator of the Holy Synod, Pobedonostsev, plainly and cynically declared that an illiterate people were easier to rule. A fundamental feature of the policy was complete Russification, to be brought about by compulsion if necessary. This covered all phases of life, including language and religion. That brought the Jews within the circle of governmental action. Not only were they of another religious faith, but they formed a community, separate and exclusive, which would not assimilate with the Gentiles. They had never had a happy time, but it was not until the early 1880's that bloody persecution began. Before that restrictive measures kept them strictly within bounds. In the eighteenth century many Jews had been brought within the borders of the Russian state by the partition of Poland and the annexation of territories in the southwest. A law was promulgated in 1804, forbidding the Jews to settle in central Russia and fixing a "pale of settlement" within which the Jews must live. Later the regulations were made more stringent, the Jews being forbidden to settle outside the towns and villages even in the sections where they were allowed to locate. The statutes became steadily more severe during the nineteenth century. Only a limited number of Jews could matriculate in government educational institutions, and with few exceptions none were admitted to government service.[10]

These restrictions and frustrations were only the beginning of troubles. The Czar Alexander II was assassinated in 1881, after many previous attempts to put an end to his life.[11] This naturally led his son and successor Alexander III to frown on, and disrupt if possible, any liberal movement. But it was particularly calamitous for the Jews, for the report was circulated that they were responsible for the attack on the late czar. This was followed by a period of extreme anti-Semitism. The new czar, together with several

[10] George Vernasky, *op. cit.*, pp. 174 f.
[11] *Ibid.*, p. 171.

counselors, among them the cynical "Grand Inquisitor" Pobedonostsev, inaugurated a policy aimed at the destruction of the Jews.
Then followed at intervals bloody pogroms, or organized massacres of helpless Jews in various parts of the country. These pogroms
were sponsored by the government, though the officials at headquarters would make the announcement that they were

spontaneous expressions of the resentment of the populace against
the hated and despised Jews. In 1888 a group of government officials
condemned the policy of persecution but to no avail. Alexander III
and his successor, Nicholas II, were bent on ruining the Jewish communities so the pogroms continued and the Jews suffered and died.
Again in 1890 other Russian leaders sought to influence the tzar but
could accomplish nothing. Finally Pleve, who became Minister of the
Interior in 1902, definitely adopted a policy of persecution against the
Jews, blaming them for the revolutionary movements against the
government.[12]

It is not essential to give a complete recital of the years during
which the bloody work went on. Voices were raised against the
drastic policy, but they were unheeded. The first Duma met in
1906, with twelve Jews representing their communities. This body
went so far as to condemn the government for its part in the
pogrom at Bolastok, and within two days the Duma was dissolved
by the czar. The later Dumas were more subservient to the authorities and even became strongly anti-Semitic. Thus the opposition
continued until the end of the old regime. Russia entered World
War I, and during this period the pogroms went on unabated.
The Jews were distrusted because of their "international sympathies," and many were punished for treason despite the fact
that they supported the war. When the Russian forces were retreating after the humiliating defeat of Tannenberg, their anger
and resentment were vented upon the Jews. Much blood was shed,

[12] Leonard Detweiler, "The Jew in Russia" (unpublished), is authority for this and
other statements in this section.

and a half million Jews were torn away from their homes and deported to other parts of the country.

Then came the Bolshevik revolution under Lenin in 1917. While this was the turning point and the beginning of a new era, it took years before the Jews could find rest and security. They were caught between the conflicting parties and were blamed for subversive activities by both the Bolsheviks and the White Army. In the Ukraine and Belorussia, at least 100,000 Jews were killed during the civil war—some say as many as 200,000. Jews were not killed because they belonged to the Jewish religion, but because they—as was true of many others—were not in harmony with Bolshevik ideals. The Jewish section of the Communist party, called the Yevsektsia (better known as Yevkom), was set up to handle the many problems which the Jews presented in the new economy. In this purpose they were in full accord with the Communist plans for all Russia. What was proposed for Judaism was in line with the procedure with respect to Christianity. Synagogues were transformed into clubs. Cultural and philanthropic institutions were destroyed. The Hebrew language was not to be taught in elementary and middle schools, though it was allowed in higher schools and in the home. This was in accord with the law of 1918 which completely secularized education. Hebrew was looked upon as the language of a cult or a luxury product of a bourgeois society. Consequently, Hebrew books and newspapers were prohibited, regardless of their content, and in particular the Zionist movement was condemned as a middleclass reactionary movement.

The Yevsektsia was dissolved in 1930. It must be made clear that the activity of this organization was a part of the Communist program to destroy all organizations and activities which were opposed to the revolution and its purpose. It did not aim at a persecution of the Jews because they belonged to an alien race but because they were a religious body not in harmony with the aims of the Communists. This may have been poor comfort to the Jews while the persecution was in progress; but they saw, as we can see now, that a different principle was at work which in the end

78

would mean a different outlook for the Jewish inhabitants of the country.

From this point the story of the Jews in relation to the Russian state merges in the wider record of the changes which have taken place with respect to all minority groups in the Soviet Union. One or two statements must be added because the Jews are different and have had, and continue to have, problems which are peculiar to themselves. They, with other minority peoples, have been encouraged to form locally autonomous groups. These have been formed in the Ukraine, the Crimea, and eastern Siberia. A quotation from Sidney and Beatrice Webb will add needed information:

> Nevertheless, it cannot be denied that all the blessings of security from pogroms and freedom to enter the professions that the USSR accords to the Jews involve in practice their acceptance of the Soviet regime, and make, on the whole, for assimilation. The policy of the Soviet Union accordingly meets with persistent opposition and even denigration from the world wide organization of Zionists, among whom the building up of the "national home" in Palestine brooks no rival.[13]

We have for obvious reasons given special attention to the Jewish minority in the Soviet Union, but there are other and important minorities which have been subject to a new kind of handling. The czarist policy was one of complete Russification. This included all the minority groups. They were to conform in language, political loyalty, and organization, as well as in religion, to the overwhelming Russian majority. The annoying fact that conformity did not result did not dampen the ardor of the czar and his associates. Their stubbornness and blindness at this and a hundred other points resulted in their complete elimination in 1917.

Looking at the new policy as a whole, one is struck with the wide difference between what the Soviet Union is putting into effect and the policy of the United States with its minority groups.

---

[13] *Soviet Communism: a New Civilization,* as quoted in *When Peoples Meet,* ed. Alain Locke and Bernard J. Stern, p. 679.

Our country has been dubbed the "melting pot," in which the different groups are expected to merge, lose their former distinctive features, and become completely amalgamated with Americans in all their ways. It may take time to bring this about, but nevertheless it is the only thought about minority groups in the minds of most Americans. On the other hand the policy of the Soviets has been to allow local and racial autonomy, the government standing by each separate group in its purpose to retain its own distinctiveness, language, traditions, and customs—with the understanding of course that there must be complete acceptance of, and adherence to, the fundamental tenets of the Communist regime.

The Soviet constitution of 1936 is the latest pronouncement with respect to racial and minority groups:

Equality of rights of citizens of the U. S. S. R. irrespective of their nationality or race in all spheres of economic, state, cultural, social and political life is an indefeasible law. Any direct or indirect restriction of the rights, or conversely, and establishment of direct or indirect privileges for citizens on account of their race or nationality, as well as any advocacy of racial or national exclusiveness or hatred and contempt, is punishable by law.[14]

Our chief interest in this volume is the relation of one racial group to another, and one does not get very far into an investigation of the Soviet Union without beginning to realize that the racial problem is not a problem by itself but one which is a part of another, that of basic human rights. When the Russian Revolution did away with all special privilege and asserted the rights of all men as being fundamentally equal, it swept away the greatest barrier to human progress. We revolt at the ruthlessness of the revolution, the denial of God, and the attempt to do away with religion, together with other aspects of its Communist program; but, when all is said and done, we must recognize the overwhelm-

[14] Louis Wirth, "The Problem of Minority Groups," *The Science of Man in the World Crisis,* ed. Ralph Linton, p. 3718. See also Corlis Lamont, *op. cit.,* p. 1498.

ing fact that one of the greatest steps forward in human progress is to be credited to what the Soviet Union has accomplished. It was man, the common man, equal and free, who was placed in the center of the entire program. Lenin and his corevolutionists did not set out to solve the race problem as such; they were dealing with what was more basic. There are countries in which there is no clash of races but in which man as man has not come to his own, for the simple reason that society has been stratified horizontally with great inequalities between men at different levels. Our American problem of industrial unrest is an illustration in point. Race is one aspect of this larger and more basic problem. The Russian Revolution was aimed at the citadel of privilege and rank, and when men were recognized as men, with no man inherently higher or lower than another, the race problem was settled almost automatically. Racism, the assumption of inherent superiority of one group over another, was officially banned by governmental action. It lost its significance with the disappearance of privilege.

The most evident aspect of the application of the new idea is the political organization of the Soviet Union. The very name of the new political entity is illuminating, Union of Soviet Socialist Republics, a union of more or less separate and different states. A soviet in its simplest form, the village and town soviet, is a local governing body consisting of representatives of workmen, soldiers, and peasants. At bottom, then, there is real democracy. This must ever be kept in mind. It can readily be forgotten in the fact that at the top democratic forms of administration have not as yet been achieved. Joseph Stalin is virtually a dictator despite the formal election to his position as head of the government. This is a weakness which must ultimately be changed, or the whole structure will be in danger of collapse. But underneath this superstructure of an imposed dictatorship lies the foundation of essential local democracy, and in that lies the hope of the future.

On the basis of the differences between the various sections of the vast domain of the Soviet Union, separate and more or less independent republics were set up, much like the states of the United

81

States of America. There are sixteen of these constituent republics, ranging in population from 114,337,428 in the largest, Soviet Russia proper, to 469,000 in the smallest, the Karelo-Finnish Republic. But it is even more remarkable that in the large states local groups which are different from the surrounding population are encouraged to form themselves into self-governing units with a very considerable degree of freedom of action and local responsibility. This is one of the most important and significant features of the whole Soviet idea. To quote:

But the widest departure from the prevailing pattern of ethnic nationalism is the Soviet program of minority cultural autonomy. Here the principle of self-determination has been incorporated into the basic structure of the state, which is considered permanently multinational on a cultural, religious, and institutional basis, and only politically and economically federated.[15]

Another testimony may be given:

This recognition on the part of the Soviet government of the right to self-determination for minority groups of whatever category has been and continues to be the strength of the Soviet Union.[16]

There is genuine equality in political rights "irrespective of color, race, creed or language." To see to it that this policy shall become permanent, and that it shall be the possession of all, the schools have been charged with the solemn obligation to make the facts of race and human equality an integral part of their curriculum. History, geography, and literature are taught with this in mind. The younger generation is not to lose the outlook and vision of those who passed through the revolution and caught its enthusiasm. There seem to be no loopholes in this attempt to bring about a new era of racial understanding.

Is this too roseate a picture of the situation in the Soviet Union?

[15] *When Peoples Meet,* ed. Locke and Stern, p. 654.
[16] Hiton Hanna, "Russia and Inter-Race Relations." (Unpublished.)

It certainly represents the official attitude and the ideal which the leaders of the revolution had in view. But does it represent the actual condition which exists among the peoples of Russia at the present time? Many times over since the great change in government three decades ago, force has been used to bring about unity. It might be called civil war, but in reality it was the forcible subjection of groups of people to Communist principles. The Cossacks were thus subjugated, and so were the Jews. That is, there was intolerance of views which were in any way subversive of the political, economic, social, educational, and religious purposes of the Bolsheviks. This rough handling of any kind of opposition has been continued and is being shown in the relations of the Soviet Union to the people of the Baltic states. How such coercion, resulting in suppression and expulsion of thousands of people from their homes, can be squared with any profession of belief in the rights of man is difficult to see.

Again the Bolshevik theory that all issues can be solved by inaugurating an official program of political, economic, and social reform fails to probe to the center of the problem of human relations. While it is possible to point to laws and regulations which clearly demand racial equality, the question arises whether the minds and hearts of the people have been changed so that they have really become friendly toward those whom they formerly persecuted and so that we can count on a continuation of relations which now on the surface are happy but which might be very difficult if conditions should change.

Yet great wisdom is being shown. The smaller groups in the Soviet republics are encouraged to develop their own distinctive customs and traditional characteristics. They are all required to learn Russian as the common language of the entire Soviet Union, but they are urged to cultivate the use of their own languages and literatures among themselves. No more important single policy could have been inaugurated. The Poles through a hundred years and more retained their essential cohesion as a nation, though partitioned off as parts of three different nations, through the bonds of language and religion. Both of these were cherished as priceless possessions. The Soviets have learned this lesson and have wisely fostered language autonomy. Slowly but surely they are coming to the same conclusion in respect of religion, especially among the minority groups such as the Jews, Moslems, Buddhists, and others.

Much remains to be done. Religion must be recognized as is not the case at the present time. Democracy must be carried to the higher levels of governmental organization. Socialism has yet to be adjusted to the different levels of human ability. But with all this the Soviet Union stands before the world as the only land, with the exception of Brazil, where racism is completely repudiated; where no assumption of inherent superiority of any group over any other is allowed; where the minority groups are possessed of a new self-respect; where youth can allow their ambitions to soar, knowing that there is no extraneous, arbitrary barrier to fulfillment, except the limits of their own abilities and perseverance. When this condition—even with all its drawbacks —is reviewed against the background of the Russian past it fills one with hope for other lands where similar conditions do not exist. It also makes certain that no fundamental change can be expected in these other countries without some powerful motivation, far more persuasive than that which to the present has been exercising its influence in these places among the people as a whole.

Chapter V

Group and Race Tensions in India

It will be recalled that Ales Hrdlicka in his classification of the races did not know what to do with the Indian people. He could not find a place for them in any of the three great divisions into which most of the people of the world could be more or less comfortably fitted.[1] And yet here is a land with a population of about 389,000,000 according to the 1941 census, so complex in its ethnic mixtures that it must be set off by itself. Eugene Pittard states "that from the high Himalaya valleys to Cape Comorin and Ceylon there is complete lack of morphological unity" and that "India appears as an isolated anthropological province with her own particular characters in the great Asiatic ensemble." He hazards the conjecture that "India will appear as one of the most ancient of human territories; on Indian soil primitive humanity must have evolved through the same stages as those represented by the European civilizations."[2] What is quite evident is that we have to deal with a population problem quite different from that in any other great land surface on the earth.

But with all the difficulties involved much progress has been made in recent years. Discoveries in the valley of the Indus since the turn of the century have quite upset theories which had previously been held with no thought of successful contradiction. These new finds will be considered in their place but are mentioned now because they have made necessary new hypotheses as to the way in which the Indian population came to be what it is at the present time. Many racial and subracial groups have poured into India in the past four or five thousand years—it may

[1] *The Scientific Aspects of the Race Problem*, p. 186.
[2] *Race and History*, pp. 390, 391, 388.

be that some came even earlier. Negrito, Mongoloid, Mediterranean, Aryan, Hun, Turk, Jew, Persian, Mongol, and Nordic are included in the list, with the possibility of one or two others.

We can see at once that representatives of all the three great racial stocks have made their contribution, whites, yellow-browns, and blacks. The ethnic history of India is in reality that of a succession of waves of immigrants coming into the land from the north, and possibly by sea from the west. They waged war with those who had come before, driving them to the south and mingling with them, so that the races became inextricably confused. Since the direction of the successive irruptions was from the north to the south, it is to be expected that the purer strains will be found in the north, especially among the peoples who came in after the former groups had been more or less amalgamated. We shall see that this is the case, at least with those peoples whose coming can be traced with a comparatively high degree of probability.[3]

The Negritos came into India and passed through, going south and east into the island world of the Indian and Pacific Oceans, but leaving some of their number like driftwood along the seashore. They are to be found scattered in the central and southern parts of India, in the mountains and hills, far from the teeming populations of the plains and river valleys, hidden off in the jungles, and having little to do with their fellows. The Kadara, Malasaras, and others are known and have been studied. Only 14,631 tribesmen of Negrito blood have been listed in the recent census, but undoubtedly they were far more numerous in the past and have made their contribution to India's racial complex.

Not many years ago Indian historians and anthropologists spoke of the Dravidians as being the basic stock before the coming of the Aryan. Now it is believed that the Dravidian was preceded by the so-called proto-Dravidian or the proto-Australoid. Neglected until recently by students, many tribes are now identified as belonging to these early immigrants. They are found in various

---

[3] I am indebted in this section to a paper by Donald F. Ebright, "India's Population and Racial Elements." (Unpublished.)

parts of the country and are known as "hill tribes." Their names are too numerous to list here, but again they are noted because they too mingled their blood with the blood of those who came after them and helped to make the Indian what he is today. At this early stage people of the Mongoloid stock trickled into the country from the northeast down through the jungles of Assam and formed the substratum of the population of Bengal in and around the lower reaches of the Ganges and Brahmaputra rivers.

When we come to the genuine Dravidian, we are in another world. "Dravida" is a Sanskrit word meaning "southern," and such they were to the Aryans who came into India from the north and drove these people southward, looking down upon them and yet mingling with them to produce the typical Indian of the central and upper Ganges Valley. Who were these Dravidian people, who came into the country in waves probably by both land and sea? The surprising verdict is that they were members of the Mediterranean peoples of southern Europe, early wanderers who, daring to leave their fatherland far behind, came to distant India and became the most important racial stock in that country. These men had wavy or even curly black hair, were of medium stature, had narrow heads and faces, generally dark eyes, and white though swarthy skin with a marked tendency to become dark under the action of the sun. The third and most remarkable wave of these intruders has been identified by some scholars with the makers of the Indus Valley civilization and the building of the ancient and now destroyed cities of Mohenjodaro and Harrapa, one near the mouth and the other on the upper reaches of the Indus River in western India. This civilization has been recovered and made known by the archaeological work of Sir John Marshall. Much still remains to be done; much will never be known; but the facts which have come to light indicate that centuries—how long no one knows—before the coming of the Aryan a civilization had been developed which bears favorable comparison with that which existed at the same period in Mesopotamia, which in turn was dug out of the ground and made known during the nineteenth century. The only statement which is relevant to our purpose here is that one Indian people had developed a worthy culture before the coming of the Aryans and doubtless influenced the development of the culture of the later immigrants.

Until recently the history of India has been thought to begin with the coming of the Aryans. We do not know when they arrived, but they probably came in small groups about 1800 B.C. or even later. They evidently belonged to the widely scattered group of peoples who for ages roamed the grassy pasture lands extending from west central Asia to the shores of the Baltic. "Aryan" is the name given to that branch of the Indo-Europeans which was separated for a long period from the main body and which in turn became divided, one branch penetrating Persia and becoming the Iranians of history, the people from whom came the prophet Zoroaster, and the other coming down through the northwest passes into India and spreading out fanlike in the Land of the Five Rivers, the Punjab, and later far down into the Ganges Valley. They were tall white men with narrow skulls, very courageous and daring, speaking the Sanskrit language and worshiping the gods of high heaven, the atmosphere, and the earth. They were extremely religious and early developed a priesthood, the Brahmans, who to this day exercise a most powerful influence on the life of India, social and economic as well as religious. These priests soon began to compose hymns of praise addressed to their gods. The collection of over a thousand of these hymns has come down to us as the Rig-Veda, the oldest literary product of any of the Indo-European peoples, east or west.

The coming of the Aryans did not end migrations into India. India has known repeated inroads since that distant day—sporadic raids, which were only temporary in character, by Huns and Tatars from across the mountains, and two conquests which have influenced all subsequent Indian history. The first was that of the Moslems, beginning with the raids of Mahmud of Ghazni from Afghanistan about A.D. 1000. This finally eventuated in the famed glories of the Mogul Dynasty, culminating in the reign of Akbar the Great (1556-1605), one of the greatest rulers in Indian history. During the palmy days of this dynasty almost all India was united under one sway. These Moguls came in as conquerors and made hundreds of thousands of converts to the Islamic faith, so that as a result of their initial impulse and later aggression Moslems number 90,000,000 in India today. But with all these political, social and religious developments, there was little change in the racial texture of Indian society. The original invaders, comparatively few in number, intermarried with the native population, thus affecting the racial type; but the Moslems in India for the most part are of the same race as the Hindus, with whom they live in close contact in almost every part of North India. In the Punjab the foreign element is only 15 per cent.

Somewhat different is the story of the second conquest, that of the European, which began with the landing of the Portuguese Vasco da Gama on the southwest coast in 1498 and has continued until our day. The Dutch, French, British, and even the Danish have had their part in the conquest and domination of India. The number of Europeans has never at one time been large. Each of the major groups mingled with the native population, but the British mingling with the Indians has been far more noticeable and significant, so that the Anglo-Indian group, though it is inconsiderable in size, must be taken into account as a source of social tension wherever found.

This fairly extended presentation of India's racial constitution seems necessary not only because it is a unique phenomenon but because the problems of racism in that country have been produced by it. We do not know what tensions existed during the earlier ages of contact. We can only imagine that they must have been severe and long continued. Limited knowledge extends back only to the time when the Aryans came into contact with the Dravidians about 1800 B.C., and even for the centuries which followed exact knowledge is scarce and fragmentary. What is sure is that the proud Aryans looked down upon the dark-skinned and smaller Dravidians, but could not resist the impulse to mingle with them. The result was the Aryo-Dravidian, whiter in the north and shading off into the darker hues as one advances into the south where the Dravidian blood more and more predominated. This mingling, however, must have taken place against violent opposition. The line was clearly drawn between Aryans and Dravidians and a strong attempt must have been made to prevent intermarriage. The Sanskrit word for caste is *varna,* whose primary meaning is "color." The use of that word reveals much. What evidently happened was that the white Aryans essayed to preserve the color of their skin, or in other words the purity of their blood, by erecting a "color bar." They were proud of their race and wanted to continue to be separate and distinct from the dusky Dravidians. The effort was a complete failure. In course of time—we do not know how long—the distinction between the colors was blotted out, and the races mingled freely. The Aryan strain was naturally more pronounced in the north, while in the far south the Dravidian remained almost, if not entirely unmixed.

The Caste System and Untouchability

One of the first things of which a visitor to India becomes conscious is the division of the people into castes. This applies of course to the Hindu community alone and not to the Moslems or other lesser groups. What is a caste? It is a group of people separated from others by several well-recognized marks. One among these is occupation, but this is by no means distinctive of many castes, whose members are found in various occupations or in professional life. Another and more important mark of caste is the regulation forbidding members of different castes to eat together, that is, to have social fellowship. This is adhered to very strictly in many cases, though it is customary for professional men—and others—in the higher castes to mingle in business and official life and come to know each other very well. Unfortunately this does not affect the women, who are secluded and are allowed to see only men belonging to their own immediate families. By far the strictest caste regulation is that which forbids intermarriage between members of different castes and subcastes. Here the rules are adamant and are adhered to when the less important regulations are relaxed. It is on this point that caste holds its deathlike grip upon the Hindus, with little prospect of change. The result is that caste is a divisive factor in Indian life and makes more difficult the national unity which the thoughtful people so much desire.

The origin and development of the caste system are more or less a mystery, and no theory has made its way to anything like universal acceptance. There is no indication that caste distinctions were known in the days when the songs of the Rig-Veda were written. In the latest part of the collections of hymns mention is made of four classes into which the population began to be divided. They were the Brahman priests, the warriors, the farmers, and the menials or Sudras. From analogy it would seem that this division took place gradually as the Aryans ceased to be nomadic or seminomadic and settled down as permanent dwellers on the land. We find the same phenomenon among the Israelites as they came into the land of Canaan. As desert dwellers they had been nomads; they became farmers and people of cities and towns. With this change social stratification took the place of the old, simple, democratic life in the desert, where no man was better than his neighbor and all performed the same tasks. There came into existence a king and a nobility, together with the warrior, the farmer, the artisan, and also the merchant.

We cannot trace as clearly the same process among the early Aryans, but the inevitable change in social and economic standing is surely indicated by the recorded division of the people into the four classes just mentioned. The Indian caste system is thus seen to have—partly at least—an economic origin. It took the firmer hold upon these people, however, because it soon became a part of their religious belief that caste regulations were based on divine commands. The Brahman priesthood at the top made their own position secure and fastened the system on the people so that it became fundamental to their whole outlook on life. Many harsh things have been said about caste, accusations which are warranted by the facts. Brotherhood and a feeling of national solidarity have fared badly in the presence of a system which locks people up into more or less watertight compartments and prevents the free intercourse of men of all classes in dealing with problems of common concern. What has been effected in recent decades of common purpose and unified planning for the future is a remarkable demonstration of a more fundamental solidarity underlying caste distinctions.

Caste has done well by the Hindu people at a number of points. It has acted as a system of social security and has prevented famine and starvation from taking the toll which might otherwise have followed drought and flood. The system has acted as a kind of trade guild and has kept up standards of workmanship. It "regulates prices, preventing cornering of commodities, and so forth." [4] Indeed, it may be shown that the system has actually "prevented the emergence of a class-problem. . . . The tremendous strength of the caste-organization in the economic field has prevented industrial exploitation developing to anything like a formidable degree." [5] All this and other favorable estimates have been made and cannot be gainsaid despite the unfavorable elements which reside in such a system. The fact is, however, that we have not yet touched one feature of the system which is truly reprehensible and casts a dark shadow over the Indian social system.

Allusion was made to the fact that the Sanskrit word for caste is *varna,* which means "color," and that in the fourfold division of the people as found toward the end of the Rig-Veda one

[4] John S. Hayland, *Indian Crisis,* p. 54.
[5] *Ibid.* pp. 55 f.

group, the Sudras, was spoken of as menials. Here we touch an entirely different feature of the Hindu social structure. All that has been said of caste up to the present has not been a matter so much of interracial tension as of class stratification among people racially homogeneous. We know something of such stratification in our Western society with its unfortunate ramifications. The originators of caste in India were white Aryans. They developed a social system which applied to their own people, but there were the dusky Dravidians. What were they to do with them? Aryans must preserve the whiteness of their skin and also use the dark-skinned people as servants and menials; but they failed in both aims, for in the course of times, as intermarriage between the two races became more and more common, a new racial type was produced. All the people came to be dusky so that the distinctions tended to fade out.

But a very remarkable thing took place. The menials, who at first belonged to a different race, in the course of the years could not be distinguished racially from those above them in the social scale. What eventually happened was that they became outcastes, with no place in the social and religious life of the recognized castes. So the division which was originally made to keep the races apart still obtained—with an intensity not known in the early days—but now it kept apart two groups who belonged to the same race. What was once true racism, the assumption of inherent superiority of one race over another, was transmuted into class animosity and antagonism, the assumption of inherent superiority of one group of the same race over another. Religious conviction intensified the sense of superiority, for according to the universally accepted doctrine of karma the man at the bottom of the social ladder deserved the treatment he received as much as the Brahman at the top, who felt that his exalted position was in accord with the very order of the universe. Each was reaping the reward which was due because of his deeds in countless previous lives.

A quotation from an Englishman long resident in India, J. S.

Hoyland, will present succinctly yet powerfully the condition of these unfortunate people:

> The first thing to recognize is that here is a mass of some fifty million of our fellowcitizens in the British Commonwealth who by immemorial social and religious sanctions are denied the elementary rights of human beings. Economically they are condemned to a miserable existence as village serfs, or as scavengers in the towns. They can only gain a livelihood through performing functions of an indescribable nature, which often involve close personal contact all day long with human filth. The only food they can get is often what others would regard as carrion. Worse still are their psychological sufferings, the knowledge that the great mass of their fellow-countrymen look upon them as defiling, and the permanent condition of fear which such an environment imposes upon them.[6]

It is difficult to exaggerate the condition in which these people find themselves. They are known as untouchables, a correct description of the attitude of caste men and women to these people of their own race who for many centuries have been subjected to this abusive treatment. This disdainful attitude started as racism, but no claim is made now that these people belong to a different ethnic group from the surrounding population. The original racism has been carried over, not only with unabated intensity but with greater poignancy, caused by the religious conviction that these people are inherently inferior and polluting by cosmic decree, which works out from one rebirth to another by the inexorable law of karma.

No wrong has ever been perpetrated upon a people worse than this. These outcastes are not within the pale of Hindu religious life and are not permitted access to the temples. An attempt has been made to change this condition but with little or no success. Because of the almost universal attitude of hostility to the outcastes great honor is due Mr. Gandhi and a resolute group of reformers among the Hindus themselves who have set themselves to re-

[6] *Ibid.*, p. 62.

duce the pitiableness of untouchability. They have been so far successful that various political parties in India have made the mitigation of untouchability a plank in their platforms. The highest praise, however, must be given to the Christian missionaries who in the past half century have devoted much of their energy to work among the depressed classes. They have demonstrated that these most abjectly despised people can be lifted up and set upon their feet and given hope and confidence for the future. When an outcaste, only one or two generations removed from the miserable condition in which his forebears have lived for centuries, sits at a desk in a government office next to a proud, high-caste Brahman, something begins to work in the Brahman's mind. He may continue to look down on his fellow-worker as inherently inferior, but he is compelled to recognize that something profoundly significant, fraught with immeasurable possibilities for the future, has taken place.

One of the most notable phases of the present situation is that the outcaste has begun to feel a sense of new possibilities lying before him. This naturally makes him restless and dissatisfied. He has found a mouthpiece in B. R. Ambedkar, an outcaste himself, but one who received the best education the West as well as India had to offer. To the surprise of the entire Indian community he was made dean of the faculty of law in Bombay University on the basis of winning out in a competitive examination for the position. In 1943 he was appointed minister of labor in the Indian Cabinet. His rise to so prominent a position of leadership, together with the new life in the outcaste community and the convictions of Indian reformers and Christian missionaries, argues well for a new life for as wretched a community as can be found in any country anywhere.

From the beginning the Christian mission has been compelled to deal with the problem of caste and untouchability in one way or another. One of the earliest Jesuit missionaries in India was Robert de Nobile, who reached his field in 1605. This priest studied the situation and soon decided to make the upper classes the object of his efforts. To do this he came to the conclusion that he must leave "the whole caste system unassailed and untouched." [7] With this settled, Nobile took the consequences and was willing that in the Christian church caste regulations should be recognized. This meant segregation in worship, the mass, and other forms of ministration. All the evils of the caste system thus came trooping into the Roman Catholic Church and have continued to be tolerated from that day to this. Speaking of the work of this church in recent days, Latourette summarizes the situation briefly: "India continued to place its stamp on Roman Catholics. Caste differences persisted and brought down on the Church the criticism of at least one radical Indian group." [8] The policy of the Protestant missionaries has been different. Realizing that caste is contrary to the fundamental principles of brotherhood, they have resolutely set themslves against this evil. It is a continuous battle, not always successfully waged. The first test comes when a high-caste convert is invited to kneel at the altar and partake of the elements at the same Communion table with the oucaste convert. Other tests inevitably follow, and they are met in the spirit of Christian fellowship. Too much is at stake, these missionaries realize, to fail at points which involve the whole conception of brotherhood in the church of Christ.

The British Occupation

The age-old evil of untouchability is purely Indian, but that troubled land is in the throes of another form of tension caused by the presence of the British as the dominant power. It is manifestly impossible to present here, even in outline, the story of the origins, growth, and recent situation of the British overlordship in India. It is sufficient to say that until 1859 the British connection with India was through the East India Company. This huge corporation started out as a business venture pure and

---

[7] Julius Richter, *A History of Missions in India*, p. 60.

[8] K. S. Latourette, *A History of the Expansion of Christianity*, VII (*Advance Through Storm*), 286.

simple, receiving its charter from time to time from Parliament; but as the decades passed, it took on more and more of the functions of government, with an increasing standing army composed of British and Indian soldiers commanded by British officers. The object of the company was to make as much money as possible for the stockholders at home, without the slightest tinge of altruism in their minds. In consequence the people of India were exploited. Enormous sums were made. Officers of the company could amass a fortune in twenty years in India, then return to Great Britain and live in luxury for the rest of their days. With exploitation went depreciation of the people. They were "natives," which came soon to be a term of contempt. All the evils of racism began to show themselves. There was, however, no slavery. The British, after a long period in which they were assiduous slavers and brought most of the Negro slaves from Africa to the United States, turned against the trade and did more than any other people to end the nefarious traffic. But except for holding human beings as chattels the British East India Company used India and the peoples of India as a means of their own enrichment.

In 1857 the Sepoy Rebellion broke out. Indian soldiers (sepoys) in the company's army revolted, in many cases killed their British officers, and tried to end foreign rule in India. The rebellion failed, but it had its effect, leading the British Parliament to put the old "John Company" out of existence and take over the control of India directly through a member of the cabinet and his staff. Queen Victoria became the empress of India and issued a celebrated proclamation "to the Princes, Chiefs, and People of India." In this document the queen states, *inter alia:*

We hold ourselves bound to the natives of our Indian territories by the same obligations of duty which bind us to all our other subjects. . . . Firmly relying ourselves on the truth of Christianity, and acknowledging with gratitude the solace of religion, we disclaim alike the right or desire to impose our convictions on any of our subjects. . . . And it is our further will that, so far as may be our subjects of whatever race or creed, be freely and impartially admitted to office in our service. . . . . It is our earnest desire to stimulate the peaceful industry of India, to promote works of public utility and improvement, and to administer the government for the benefit of all our subjects therein.[9]

This truly noble pronouncement introduced a new era in the life of India.

That era may be said to have lasted until 1905. It was a half century of peace and prosperity such as India had never known before, at least in modern times. The *Pax Britannica* was the background and atmosphere in which progress was possible. For the first time in her history India learned what impartial justice in courts of law meant. It made no difference whether the defendant was a Brahman or an outcaste; he knew that he would receive equal treatment under the law. The British administrator, from the viceroy at the top to the local magistrate in a small district, was known as a man of honor and official integrity. Such was the high level of British public service that in the colonial empire everywhere confidence could be placed in the honesty of the local representative. The postal and telegraph systems, roads, and transportation by rail became excellent. Public works like canals and irrigation systems were built where they were needed. By these methods the dreadful effects of famine were mitigated, for men and women could be put to work and food could be conveyed to them with relative ease. Schools were introduced. By a grant-in-aid system mission schools were able to minister to a far greater number of people than their own funds would allow. Other items might be mentioned, but these are recounted in the attempt to be fair to the British administration against which so much is being rightly charged by Indian nationalists.

But in spite of all this and more, the Indians have felt that there was another side to the story, which was not appreciated by most of those who looked on from the outside. Gradually but

---

[9] Vincent A. Smith, *The Oxford Student's History of India*, Appendix A, pp. 366 f.

with increasing bitterness, during the long reign of Queen Victoria, Indians began to chafe under the overbearing attitude of British officials and businessmen. They realized that they were being denied certain human and social privileges which they had the right to expect. How this feeling would have developed and what the outcome would have been is problematical. An event did take place, however, which changed the entire situation and brought all the strands of ill feeling and criticism to a sudden focus. It was the victory of Japan over Russia in 1904-5. The outcome of this conflict was decisive and clear-cut—a powerful European power had been defeated and humiliated by a little nation in the East. Nothing like it had ever taken place. For over four hundred years the West had been increasingly and ever more aggressively dominant in Asia. The story must be read at length to be appreciated fully. But this era of aggression came to an end. Since 1905 the West has been on the defensive in the East. Nowhere was the effect of this victory more deeply significant than in India. The Indians had been made to believe that they could not resist successfully the might of Britain. They were not equal to the British—that had been made clear. So why should they wish to assert themselves? Such was the attitude which an Indian was supposed to have. All this was changed as in the twinkling of an eye. The Japanese were of the East, as were the Indians, and they had demonstrated their ability to cope with the West. Why could not the Indians do the same? Louis Fischer gives it as his own experience that "in one out of every three political conversations in India, the Indian I was talking to would mention the Russo-Japanese War of 1904-5." [10]

The agitation was deep and widespread. Within two years, in 1907, what was known as the Indian Unrest united the people in protest against certain aspects of British rule. From that beginning almost forty years ago a series of protests and demands have followed one after another, each going farther than the one preceding, until now the people of India are united in the de-

[10] *Empire*, p. 10.

mand for complete independence. This is not the place to deal with Indian nationalism and the problems that are involved in arriving at the goal of independence, but nationalism is so closely connected with our central theme of racism that some reference to it here cannot be avoided.

Many counts are listed against the presence of the British in India. Too much money is spent on the army and too little on education. The government is not exerting itself sufficiently to deal with the fundamental economic problem, India's poverty; it seems more intent on good returns to the British investor than on the conditions of the poor peasant in India. Indian leaders acknowledge that one half of the civil servants are now Indians, but they are deeply humiliated because the choice positions at the top are always reserved for the British. They may have their hand on many phases of the administration, but the British see to it that they themselves control the army, finance, and all relations with other countries. So the story goes, and it is very convincing. The Indian leaders have made good with the people, and unitedly they voice their protest and demand that they be free, with every function of government completely in Indian hands.

But the chief indictment and their most galling experience is the overbearing display of racial superiority on the part of the British official and businessman in their country. There are clubs to which the Indians cannot belong solely because they are Indians. This exclusiveness has been modified in recent years, but in a hundred ways, mostly small and each by itself insignificant, the Indians are made to feel that they are inferior because they are not British and their skin is of another color. One observer sums the whole matter up by a definite statement, "If a reference were taken among the people of India today on their chief grievance against the English the majority would undoubtedly say, it is racial and social discrimination." [11] Louis Fischer declares:

When I pinned him and other Indians down and demanded why, concretely, they objected to the British, the usual answer was that

[11] Paul Burt, "Racism in India." (Unpublished.)

the British regarded Indians and treated Indians as inferiors. Nobody likes being treated as an inferior by an intruder whose claim to ascendandancy rests on his strong right arm and the white color of his skin.[12]

With no attempt to enter deeply into the complicated problems of India's longed-for independence we may call attention to certain difficulties which arise, partly out of the race and group tensions we have been considering. Indians are seriously divided into innumerable groupings which jeopardize at the start the unity which must accompany political freedom if it is to endure. The caste system is very evidently a barrier to the possibility of a compact state, especially since the untouchables must become a part of that state. But other cleavages are equally difficult to overcome. Over two hundred languages and dialects keep the people apart. Even in the Indian National Congress, which is the very heart and center of the independence movement, the only means of communication which can be used is the tongue of their hatred overlords, the English language! In addition, over two hundred native states, large and small, are scattered over the country, each with its own ruler, its laws, and even its customs, thus forming a formidable bar to the greatly needed unity. And, finally, over and above all these is the overwhelming cleavage between Hindus and Mohammedans, which more than any other would seem to be unsurmountable as India draws closer and closer to the independence which all desire, which will undoubtedly come, but which no one seems to know how to handle for the best interests of all the people. A great change took place in the situation in India in the late spring and summer of 1946. A parliamentary commission, acting under the direct authority of the labor government in London, offered India political freedom even to the point of deciding for itself whether it would remain a self-governing dominion in the British Commonwealth of Nations or separate itself completely and become an independent nation. The sincerity of the offer

[12] *Op. cit.,* pp. 9 f.

and the subsequent transfer of authority to an interim Indian government under the leadership of Jawaharlal Nehru has cleared the atmosphere, and India looks forward with enthusiasm to the fulfillment of its long-cherished hope. The difficulties ahead are enormous and baffling. The initial difficulty seems to be in process of solution. Mr. Jinnah and his Moslem leaders have recently (October, 1945) consented to join the Hindus and other groups in setting up the interim government. They have accepted control of five bureaus and give promise of further co-operation.

It does not come within the compass of this book to deal with questions not connected with the relation of racial groups. The bitter struggles beween Hindu and Moslem in India is one between adherents of two religions who belong for the most part to the same racial group. We come, however, much closer to our chief issue when we discover that the tension between the British and the Indian has been considerably eased. Many Indians who only a few months ago, bitterly critical of their hated overlords, placed all the responsibility for India's ills on the British are now willing to concede that the British record is not all evil, that many good and indispensable things have come to India through Great Britain.

Two final outcroppings of racism will shed light on the main problem as it is faced in India. Everywhere in the cities is to be found a small group of "Anglo-Indians," which is the name used to designate those of mixed Indian and British blood. They number only a little over 100,000 and so do not bulk large in India's enormous population, yet they are important because of the position they occupy and the attitudes they represent. They are said to be "the most pathetic of India's minority groups." The British will have nothing to do with them socially; neither will the Indians. They on their part look down on the Indian seemingly more than the British do. They try to act, and want to be recognized and treated, like their British forebears. The worst features of racism come to the surface in their attitudes. They treat their

102

Indian servants more shabbily than others, venting their resentment and bitterness on those whom they consider their inferiors. Their position is not improving. Until recently they had almost the monopoly on certain lower government positions, on the railroads and in the telegraph and postal systems, but now that Indians are taking over most of the administration, they are losing out. Their only future economically would seem to lie in identification with the Indian community, whereas every aspiration they have leads them in the opposite direction. This summary description does not present the many exceptions to the various attitudes which have been presented.

The other special feature to be mentioned is the Indian abroad. This subject deserves much more space than can be allowed; it will appear again as we study South Africa and some of the islands of the South Seas. The exact number of Indians who have migrated is not known. The *Indian Year Book* for 1942-43 gives a total of over 3,750,000. The largest groups are naturally in near-by Burma, Ceylon, and British Malaya; but they have gone to South and East Africa, the West Indies, Fiji, Guiana, both British and Dutch, and to many other parts of the empire. Our reason for mentioning these immigrants here is twofold. In the first place they have not greatly improved their lot by journeying to distant lands. Caste regulations have been relaxed, and religious anatgonism is not so keenly felt, but financially and economically they are still at the bottom of the economic and social ladder. The other aspect of the situation is the estimate in which they are held by the white Britisher, and that is the same elsewhere as it is in India. The Indians are considered inferior and are treated as such. Only because of their labor are they wanted, and when there is no demand for that, they are excluded. What is ominous in the eyes of the Indian leaders is that, while India is a part of the British Empire, the Indians themselves have no status as citizens in many parts of the empire. Of the 11,000,000 square miles of territory in the em-

103

pire 8,000,000 are closed against the coming of the Indian emigrant. What conclusion is to be drawn? Only one for the Indians, namely, that they are not wanted in most parts of the empire to which they are forced to belong and from which they are eager to be separated. No stronger evidence can be given of the place which racism holds in the relations of two peoples than this most unfortunate cleavage in the British Empire.

Chapter VI

The Far East and the West

By the "Far East" we mean China and Japan. Unlike India, which is so heterogeneous racially that its people cannot be listed as belonging to any one of the main racial stems, the peoples of the Far East are clearly a branch of the yellow-brown peoples commonly designated as Mongoloid. This does not mean that the Chinese and the Japanese are exactly alike. They are to be distinguished not only by dress, customs, and language, but also by physical features. They are so much alike, however, that unless the peculiar physical features are well developed it is at times difficult to be sure whether the man who stands before you is a Chinese or a Japanese.

China

Among the Chinese there are different types. The most evident difference is that the man of the north is taller and larger than the man of the south. A more disconcerting difference is that of language. Three fourths of the Chinese, roughly those in the north, the west, and the east as far south as the Yangtze, speak the Mandarin dialect. It is the same tongue in all these areas with very slight regional differences between the Mandarin as spoken in Peiping, Nanking, and Chengtu. But in the southeastern part of the country a large number of dialects are found, some of which have a range of only a few miles, are spoken by a relatively small group of only a million or so people, and cannot be understood by neighboring Chinese. What these differences—and others which need not be mentioned here—indicate is that, while all the people in China are Mongoloid, the civilization which we think of as Chinese was originally that of the people in the north and northwest who carried their conquests into the south. What we know

105

as Chinese civilization came into being very gradually. It was not until a short time before the opening of our era that the people south of the Yangtze were included in the Chinese state. Very fortunately a common written language holds the peoples of the different sections together despite the differences in the spoken language. The magic of the written Chinese character is one of the bonds which has unified the culture of the entire Far East. An educated Korean or Japanese reads the Chinese character as readily as a Chinese.

So short a time ago as 1927 Eugene Pittard could say, "We know nothing about Chinese prehistory." [1] Archaeological research in north China in very recent years has disclosed an amazing number of facts which shed light on the origins of the culture and civilization of the entire region we are surveying. Chinese and Western students have uncovered evidence which makes clear that in northwest China one of the great world cultures had its origin. It seems to be native to this center and not dependent on any of the other world culture centers. One of these investigators declares that "as civilization advanced in the Old World it developed not one but two great centers of culture diffusion—the Near East on the one hand, China on the other. The latter country has in fact played a civilizing role in eastern Asia quite worthy of comparison with the better-known one assumed in the Occident by Babylonia and Egypt, by Greece and Rome." [2]

China being the culture source and center of a growingly splendid civilization, which at a number of periods in its long history surpassed that of Europe, what of the attitude toward other peoples and cultures? China grew up separated from other great nations, and looked upon herself as the "Middle Kingdom," the center of the earth and of all worth-while culture. There were other peoples around the boundaries, but they were manifestly of inferior culture—so the Chinese thought. This attitude of superiority became more pronounced during the period of the Man-

---

[1] *Race and History*, p. 397.

[2] Carl Whiting Bishop, *Origin of the Far Eastern Civilization: A Brief Handbook*, p. 51.

chu domination (1644-1912) than it had been in earlier ages. Despite sea and desert China had for many centuries carried on trade with peoples far distant. Chinese silks were known in Rome in the reign of Tiberius Caesar (A.D. 14-37), and trade in silk was carried on with Europe in the Middle Ages, [3] and so it continued for centuries. The chief route was that by way of the desert, although Chinese merchantmen were not unknown in the distant seas beyond India.

Not much can be learned from the Chinese sages about the attitude of the people in ancient times toward other races, but there are at least two illustrations of a liberal attitude on the part of the wise men themselves. One of these is to be found in the *Analects* of Confucius (Book XII, Chap. V). In a conversation one of his friends remarks that he is unfortunate in having no brothers. He is comforted by this noble response, "When the man of noble mind unfailingly conducts himself with self-respect, and is courteous and well-behaved with others, then all within the four seas are his brothers." [4] Some question has been raised about the inclusiveness of this statement, but we may take the interpretation of Arthur Waley as authoritative. His comment is that the four seas "bound the universe." [5] Thus we have from the fifth century before our era an expression of the possibility of brotherhood extending out as far as men are found.

The other illustration is taken from one of the most pronounced convictions of the philosopher Motse (also transliterated Mu-tze, Mu Ti, Mo Ti, etc.), who lived during the century after Confucius but before the time of Mencius, the greatest exponent of Confucius and his teaching. One of the cardinal doctrines of Motse was "universal love." He said:

[3] L. Carrington Goodrich, *A Short History of the Chinese People*, p. 41.

[4] Trans. William E. Soothill, p. 117.

[5] *The Analects of Confucius*, p. 164. This interpretation is endorsed by Dr. Hu Shih, the eminent authority on things Confucian, who in a personal note says, " 'Within the four seas' is the then known world, which included the barbarians," those who lived outside of China.

Partiality is to be replaced by universality. But how is it that partiality can be replaced by universality? Now, when every one regards the states of others as he regards his own, who would attack the other's states? Others are regarded like self. . . . Now, since universal love is the cause of the major benefits in the world, therefore, Motse proclaims universal love is right.[6]

It seems strange to us that this teacher should have been so strenuously opposed by Mencius that his doctrines have been sentenced "to the dark dungeon of obscurity for almost two millenniums."[7] Confucius and Motse were not as far apart in their sense of brotherhood as Motse's repudiation by Mencius would indicate. He was "snuffed out," as Herbert A. Giles put it, because he attacked Confucius at a number of other points and was looked upon as dangerous to his master's reputation by Mencius.[8] Yet now this old sage with his marvelous ideal seems to be coming into his own. Chinese may well be proud that so long ago one of their own race repudiated racism so completely.

The contact of the Far East with the Occident which especially concerns us is fairly recent. China had commercial relations with Europe for hundreds of years, and then came a time when she was cut off or cut herself off from such contacts. In addition to traders, Nestorian missionaries came into the country as early it may be as A.D. 505. Their great representative Alopen reached China in 635. In about two hundred years the Nestorian mission failed and left almost no traces, only to be brought out of oblivion by the discovery in north China in 1625 of what is known as the Nestorian tablet, which tells the story of the mission until 781. A Roman Catholic, John of Montecorvino, came to China in 1292 and was for a time successful, but when persecution arose, the work disappeared entirely. In the sixteenth century the Jesuits arrived and because of their mathematical and astronomical skill gained the good graces of the emperor. They retained their hold

[6] Yi-Pao Mei, *The Ethical and Political Works of Motse*, p. 88.

[7] Yi-Pao Mei, *Motse, the Neglected Rival of Confucius*, p. 87.

[8] *Confucianism and Its Rivals*, p. 107.

for 150 years, but between 1724 and 1858 they were practically out of the picture. The Chinese preferred to be left alone religiously as well as commercially. These were the only contacts with the West until a century and a half ago.

In the early nineteenth century England came knocking at the door and finally forced an entrance. The Russians also sought trade relations. The early embassies of these two powers reached an impasse over the *kowtow*. Chinese custom demanded that a foreign envoy should *kowtow* as he came into the presence of the emperor. This meant approaching the throne on hands and knees and at intervals touching the forehead to the floor. The Russians and the English would not conform. When it is realized that everyone who came into the august presence of the emperor, even the highest minister in the Chinese state, was obliged thus to *kowtow,* the reason for the requirement with respect to representatives of foreign powers is seen in clearer light. This act did not in itself indicate that these foreign ministers were looked upon as inferior to a Chinese prime minister. But, of course, to the English and Russian envoys it was humiliating in the extreme and could not be tolerated. As a result the English envoy "was dismissed without an audience and with a haughty mandate which clearly indicated that the Emperor regarded the King of England as the prince of a tributary state." [9] The Opium War was fought in 1839-40 between England and China, as a result of which China was compelled to open certain ports to trade and to deal with the disliked and (to them) inferior strangers from afar.

One of the earliest provisions demanded by the Western powers was "extraterritoriality" (sometimes shortened into "extrality"). The agreement, embodied in all the early treaties, was that citizens of Western nations were not amenable to the laws of China nor could they be tried in, or be compelled to carry cases to, Chinese courts of law. They were under the law of the land from which they came, administered by consuls and other agents of the various powers. It is hard to see how the Western governments could have

[9] K. S. Latourette, *The Chinese: Their History and Culture,* I, 347.

done otherwise at that time. Court and legal procedures were unlike those in Western countries; the judges in many cases were venal and expected to receive a bribe for favorable decisions; a witness could be put to torture to compel him to make confession or to testify; the punishments inflicted were frequently barbarous; the law was not uniform and could be manipulated at the will of the judge. No civilized foreign government could consent to subject one of its citizens to such treatment and to such uncertain procedure. Undoubtedly racism played its part in that the sense of superiority of European nations made it much easier to demand extraterritoriality of a people who were unable to defend themselves against Western armaments. It placed the badge of inferiority upon the Chinese, a mark of humiliation which they were compelled to bear for decades. It is now a thing of the past, and foreigners are subject to Chinese courts as Chinese are to the courts of the countries to which they go.

Closely connected with extraterritoriality was the founding of settlements in treaty ports in which China had no jurisdiction. There were a number of these, the chief examples being the international settlements in Shanghai and Tientsin. These small bits of territory in the midst of China, controlled by joint action of foreign powers, were also a sign of weakness and continued to exist until the Japanese occupation of all the centers where they were located. The United States possessed the benefits of the extraterritoriality clause in the treaties and in the joint control of settlements in China, and thus shared in the general attitude of a superior power dealing with China.

But of all the relations of the Western powers with China, that which has been most humiliating has been the exclusion of Chinese from Western countries. This is a problem shared by Australia and Canada, but has had its chief development in the United States. The first Chinese came to America in connection with the California gold rush, following the discovery of gold in 1848. They were well received, for they provided the cheap labor which was needed. Chinese laborers built the Central Pacific Railroad from

San Francisco to Ogden, Utah, the last link in binding east and west in the United States. But when they came in greater numbers and a workingman's party was organized in California, there began to be trouble, which led to a race riot as early as 1871. The first exclusion bill was passed in 1882, barring Chinese laborers from entering the United States for a period of ten years. This attitude continued until 1902 when a new exclusion bill was passed, not for a term of years, but with the intention that it should be perpetual. As in most expressions of racism so in the case of Chinese exclusion, the economic motive played an important role, but it is always easier to carry the economic motive to a more drastic outcome when racial differences and antipathies can be called in to add bitterness and prejudice against what is strange and foreign. It should of course be realized that exclusion was not complete. Diplomatic agents of the Chinese government, students, visitors, and businessmen were allowed to enter on special passport visas. What the exclusion bill aimed at was to prevent the coming of Chinese who would become permanent residents.

Fortunately the exclusion of Chinese is now a thing of the past. The last governmental measure which excluded the Chinese was the Immigration Bill which went into effect in 1924. Further mention will be made of this when we deal with the Japanese, with whom it caused far more difficulty. There was little reason to think that the United States was ready for repeal of Chinese exclusion when it came with surprising rapidity in the autumn of 1943. Even so keen a student of world affairs as Dr. Paul Hutchinson could be led to write earlier that year:

Yet not only are those members of Congress who are most eager to see all marks of racial discrimination wiped from our statutes unanimously of the opinion that it would be impossible at this time to introduce such legislation with the slightest hope of success, but some whose judgment carries great weight believe that if such a bill confining the effort to do racial justice to the Chinese would reach the floor, it will be seized on by some Congressman as a pretext for an outburst of racial vituperation which will do irreparable damage to America's standing with the peoples of the East.[10]

This writer cautiously says in his preface:

It may easily prove that there will be developments between the day when the manuscript leaves my hands and the day when it appears as a published book that will force changes in judgment on details of the world situation.[11]

He wrote more truly than he knew, for almost at the moment the book was published a Congressional enactment became law which placed the Chinese on the same quota basis with European immigrants. They could now come into our country as permanent residents at the rate of 106 or 107 a year—not enough surely to do serious damage to our American civilization! Chinese born outside the United States might also become American citizens. It is impossible to overestimate the ultimate effect of these legislative changes. They are not much more than gestures, but gestures at such a time as this and in relation to such a vital issue are most significant. How was it possible for such a radical change to be brought about and that without "an outburst of racial vituperation" which some members of Congress envisaged? Several causes can be identified. China was our ally in war against Japan and was having a very difficult time; public opinion in the United States, especially among the intelligent leaders of thought, had been aroused by propaganda of a high type; Wendell Willkie's book *One World* had had a phenomenal circulation; and last but not least Madame Chiang Kai-shek had been touring America, making most effective addresses, one of which was before a joint session of the two houses of Congress. To exclude a people on the basis of racial inferiority could be nothing less than the height of absurdity when that people was so magnificently represented by a woman of refinement, culture, intelligence, and moral and spirit-

[10] *From Victory to Peace*, p. 115.
[11] *Ibid.*, p. viii.

ual power. At any rate by a happy combination of circumstances a new policy was inaugurated, the effect of which during the years to come must be an extension of the same policy to other Asiatic races and nations.

Japan

When it comes to the racial affiliations of the Japanese, we are to a considerable extent in the dark. We do not know the racial strain or strains which distinguish them from the Koreans and the Chinese. So far as their racial substratum is concerned it is clearly Mongoloid, thus linking the Japanese closely with their fellow Mongoloids on the mainland. But several questions come immediately to mind. Were the Mongoloids who came to Japan mingled with a race already in Japan and were these previous immigrants people from the mainland or Malays from the island world to the south? No authoritative answer can be given. To many it seems likely that they were Malays, who could easily have been carried up from the south by the Kuroshio, or Black Current, which sweeps up along the coast of Asia like the Gulf Stream in the Atlantic. But any answer comes into contact with disconcerting facts. Even a brief acquaintance with these people will disclose the fact that, while most of the Japanese are short in stature and have flat noses and wide, short hands and feet, there are Japanese, frequently those who belong to the upper classes, who are tall and have delicate features with high noses and long, narrow hands and feet. We can do little more than note this fact without being able to account for the origin of those who thus differ from their fellow Japanese.

Besides the Japanese there is the remnant of another stock, the Ainu, now found in the far north on the island of Hokkaido. These people, now numbering only about 25,000, are very distinct from the Japanese and have no racial affiliation with them. One theory, different from those just mentioned, is that the Mongoloids who came over from the continent mingled with the aboriginal Ainus to form the Japanese type, but this is unlikely. The

113

Japanese are too nearly like their neighbors in Korea and China to have intermarried freely with a people like the Ainus who are so different. The Ainus have lighter skin and profuse beards, which are almost unknown among the Japanese. In language, religion, habits, customs, and folklore they are distinct. There seems to be little in the future for these hunters and fishermen unless they give up their tribal life and become completely assimilated with the Japanese. Be that as it may, the question arises, Who are these interesting and strange people? Are they prehistoric wanderers who traveled far from their original haunts, lost their way, and became stranded on these islands? That may be—indeed it is more than likely. About the best the anthropologist can do is to say that the Ainus belong to the white or Caucasian race and in their migration picked up other traits as they mingled with various peoples. At the time of the conquest of the islands by the Japanese the Ainus occupied more or less the entire country and were driven east and north by the invaders very much as the Indians were driven west by the American colonists. They fared very much as did the Indians. They were looked down upon as inferiors by the Japanese who, when the Ainus were out of the way, paid little attention to them. Thus we find the beginnings of the assumption of inherent superiority displayed by the Japanese in their relations with a weaker and subjugated people.

Japanese traditions give us little or no help. Mythology and folklore show no trace of continental origin. Two ancient writings which embody material that is much older have come down from the early part of the eighth century of our era. They are known as the *Kojiki*, "Record of Ancient Matters," and the *Nihongi*, "Chronicles of Japan." Their purpose was to trace the history of Japan back to the beginnings, but they were written very definitely to demonstrate the supreme place which the ruling house had, and should continue to have, in the esteem of the Japanese people. The chief burden of the writers was to trace the descent of the emperors in unbroken line from Jimmu Tenno, the first emperor, who was said to have ascended the throne in 660 B.C. Now this first emperor, the progenitor of the imperial line, was said to be the "grandson" of Amaterasu-Omikami, the sun-goddess, the most powerful deity in the pantheon of Shinto, the primitive religion of Japan. This relationship with divinity made the first emperor himself a divine being, and, since the line of descent has not been broken, all the later occupants of the throne have been of the same divine nature and origin. This was not only the doctrine of the early books; it was the official belief until 1945. In fact, it was the essence of the creed of modern Japan, the touchstone of loyalty to the empire.

These ancient documents go farther. They tell the tale of two divinities, Izanagi and Izanami, male and female, who came down from the heavenly regions and as a result of their union brought into being the islands which we know as Japan. But the tale does not stop there. The modern Japanese are taught to believe that they themselves are also descended from divine beings. As the result of these myths and the doctrines which are deduced from them, we come to the amazing claim that in dealing with the Japanese we have to do with a people who are themselves of divine origin, who live on divine soil, and who are ruled over by a divine emperor, a direct descendant of their most exalted goddess Amaterasu. This dogma goes far to explain the peculiar pride of the Japanese and their feeling of superiority over other peoples. The great Emperor Mutsuhito (reigned 1868-1912) gave a constitution to Japan in 1889. The first article reads, "The Empire of Japan shall be reigned over and governed by a line of Emperors unbroken for ages eternal." The document continues, "The Emperor is sacred and inviolable. . . . The Sacred Throne was established at the time when the heavens and the earth became separated. The Emperor is Heaven descended, divine and sacred."

The schools were given the task of making these doctrines real. Until the end of the old regime with the surrender of Japan in August, 1945, they taught:

The protection and advancement of the country are in the care of the ancestral spirits and their power resides in the Emperor. The use of that power is the work of the Imperial Throne. . . . The central idea of the Japanese State is the belief that the spirits of the Imperial ancestors continue to rule through their living representatives, and from this belief springs the singular national spirit of the Japanese People.[12]

The fall of Singapore before the Japanese armies was a notable event which occasioned six radio broadcasts by S. Komaki. He dealt not only with geopolitics but with the distinctively Japanese theory of race:

The Asiatic races originated from the Japanese race. The Emperor of all nations, the Japanese Emperor, is the ruler of all nations. . . . The main Asiatic race is a composite of people from the south, east, west and north. The Japanese race is the essence of all these races. That Japanese race is called the Yamato race which means "great and peaceful." To bring the world into eternal peace is Japan's duty and privilege. . . . The world must be unified around Japan.[13]

Former ambassador of the United States to Japan, Joseph C. Grew, asserts:

The Japanese have preached the racialism of their own utter superiority to the rest of mankind, and have also preached the racialism of all Asia against the Western peoples. . . . The Japanese have made enemies of the peoples whom they profess to lead in a crusade. This came because of their unbearable attitude of superiority and because of the violence and unfairness which are always resorted to by those who seek to bolster up such pretensions to superiority.[14]

No further word is needed to show the nature of Japanese racism and the ambitions to which it gave birth.

[12] *The Japanese Advertiser*, Nov. 3, 1916, as quoted by D. C. Holtom, *Modern Japan and Shinto Nationalism*, p. 10.

[13] S. C. Menefee, "Japan's Global Conceit," *Asia*, June, 1943, pp. 330-32.

[14] *Report from Tokyo*, p. 65; see also *Ten Years in Japan*, *passim*.

On January 1, 1946, the Emperor Hirohito made an official pronouncement renouncing his divinity and the pretensions of the Japanese people to racial superiority over other peoples. The effect of this amazing and surprising announcement is as yet incalculable. Time only will disclose the far-reaching influence of so revolutionary a position, the more marvelous because taken by the person most deeply affected. One result which can already be recorded is that on February 6, 1946, a new constitution was proposed which at one stroke divests the emperor of the divinity claimed for him in the constitution of 1889. It also reduces him to little more than a figurehead of the national life and unity, with prerogatives which are of a formal and ceremonial character only. The sovereignty will no longer be his by divine right. That choice will be placed upon the people of Japan, who will possess the right to decide for themselves the question of the person and prerogatives of their ruler. Undoubtedly he will continue to have the admiration and loyalty of his people, but the entire situation will be changed—he is to be subservient to his people and not their divine and irremovable ruler. This constitution has been accepted by the Imperial Diet and promulgated by the emperor as the basic law of the land.

During the latter part of the sixteenth and the early part of the seventeenth centuries Japan had become acquainted with Europe through Spanish merchantmen and Roman Catholic missionaries, who had been received cordially and whose work had resulted in the conversion of hundreds of thousands of Japanese to the Christian faith. But catastrophe came quickly. Ieyasu, the shogun who ruled the country with an iron will, became convinced that the ultimate purpose of the missionaries meant no good to Japan, that in reality they were the emissaries of the king of Spain who would in time attempt the conquest of the country. He drove the missionaries out and attempted to supress Christianity. He almost succeeded. The only Christians who remained were driven under cover and practiced the rites of their religion in secret. With this drastic action is to be coupled the isolation of the entire land, which lasted for two centuries and a half. No foreigners were allowed to come in, and no Japanese could go out. One or two Dutch ships were permitted to come for the purposes of trade each year to the port city of Nagasaki. This rigid exclusion of foreigners and foreign influence remained in force until a remarkable happening in 1853-54.

During the first of those years the quiet of the Japanese waters was ruffled by the coming of American warships under the command of Commodore Matthew Calbraith Perry, who had been commissioned by the president of the United States to open Japan to friendly relations with the world. He was asked by the Japanese to give the authorities time to consider the momentous step. So he sailed away to the south seas, returning in 1854 to receive an answer. It was favorable, and in due time, not without difficulties, Japan entered into the full stream of the life of the world. The Japanese never ceased to be grateful to America for opening their country and for doing it without the firing of a hostile gun. Their gratitude was intensified by the helpful advice and kindly interest in their affairs which were unfailingly shown by the first American representative, Townsend Harris. He was a true friend, and they learned to trust him. This happy relation continued almost without friction until after the close of the Russo-Japanese war.

I remember vividly my experiences as a boy in Tokyo and in other parts of Japan. Unfailing courtesy and genuine friendship were extended. No thought of racism marred the happy relationship. On both sides there was only good will with no thought of superiority or inferiority. But serious difficulty was encountered when Japan, which had with China been compelled to accept extraterritoriality, became restive after her leaders had made a clean sweep of old legal and court procedures. The Japanese could not understand why the United States and other nations did not at once revise their treaties and allow Japan to stand up as an equal member of the family of nations. When the change was finally made, the Japanese could not forget that it was our country that first removed the hated restrictions. A new treaty was signed

118

in 1894 which stated: "The citizens of each of the High Contracting Parties shall have the full liberty to enter, travel or reside in any part of the territories of the other Contracting Party, and shall enjoy full and perfect protection of their persons and property." [15] No racial discrimination shows it head here. The Japanese were satisfied, little knowing what the years ahead had in store.

When Japan was in the midst of her mighty struggle with Russia in 1904-5, the people of the United States were with her heart and soul. They wanted to see this little David humiliate the mighty Goliath, the country of oppression, Russia, which just at that time was visiting the Jews with bloody pogroms. So fully did Japan feel that she could count on American friendship that "within four days of Admiral Togo's great victory over the Russian fleet in the sea of Japan, the Japanese intimated to President [Theodore] Roosevelt that if he would please invite them to a peace conference, they would be glad to accept." [16] There seemed to be no reason why this happy accord should have been broken, but several untoward events took place, and our relations with Japan since then have never been the same.

In October, 1906, only a year after President Roosevelt's invitation of the two powers to the peace conference which ended the Russo-Japanese War, the San Francisco school board took the unprecedented action of requiring all Japanese pupils in the public schools of the city to attend separate Oriental schools. There were only ninety-three Japanese pupils in the entire school system, scattered in twenty-three separate buildings. Here were discrimination and segregation for reasons of race and race only. President Roosevelt was indignant and called the action of the board a "wicked absurdity." [17] An outburst of protest broke out in Japan. The president did all in his power to ease the situation but found that there was little prospect of formal legislative action, so "Japan and the United States entered into the famous

[15] R. G. Adams, *A History of the Foreign Policy of the United States*, p. 348.

[16] *Ibid.*, p. 344.

[17] George H. Blakeslee, *The Recent Foreign Policy of the United States*, p. 243.

Gentlemen's Agreement, which provided that the Japanese government would itself refuse passports to laborers skilled or unskilled, who wished to go to the continental United States." [18] By this agreement also "Japanese children under sixteen years of age were admitted to the regular public schools." [19] The United States government attempted to keep things steady, but in 1913 the California legislature, against the full weight of the opposition of the national government, passed legislation which allowed "only aliens 'eligible to citizenship' to own certain classes of land, which would bar Japanese." [20] The unfortunate disagreements between California and the federal government continued for a number of years, Washington seeking to avoid a serious clash with Japan because of acts of the California legislature in violation of treaty rights.

Again at the peace conference after World War I a most serious event took place. The Japanese delegation sought "to have inserted in the Covenant of the League of Nations a clause granting 'to all alien nationals of States members of the League, equal and just treatment in every respect, making no distinction either in law or fact, on account of their race or nationality.' " [21] The Japanese ambassador had previously handed a note to President Wilson in Washington which stated: "The Japanese Government regards as of first importance the establishment of the principle that the difference of race should in no case constitute a basis of discriminatory treatment under the law of our country." [22] Some time after the Japanese delegation at Versailles had presented the request just mentioned, it "modified its request asking only for a mere phrase in the preamble endorsing 'the principle of the equality of nations and the just treatment of the nationals.' " [23] The motion to

---

[18] *Ibid.*

[19] D. S. Muzzey, *A History of Our Country*, p. 577.

[20] George H. Blakeslee, *op. cit.*, p. 245.

[21] *Ibid.*, p. 261.

[22] *Ibid.*, p. 262.

[23] *Ibid.*

insert the clause received the majority of votes in the League of Nations' Commission but not the necessary unanimous vote, and so it was lost. Great Britain and the United States were among those nations voting against the clause. Japan and all the other Eastern nations were thus rebuked and given to understand that racial discrimination would still be allowed to play its blighting role in international relations.

This blow was soon followed by another. A new Immigration Bill was passed by the Congress of the United States and signed by President Calvin Coolidge on May 24, 1924, to become effective on July 1, 1924. There is no doubt that it was needed. The United States faced the prospect of being swamped by an inrush of people from poverty-stricken Europe. The bill as finally passed limited the "annual immigration from a given country to 2% of the nationals of the country in the United States in 1890." [24] So far the bill was not seriously to be criticized, but it went on to provide for the *total exclusion* of all Orientals. This of course included the Japanese and automatically abrogated the Gentlemen's Agreement of 1907. President Coolidge disapproved of this part of the bill but signed it because he felt the need of an immigration bill and could see no hope of anything better with Congress and the country in a very reactionary state of mind.

The protest from Japan was violent and truculent. There was some amelioration when thoughtful Japanese came to know that countless chambers of commerce, luncheon clubs, and church organizations had repudiated this provision of the bill. The fact is that every major church body took action condemning the short-sighted, narrow action of Congress. But what did all that amount to? The law was on the statute book and would be enforced. America had gone back on Japan and was excluding Japanese from her shores because they belonged to an inferior race. There were many in America who realized that unlimited immigration of the Japanese—or any other alien people—would be unfortunate. But did not the 2 per cent quote provide for that? Accord-

[24] *An Encyclopedia of World History*, p. 1051.

ing to that quota less than 150 Japanese could come to our shores each year, a mere trickle with no possibility of doing irreparable damage to our institutions. And if even this small number would give offense, the Japanese declared that they would themselves prevent the legal number from leaving Japan. The Japanese resented not only being discriminated against as an inferior people but the manner in which the action was taken, which could be interpreted only as a deliberate affront.

On July 1, 1924, placards were displayed in Tokyo reading, "Japanese must never forget July 1st, when American inflicted an intolerable insult on Japan." [25] A Japanese newspaper carried these words, "If diplomacy be misguided in handling that problem, mankind is bound to be led to the greatest tragedy the world could know—the conflict of the East and West." [26] Professor M. Anesaki, of the Imperial University in Tokyo, well known in the United States, spoke of two alternatives for Japan, to continue to be "a harmonizing factor in the peaceful program of humanity, or to accept the challenge and to trust her fate to the cause of 'Asia for Asiatics'; that is, to lead a life-or-death struggle of the Orientals against the Occidentals." [27] There are those who, taking these facts into consideration, have declared that the Immigration Bill excluding the Japanese was the cause of World War II so far as the United States and Japan were concerned. I cannot share this opinion. The plans for the struggle just ended antedated this particular act and were based on many other factors, but I know as do all others who have tried to understand Japan and the Japanese that exclusion and the resentment and bitterness which followed in its train offered the militaristic clique a splendid opportunity to foment hatred against Americans and everything Western.

So much for the events which preceded the declaration of war which followed the attack on Pearl Harbor, December 7, 1941.

[25] George H. Blakeslee, *op. cit.*, p. 283.

[26] *Ibid.*, p 288.

[27] *Ibid.*, p. 289.

Japan was in the clutches of violent racism and in addition was obsessed with the passion to conquer Asia and make all its peoples subservient to her domination, and then go on to conquer the world. By so doing she expected to show herself superior to other nations, the lord and master of mankind.

And now the war is over. The end came quickly after the atomic bombing of Hiroshima and Nagasaki. General Douglas MacArthur, as the representative of the allied nations, is the virtual ruler of Japan. He has shown rare tact and understanding in dealing with the completely defeated and humiliated nation. It is too soon as yet to be able to predict what conditions will be in Japan as the people gather themselves together and reconstruct their life in a situation far different from that which they had expected. They have shown themselves altogether ready to fit in with the dictates of General MacArthur, realizing that their military leaders led them into a war which ruined them. It is no time to attempt to predict what the relations of the Japanese government and people to the other nations of the world will be. One very favorable sign is the cordiality which has been shown by Japanese Christian leaders who have welcomed American Christian leaders and given assurance that they will cooperate fully with their American friends, with the understanding, of course, that all their relations shall be conducted on the basis of Christian brotherhood with no distinction based on racial and national differences.

Chapter VII

The Island World of the Pacific

Geographically, politically, and racially this vast region is crowded with dissimilarities. We might easily be lost in a maze of details and contradictory situations and relationships. Our hope of a more or less unified study lies in the limitation of our subject. We are set to investigate the relations of the various ethnic groups and to discover the manifestations of racism which may be found.

The peoples of this area are divided into a number of groups, which do not coincide with their political affiliations. The Netherlands Indies comprise peoples belonging to at least two of the fundamental racial groups, and the same can be said of the peoples under the dominion of Great Britain and France. We shall first survey the racial alignments and then consider the relationships in each of the major political spheres.

The inhabitants of the island world of the Pacific are to be distinguished under four designations:

1. Malaysians or Indonesians, who comprise the inhabitants of the Malay peninsula and the islands of the Netherlands Indies. This is not a strictly racial classification, as we shall see. Aside from the Malay peninsula, which is under British protection or control, this alignment is political, gathering together the islands which are ruled by the Dutch government. This colonial empire includes the islands of Sumatra, Java, Celebes, most of Borneo, the western half of New Guinea, and has a population of 72,000,000 (estimated in 1944), the five islands just mentioned containing all but 5,000,000. Java is the smallest of the large islands but has (with Madura) a population of 46,000,000; it is one of the most densely populated regions in the world.

2. Melanesians. These "Black Islands," as their name indicates, are inhabited by the darkest people in this entire area and are classified together because of this fact. The islands on which these people live are New Guinea, New Ireland, the Solomons, the New Hebrides, New Caledonia, the Fiji Islands, and many others in the same region. These names have became household words in America through the early campaigns of World War II in the Southwest Pacific.

3. Micronesians. These people live on the "Small Islands" north of the Melanesians. The total population is only a little over 100,-000. The islands could scarcely support a larger number, being coral reefs with little cultivable soil. Again their names have become very familiar during recent years. They include the Marshalls, the Gilberts, the Marianas (one of which is Guam), the Carolines (with Truk), and the Ellice Islands. After World War I they were mandated to Japan, who fortified them in anticipation of her coming conquests.

4. Polynesians, who live on the "Many Islands" which are widely scattered over the Pacific east of the other island groups just mentioned. The area in which they are found might be described as a mighty triangle with its apex at the Hawaiian Islands, its southwest angle at New Zealand, and its other extreme point at Easter Island far out in the Pacific toward South America. The size of this area can be realized from the fact that each side of the triangle is approximately 4,500 miles. Countless islands are dotted over this huge area, the best known of which are Samoa (partly under the control of the United States), Tahiti, Pitcairn (made famous by the thrilling story of *The Mutiny on the Bounty*). The largest in the group is of course New Zealand, with which the total area of Polynesia is about that of Arizona and without which it shrinks to the size of Vermont. The total Polynesian native population is about 300,000, of which the Maoris of New Zealand number in excess of 90,000. The entire area with which we are dealing, with the exception of the Netherlands Indies, is frequently referred to as Oceania.

Who are all these island people, not great in number yet scattered widely over the surface of the world's greatest ocean? It is generally agreed by anthropologists that the people who now inhabit these islands were emigrants from the mainland of Asia. They were adventurers or refugees or both. Crowded out of their former homes or stopping places by other peoples, they came to land's end at the tip of the Malay peninsula (or other points on the southeastern shore of the continent) and took to the sea in boats and gradually—but in most cases within historic times—spread out and traveled until some of them reached the farthest islands to the east. The story has a close likeness to that of India, which was peopled by one wave of immigrants after another, some of whom continued to travel and became the inhabitants of the South Sea Islands.

First, there were the Negroids. They were dark people, rather short, with the well-known features which mark off the black peoples from the whites and the yellow-browns. Pressure from behind drove some of them to outlying islands, while others retreated to the mountains and the jungles on the mainland and have remained there to this day, isolated and backward. This took place in India and Malaya; it also took place in the island world itself. The largest group which have been able to preserve their identity are the Melanesians, the black men with fuzzy hair in New Guinea and adjacent islands. In other places they could not resist the coming of the later groups and so betook themselves to the interior of the larger islands such as Borneo and the Philippines, where they still live quite apart from the population in the lowlands and at the mouths of rivers near the coast. Others intermingled with their supplanters and permanently affected the racial type. This was the case in Polynesia, in the Dutch East Indies, and even in Micronesia, where traces of this mingling are to be found among people who are for the most part lighter in color, taller, and have wavy hair and other features quite different from the Negroids.

A second wave followed from the mainland. They have been

called Caucasoid, another name for the Mediterranean people who became the basic stock of the Dravidian population of India. Some of them pushed on beyond India and Malaya and traveled east from island to island, driving the Negroids out or mingling with them, until they went as far as islands are to be found. This second wave of immigrants came to be a dominant people in Indonesia, but were in turn to a certain ,degree displaced by a later wave of migrants. They still exist in large numbers in all the western islands. In some, like Bali and Timor, they constitute the bulk of the population; in Polynesia they have not been displaced and are seen in more nearly their early unmixed condition. They were and are skilled seamen. With the use of that ingenious device, the outrigger, they made their narrow boats secure and, taking their wives, children, pigs, and chickens with them, braved the seas and went on and on till all the islands were occupied. They are men and women of splendid physique, with yellowish brown skin, sometimes copper-colored, brown eyes, and wavy dark hair. Some, as already noted, show Negroid traits and some Mongoloid, but the typical Polynesian is distinct from both.

And finally a third wave is believed to have come in, and again from the mainland of Asia. They were Mongoloids, whose original habitat was northeast of the Malay peninsula, presumably the same Mongoloids from whom the Chinese have come. The populations of French Indo-China, Siam, and Burma have the same origin, while the people of Bengal in eastern India also show a very marked Mongoloid strain. These people pushed on toward the south and came to land's end and, like others before them, became men of the sea and helped to populate the island world. They have been called Mongoloid-Malaysians to distinguish them from the Caucasoid-Maylaysians who preceded them in their journey south and east. These people have scant body hair, yellowish skin, slant eyes, slightness of build, like the people of South China. They constitute the present seacoast population of the larger islands of Indonesia. But here again one sees evidences of mingling with the Caucasoid and the Negroid, so that in all the islands it is difficult to find large groups which are not intermingled with other stocks. In Micronesia the people are inheritors of features which are mainly a mixture of Caucasoid and Mongoloid, without the Negroid. They have narrow noses, straight wavy hair, are lighter-skinned than their Negroid neighbors to the south, the Melanesians.

As has already been indicated of all these peoples, miscegenation has gone on in the past and is going on at present. This can be seen very clearly in Hawaii, where the native Polynesian Hawaiians comprise only 15 per cent of the population. It is a question whether they will long survive as a separate group. In the Philippines there are two native types: the Negritos, found in the mountain fastnesses mostly in Luzon; and the Mongoloid-Malaysians, who form the vast majority of the population. But since the Spanish occupation there has come into existence a mixed type of Eurasians, to which again another mixture has been added, that between the Filipinos and the Chinese, who are in the islands in large numbers.

Do we know all the facts? Most surely not. What has been presented is the best that recent anthropology has been able to devise to explain the complicated maze of life in this area. No one as yet has been able to account for the strange carved monoliths on Easter Island—those huge, gaunt statues of beings supposedly divine, which stand out on a bleak island, utterly inexplicable to any of the Polynesians in that area. Who placed them there and what do they mean? Are they the creation of a race, more advanced than the present Polynesians, which has completely disappeared? Nor do the present theories of the immigration of various ethnic groups into the island world take account of the Java man (Pithecanthropus erectus) found by the brilliant young Dutch professor Eugene DuBois. In a lava deposit fifty-two feet below the present surface of the earth, he discovered in 1891 authentic bones of a very primitive human being. It is not known how far back to place the man whose bones these are. The guesses

128

and estimates vary from a million to a quarter of a million years. All that concerns us now is to realize that long, very long before the migrations which have been sketched above took place, man or proto-man lived on some of these islands. Did the same men continue to live there, or did they die out? Have they any connection with the present inhabitants? There seems to be no way of finding out; so all we can do is to proceed on the basis of the best indications which can be found—with the caveat that other discoveries and further study based on facts not now known may alter the present more or less tentative conclusions.[1]

The problem of racial tension must now be faced. What are the relations of the various groups in the island world to each other and to the European, who has thrust himself into the picture, particularly during the past 150 years? In this region in general it may be said that we see racial relations at their worst and also at their best. Nowhere have cruelty, greed, and lust been exhibited by the man of the West more flagrantly and more unabashed than among these people. In one case at least, that of the Tasmanians, the people were exterminated. Ruthless warfare was waged; the poor creatures were hunted down like partridges; finally a remnant consisting of 203 persons was moved to an adjacent island, where they all died, the last member of the race passing away in 1876. There was provocation of course—there always is—but the policy of bloody reprisals resulted in the complete liquidation of a people whose chief crime was that they defended their homes from invaders. Almost the same was true of the Blackfellows in Australia. They too fought back when they were driven from their ancestral holdings. No one knows how many there were when the white man arrived. One estimate is that there were 150,000. Now there are about 70,000. A whole tribe is known to have been wiped out in retaliation for the stealing of sheep and cattle. Only recently has the government adopted a different policy, one of care and protection, but it remains to

[1] Cf. Fay-Cooper Cole, *The Peoples of Malaysia,* an authoritative study, not covering the entire field of this chapter.

be seen what the effect will be. Many declare that they are a doomed race and will disappear in a short time. The churches are now taking the matter seriously and are making efforts to re, habilitate the race and lead the aboriginals to adjust themselves to ways of living which promise a future of satisfaction and usefulness. The same fate almost befell the Maoris in New Zealand. These Polynesians were a hardier race, more alert and with ambition and initiative, so they could strike back harder when the white men attacked them. But the odds were against them, and they might have been destroyed had it not been for the splendid work done by Christian missionaries. They not only gave the Maoris a new outlook on life and new stamina, but brought the white men and the Polynesians into an understanding relationship which has changed the whole attitude of the natives and the white men toward each other.

When the white men did not feel impelled to resort to killing, they did what was only second in deviltry: they exploited the natives and debauched their women. No tale is more shameless than the cheating of the natives in the early day and the licentious conduct of merchants and seamen. And when the stage of petty bartering with the individual trader and ship captain had passed, large-scale exploitation of native labor and of the soil became the order of the day. Only here and there would a governor from a European country take an enlightened attitude and protect the simple-minded and easygoing natives from the unscrupulous agents of business and manufacturing interests. The natives in the eyes of a board of directors in the homeland counted for a little or nothing as compared with the profits of the investors. Few problems are more urgent in world organization after World War II than that of the treatment of subject peoples and colonies. Shall they be thought of only as a means of enriching privileged persons of a colonial power, or shall the purpose of government be primarily the happiness and development of these peoples?

On the other hand no part of the world has witnessed greater

130

self-sacrificing devotion on the part of missionaries than the islands of the Pacific. The roll of these elect men is a long one and includes the names of some of the greatest heros and martyrs in missionary annals. Attention is called to them here, not only because of what they were in their own lives, but because they exhibited a totally different spirit in their dealings with the islanders. They believed in them and were able to lift them up. The results achieved on many of the islands form an epic of human uplift almost incredible. John G. Paton's transforming work on several islands of the New Hebrides reads like a romance. The work of English and Australian Methodists in Fiji has resulted in the membership of 95 per cent of the Fijians in the Christian church and a completely different policy on the part of the government in dealing with the problems of the natives. These are two illustrations out of many. Cannibals have become peace-loving, industrious men; head-hunters have laid aside their gruesome practices; and lazy easygoing children of nature have become serious-minded workers. All that has taken place in hundreds of islands has resulted in deeper mutual respect on the part of employers and government officials and the native worker.[2] There is still much racism remaining to be overcome, but that day is more sure of coming when the islanders are given the opportunity of an education, adequate medical care, and some part in the affairs of government.

Turning from these general considerations of relationship between races we may find in this island world a number of types which are different in nature, in method of handling, and in outcome. America has taken part in two of these experiments, each of which has its lesson to teach in the relations of people of very different ethnic groups.

[2] See Henry P. Van Dusen, *They Found the Church There,* for an illuminating account of Christian missions as seen through the eyes of American soldiers, sailors, and marines either stationed in or driven by the exigencies of war to find shelter in these islands.

Hawaii

We first turn to the situation in Hawaii. Not long after the discovery of the islands by Captain James Cook in 1778 outsiders began to come to this paradise from both east and west. When the demand for sugar grew to huge dimensions and it was found that Hawaii was an advantageous place to cultivate sugar cane, the economic fate of the islands was settled. Huge plantations grew up under American ownership. The one serious problem was to secure satisfactory labor. The native Hawaiian is strong physically, courteous, and thoughtful, but he is not thrifty or ambitious. He did not make a good steady laborer: he quit work when he had enough for immediate needs, and did not go back until he felt the pinch of hunger. This explains the coming of foreign laborers. From 1865 to 1885, 27,000 Chinese were brought in, 20,000 Portuguese, and 70,000 Japanese a little later. When the immigration laws excluded the Orientals from the islands, the Filipinos came in to meet the growing demand.

The inhabitants of Hawaii are American citizens on American soil; but only two tenths are Westerners, while seven tenths are Orientals, and one tenth, the smallest percentage of all, is composed of Polynesians. But with all this there is little or no racial tension. How can this be? The suggestion has been made that, while the Polynesian Hawaiian forms so small a part of the population, his old-time sense of equality and independence has pervaded the minds of all the Hawaiians. At any rate this is the situation socially. The Hawaiians intermarry without hesitation and so do the Chinese. The Japanese do not; they hold tenaciously to family and racial solidarity. But there is no racism—all the groups accept the situation and show no bitterness with respect to others. All have equal educational opportunities. Thus an intelligent community has developed in which there is little reason for jealousy and resentment.

But still there is another side. Economic disparity exists between the owners of the great estates and the remainder of the population, which for the most part is in the employ of the landowning sugar barons. Fundamentally the tension is economic but becomes at least partially racial when the employee realizes that the man on whom he is economically dependent is an American and that the American boy with whom he, a Chinese, Japanese, or Filipino, went to school is the only one who can rise to occupy the better-paying positions. Here is an open door for bitterness, and it has not failed to provide entrance for the spirit of revolt and antagonism. Thus the problem in Hawaii merges with the world-wide problem of economic inequality.

Philippine Islands

Another and more significant experiment is in the Philippines. The islands were discovered by Magellan in 1521. He came first to the island of Leyte—where the Americans landed on their return to the islands in 1944—and was soon killed by the natives. After difficulties with Portugal, which was beginning to build up its ill-fated eastern empire, Spain came into possession of the entire archipelago and remained until Admiral George Dewey sailed into Manila Bay on May 1, 1898. As soon as the United States took the islands over in 1899, Congress passed a resolution to the effect that "the ultimate goal of the United States was not annexation, assimilation, or any type of permanent control, but eventual self-government." [3] Here was something new in colonial administration, clearly expressed from the beginning as the goal to be attained. There have been Americans on the islands who not only have felt themselves superior to the Filipinos but have acted the part, and undoubtedly there have been instances of commercial exploitation and personal abuse—unfortunately we cannot but expect such exhibitions when the West meets the East. But it is generally acknowledged that by and large the relations of our American people with the Filipinos have been on a high level of disinterested purpose to treat the people with respect

[3] *Public Education in the Philippine Islands,* U. S. Department of the Interior, Office of Education, p. 15.

based on sympathetic concern for their welfare. Not only was a promise of emancipation made, but every evidence was given of the sincerity of the pledge. Modern education has been placed within the reach of all, and in all sorts of intangible ways the Filipinos have been made to realize that they were free man, entitled to look into the future with assurance of citizenship as an independent, self-respecting member of the family of nations.

The United States in addition saved the islands from the hands of the Japanese conquerors, who came in with a very different purpose from that of the United States. And moreover America has already had an ample reward. The attitude of the Filipino people was voiced by the Honorable Sergio Osmena, who wrote:

The gap between peoples of different races can be bridged with understanding if the right policy is chosen. This was demonstrated by the happy outcome of the joint Filipino-American adventure. By first promulgating an altruistic policy, "the Philippines for the Filipinos," and then following it to the letter and the spirit, America succeeded in winning over the skeptical and antagonistic Filipinos and in changing their policy of opposition to that of cooperation. . . . The Philippines stand as a vivid example of what the nations of the West can do for all dependent peoples everywhere.[4]

On the Fourth of July, 1946, in the presence of the American representative, General Douglas MacArthur, the freedom and independence of the Philippines was proclaimed amid great jubilation. America had redeemed her promise. This was a new thing in the relations of the East and the West—and its significance will not be lost.

Netherlands Indies

We turn to the Netherlands Indies, commonly called the East Indies, with an estimated population of 70,000,000 in 1940. Rich in the raw materials needed in all civilized lands, these islands have a large part to play in world trade. In the eastern part of

---

[4] "The United Nations and the Philippines," *The Annals of the American Academy of Political and Social Science*, CCXXVIII (July, 1943), 28 f.

the archipelago the Negroid strain is found, but in Java the Mongoloid-Malaysian predominates over the earlier Caucasoid-Malaysian. Besides these there are over 1,000,000 Chinese, with some Indians and Arabs. About 250,000 Europeans complete the roll, but about 65 per cent of those so classified are Eurasians or Indo-Europeans. This very small group of Westerners is highly important, since it is they who have ruled the islands and conducted the commerce with the Western world. Except for one brief period a century and a half ago, Holland has held sway since 1650.

The Dutch government has not had an easy time. For almost a hundred years after it finally took the islands over in 1818 there was sporadic warfare here and there in the Indies. In the early days of the Netherlands East Indies Company and latterly, when the rule was taken over by the Dutch government, the policy seems always to have been that of exploiting the islands for the sake of the Dutch. Since the turn of the century a more liberal policy has prevailed, but it leaves much to be desired. Little authority has been allowed to pass into the hands of the natives. The government has been very reluctant to allow many of the people to receive an education, thus making no provision for any further assumption of authority by native leaders. An interesting fact is that, in contrast with the situation in British India, the offspring of marriages between the Dutch and native population are not ostracized. This helps to relieve the tension, but with the prevalence of illigitimacy the ideals of family life suffer.

The end of World War II has seen smoldering unrest breaking out in open, armed revolt. Ever since the victory of Japan over Russia in 1905 the spirit of independent nationalism has been perodically appearing above the surface. Desire for political freedom, resistance of economic exploitation, hatred of the Chinese moneylender, eagerness to break through the bondage of illiteracy—all of these have combined to increase a spirit of open revolt against the Dutch domination.

This situation is still (autumn, 1946) in crisis. The cohesion and strength of the native opposition have come as a surprise to the Western world. In spite of all that the Dutch, aided by the British, have been able to do, the government set up by the nationals in Java has been able to maintain itself and secure a considerable amount of recognition from the home government in Holland. What begins to be apparent is that the Netherlands government cannot expect ever again to rule the East Indies unless in co-operation with some form of national organization.

This systematic uprising of national spirit is largely confined to Java. The great bulk of the people of the Indies consists of savages and others who have made only a slight advance away from a primitive state. They comprise most of the population of that island world and are incapable of self-government and of coping with the problems of modern life. Little cohesion exists between this vast population scattered over many islands in a span of over two thousand miles east and west. If it is not Holland, it must be some other power or coalition of powers which shall be designated to take charge of these various peoples and fit them gradually for self-government. No more difficult tasks lies before the United Nations than that of providing for the uplift and advancement of the backward peoples of the earth.

Fiji

In the Fiji Islands racial tension exists in a form unknown elsewhere in the island world of the Pacific, though it is found in a similar form in a few of the West Indies, notably Trinidad. The tension exists because of the presence of Indians brought in to work in the sugar plantations. The story is somewhat like that in Hawaii. The British Colonial Sugar Refining Company must have labor, and the native Fijians did not take to the prospect of regular hours of employment under rules which kept men at their tasks. They, like the Hawaiians, had found it easy to exist in an easygoing way with little exertion and did not take kindly to any change. So as early as 1877 laborers were imported from India into Fiji and are there today. Not only are they there, but they have increased until they number as many as the native

Fijian population, about 100,000. The two groups are quite distinct, with the Indians looking down on the Fijians as an inferior people.

Changes have taken place in both groups. The Indians were either Hindus or Moslems, and they continue their ancestral religious relations; but in a foreign land far away from the centers of Indian life the two groups are more tolerant and manage to get along without the bitterness and conflict which are always in danger of flaring up between the two groups in the motherland. Likewise with caste, the Hindus were of different castes when they came to Fiji, but the barriers do not seem so high, and caste regulations are not insisted upon as strenuously as at home in India. On their side the Fijians have been compelled to change at a number of points. The land had always been held in common among them, and ownership meant nothing to the individual native. But now the Hindus have begun to buy land for occupation and cultivation, and the Fijians have become aware that they must hold on to their land and make use of it or be crowded out. The British government felt compelled to step in and prevent the further sale of native lands on the theory that it is bound to dispose of the land for the best interest of its wards, the Fijians. Working with the government, the mission schools are teaching agriculture as well as the regular academic subjects. Thus slowly a people is being drawn away from one mode of life and being introduced to another. It is their only hope of a worth-while future in the modern world, whose influence is being felt so strongly and increasingly in the South Seas. One of the most competent authorities in the field comes to this conclusion:

This, then, in our view is the goal to which we must arrive—to make the native a self-reliant, capable farmer, and not a hired serf without hope of progress. Thus shall we help to resolve a conflict of cultures and of interests.[5]

To quote again:

[5] John W. Burton, *Brown and White in the South Pacific*, p. 30.

To ensure adequate protection from without, education from within, and development in the quality of life, it would seem necessary that native races should be under the direction, however benign, of some more advanced peoples who are familiar with modern civilization and who can assist the less sophisticated to triumph over it. There seems no group in the Pacific, not even in Tonga, where the people can do without the help and guidance of European officials.[6]

The Fiji Islands are a crown colony of Great Britain. This means that they are ruled by a governor and his staff who are directly responsible to the British Parliament in London through the colonial secretary. Neither the Indians nor the Fijians have any part in their own government except in an advisory capacity. The governor is assisted by an executive council and a legislative council. Of the latter five Indians and five Fijians are members. But so far as authority is concerned, it is in the hands of a small group of British from abroad. Both the Indians and the Fijians are growing restive and are making known their desire for some authoritative control of their own affairs. Undoubtedly the hand of Britain is needed, but it must be sympathetic to the welfare of the people themselves or else the dissatisfaction will continue to grow. It remains to be seen how the new colonial policy under the labor government will affect life in Fiji.

New Zealand

The story of the relation of the immigrant British population to the native Polynesian Maoris in New Zealand is highly instructive. The earlier stage has already been alluded to as an illustration of the vicious policy of reprisals, which has ended in some cases in near or complete extermination. The later stages in New Zealand, however, present a very different, in fact a truly inspiring, picture. The population of New Zealand today is about 1,500,000, of whom all are of British descent except the Maoris, who number 90,000. No account need be taken here of the small numbers of Chinese and Indians and the tiny group from Japan. The main

---

[6] *Ibid.*, p. 61.

groups of the British and Maoris are in agreement in enforcing restrictive measures to prevent the growth of Oriental population. The result is that the Orientals are actually decreasing in number. We cannot but note that this policy of exclusion exhibits the same brand of racism as that which has dogged Canada and the United States for over half a century—and will ultimately have to be given up.

But to come back to the Maoris and the British. A half century ago the prospect was that the aboriginal New Zealander would soon be extinct; but the whole situation has changed, and the Maoris face the future with enthusiasm and hope. They have regained their high spirit and have increased from less than half their present number to the 90,000 which the census gives them today. The policy of the government has been completely revolutionized. Now the Maoris are given every possible encouragement to grow in power and influence. They have been accorded equal political, economic, and social rights, that is, so far as these can be conferred by legal enactment. They have full opportunities of securing an education. Most of them are nominal Christians. Unfortunately they are subject in their life as members of the church to extreme manifestations of fervor, and much of their old animistic outlook on life still clings to them. But what more could be expected of a people so recently delivered from fear of animistic spirits when even among members of Christian congregations in Western lands outlandish and enervating superstitions continue to have their baleful influence?

This remarkable change does not mean that all is well. It will take many decades to bridge the gap between the races, and it may be that there will long be tensions and problems. The Maoris and British are different in appearance; though the difference is not as marked as between a Negro and a white man, nevertheless it is real. This leads to discriminations of a mild kind, yet nothing like Jim Crow segregation in the southern United States. The linguistic difference is still a barrier, the Maoris clinging to their native Polynesian tongue with tenacity. Socially there is some discrimination. This leads to misunderstanding, and the result naturally is suspicion and resentment. But the Maoris are represented in the governing body and hold positions of authority. There is no racial bar to their advance to any position to which their ability entitles them. And above all these exists the fixed purpose on the part of both races to be fair, and on the part of the British to encourage the Maoris to preserve the features of their native heritage which fit in with the new life they all desire. In addition it is to be recorded that the Maoris soldiers in the New Zealand contingent played a most worthy part in World War II, especially in the campaign in the island of Crete. That will raise their prestige in their homeland.

Australia

We come finally to Australia, which has two problems, one entirely her own and the other involving her with other peoples in the East. The first is the relation of the white Australians to the Blackfellows of the interior. These despised, neglected, and ill-treated people are beginning to lie heavily on the conscience of the Australian. The beginnings of a different policy are making themselves felt, but with all that government and the churches are doing and may be able to do, doubt is expressed as to the future of these people—that is, whether they have any future at all and will not all die off in a few decades or a century at most.

The other, the really serious, problem which the Australian faces is that of population. A land almost as large as continental United States is the home of only about 7,000,000 people. Australia is the most sparsely settled of the continents, with only 2.23 people per square mile as contrasted with 689 in near-by Java, 403 in Japan, 102 in China, and 177 in India.[7] Of the total population, 97 per cent were born either in Australia of British parentage or somewhere in the United Kingdom. Here then we have a phenomenon doubly unique: an enormous territory not only

[7] "Population," sec. 2, "Density and Urbanization," *Encyclopedia Britannica* (14th ed.).

with far fewer occupants than it could easily support, and with a population wholly British, situated close to islands and a continent where population congestion is a most serious problem. The people are British, exceedingly proud of their heritage, intending to maintain themselves as a British state separate and distinct from their neighbors. Thus they have set up the "White Australia Policy."

One of the most serious factors in the history of Australia has been the failure of the various states to act together. But at this one point there has been almost complete agreement. Australians have always been at one in their adherence to the White Australia Policy. This has meant exclusion of all peoples from China and India, from which a flood of immigrants was feared. And yet Australia is in sore need of more people and yet more people. If only they would come from Great Britain or even from America, all would be well. No, they do not want others, not even Italians who might have been induced to come. The reality of this problem of population is becoming ever more consciously appreciated. Many years ago Mr. W. M. Hughes, the veteran Australian statesman, made this statement:

Australia needs a much larger population. World opinion will not tolerate much longer a dog-in-the-manger policy. We must choose between doing the thing ourselves in our own way, or letting others do it in their way. Our choice lies between filling our spaces with immigrants from Britain, and, if need be, other countries, and having the matter taken out of our hands and being swamped by the rush of peoples from the over-crowded countries of the world.[8]

An Australian writer speaks of this problem as "the hinge on which both the success and the justification of the policy must ultimately hang."[9] The tension in the minds of the Australians has not diminished but rather has increased as a result of the

[8] *The Sydney Morning Herald,* as quoted in Myra Willard, *History of the White Australia Policy,* p. 213, n. 69.

[9] Willard, *op. cit,* p. 211.

course of events at home and abroad during the last century. In defending their policy, Australians emphasize the economic and minimize the racial aspects of their attitude. "The fundamental reason for the adoption of the White Australia Policy is the preservation of a British-Australian nationality," [10] one of the chief means to accomplish this end being to hold up the standard of living by excluding cheap Oriental labor. Realizing how closely this attitude impinges on ideals of racial superiority over Orientals, Miss Willard feels compelled to say, "In the formation of their policy the leaders of the people were not actuated by any idea of the inferiority of the mentality or physique of the excluded peoples." [11] But while this was proclaimed as the official attitude, racial fear and animosity lay immediately beneath the surface. To quote again, "While this is true of the leaders it is not always true of the peoples' representatives as a whole." [12] Racial problems are almost always economic as well, made the more serious and difficult of solution because of this relation with physical well-being, but it will scarcely do to blind ourselves to the racism which is immediately at hand by seeking cover in the tangle of economic discussion.

Let us not minimize the reality of the problem which the Australians face. We must acknowledge the danger of lowering the standard of living by cheap labor, were the bars removed and Chinese and Indians allowed to come in unhindered. In the years during World War I the Anglican Bishop of Bathurst was so sure that Australians were solidly against unlimited immigration that he stated that "a change of 'opinion' is unimaginable, for this has long since been removed from the categories of fleeting political opinions." [13] But this is not the conviction of all Australians today. At least one writer looks at the matter quite differently. Dr. Charles I. McLaren, a former Australian medical

[10] *Ibid.,* pp. 188 ff.
[11] *Ibid.,* p. 191.
[12] *Ibid.,* p. 191 n. 8.
[13] "White Australia," *The East and the West,* XVII (1919), 299.

missionary in Korea faces certain sobering realities: "As the imminent threat of invasion and the deliverance therefrom by American intervention has taught us, Australia can remain inviolate only so long as her national policies commend themselves to the approval of Britain and America and win their active and costly support."[14] In addition Australia cannot afford to offend the racial susceptibilities of her 1,000,000,000 Asiatic neighbors. Putting his finger on the fundamental difficulty, this writer says, "I would say the first thing she [Australia] must do (and it will require honest effort and sustained education) is to rid herself of a 'white superiority complex'"[15] Dr. McLaren is fully alive to the danger of being swamped by cheap coolie labor. "Only sentimentalism can deny or obscure these facts. I for one would be opposed to a policy which forthwith, unconsidered and unprepared, opened Australia to an uncontrolled flood of coolie-standard Chinese or to the espionage of the agents and forerunners of Japan's military machine."[16]

Dr. McLaren knows that self-interest would dictate the policy of selection of immigrants, but he also realizes that it is difficult to devise a satisfactory practical plan of action. He feels that a deeper note needs to be struck. The Australian is in fear—that is quite evident—but it is to a considerable extent dread of the unknown, a want of faith in what the future has in store. His countrymen must rise to a new level where God's sovereignty—to use Dr. McLaren's own phrase—over nations and human life is recognized and where God's will may be done in confidence that only in doing that will can Australia come to her own.

Neither the exploiting greed of monopolists, bent on making profits by cheap imported labour and at the expense of essential human values, nor a dog-in-the-manger policy of "no-place-or-work-for-outsiders" which seeks to keep an empty continent as the vested interest of present

[14] *Preface to Peace with Japan*, p. 110.
[15] *Ibid.*, p. 111.
[16] *Ibid.*, p. 112.

occupants, neither of these conflicting selfishnesses nor both together can point the way to successful national or international solutions of Australia's major problem,—her future immigration policy. But there is a principle which is sound and it we must follow. We have a stewardship in this island continent in the Pacific.[17]

A group of Sydney ministers and laymen calling themselves the Christian Distributors' Association has issued a publication entitled *White Australia?* It shows that "the fourfold basis of the policy is conscious racialism, strong nationalism, a desire to maintain economic standards and imperial strategic realities." The publication "criticizes each of these in turn, and ends by a plea for a new immigration policy which, turning penitently away from racial exclusiveness, shall be 'a regulated yet generous opening of the doors of this land to all peoples.' " [18]

[17] *Ibid.,* p. 129.
[18] Letter from Allan T. McNaughton, *The Christian Century,* July 17, 1946, p. 902.

Chapter VIII

Black and White in Africa

Africa has had a longer period of recorded history than any other of the continents. The history of Egypt is said to have begun with the First Dynasty about 3200 B.C., but there was a long development of civilization before that time. This and other dates for over a thousand years are uncertain, but they serve to indicate that an African culture emerged out of the unknown ages of prehistory before that of any other part of the world. But besides Egypt the entire north coast of Africa has had a history going back as far, if not farther, than that of any of the European lands on the shores of the Mediterranean. In striking contrast, Africa south of the Sahara Desert continued to be the Dark Continent almost to our time. Maps of Africa made within the last eighty or ninety years were curious combinations of authentic information concerning the coast line and misinformation or no information at all about the interior. Jonathan Swift hits the situation off exactly when he writes:

> So geographers, in Afric maps,
> With savage pictures fill their gaps,
> And o'er unhabitable downs
> Place elephants for want of towns.

It is the people of that part of Africa so long unknown with whom we have to do in this study.

The continent is divided racially into two major sections, Caucasian, or white Africa, and Negro Africa. According to A. H. Keene these two races in Africa "have been conterminous throughout all known time."[1] There has been considerable mix-

---

[1] *Man: Past and Present* (rev. ed., A. H. Guggin and A. C. Haddon, 1920), p. 41.

ture of the races, yet "without any very distinct geographical frontiers, the ethnological parting line may be detected."[2] This line runs from west to east beginning at the mouth of the Senegal River in French West Africa and continuing steadily eastward across the continent as far as Khartoum on the Nile, touching the upper part of the great bend of the Niger at Timbuktu and coming close to the shores of Lake Chad in the center of the continent. From Khartoum the line turns abruptly to the south, following in general the course of the Nile as far as its sources in the great lakes in Uganda, and then again making a turn to the east and southeast until it reaches the Indian Ocean at the mouth of the Juba River exactly on the equator. All the country north of that line is inhabited by the Hamitic-Semitic section of the great Caucasian or white race, and all the lands to the south by the people of the black race. We do not know when the black man began to occupy this region. The few archaeological remains do not supply sufficient evidence to warrant any reliable estimate. What we do know is that the ancient Egyptian monuments picture the same black man who inhabits the regions to the south today.

In this vast section of the continent "there is a remarkably general similarity of type."[3] While that is true at first sight, there exist differences between the Sudanese Negroes in the north and the Bantus in the south. Again a line can be drawn with considerable accuracy between these similar yet different groups. It begins at the mouth of the Rio del Ray in the southeast corner of Nigeria on the Gulf of Guinea and runs eastward to the region of the great lakes where it meets the aforementioned line from Khartoum which separates black Africa from white. A glance at the map will quickly show how disproportionate these two sections of black Africa are. The Sudanese Negroes live in the smaller section which lies between the Sahara Desert on the north and the Atlantic Ocean and the huge Congo basin on the south.

[2] *Ibid.*
[3] *Ibid.*, p. 43.

146

All the rest of Africa down to Cape Town at the tip of the continent is Bantuland.

"In both groups the relatively full blood natives are everywhere very much alike, and the contrasts are presented chiefly among the mixed or Negroid populations." [4] This means that in the Sudan the Hamitic Berbers and Tuaregs and Semitic Arabs have mingled their blood with the Negroes. Farther to the east the Hamitic Galla, who came from northeast Africa, intermarried with the Bantus.

Wherein do the Negroes of the north differ from the Bantus of the south? Without doubt the people of the Sudan have made more cultural advance than their kinsfolk in the south, but this is not the only, nor is it the chief, difference. In one point at least "the Bantu somewhat unaccountably compare favorably with the Sudanese. . . . The less cultured Bantu populations all, without any known exception, speak dialects of a single mother-tongue, while the greatest linguistic confusion prevails amongst the semi-civilized as well as the savage peoples of Sudan." [5] The Bantu language "cannot now be even remotely affiliated to any one of the numerous distinct forms of speech current in the Sudanese domain." [6] Attention is called to this remarkable fact because it indicates that these people have lived apart through long ages.

Several other small groups belonging to the black race are found in the area inhabited by the Bantus, but are farther removed from them than the Bantus are from the Sudanese Negroes. The least important are the Negrillos, or Pygmies, those shy little men having a precarious existence in the Congo forests. They are thought to have been more widely spread in times past, but today they live only in small scattered groups in the heart of the continent between 6 degrees north and 6 degrees south of the equator, that is, about a thousand miles north and south.

[4] *Ibid.*, p. 44.
[5] *Ibid.*, p. 45.
[6] *Ibid.*

More important are the Bushmen and the Hottentots, living in the more or less desert regions in southwest Africa. In early times they were a fine race, probably widely spread over South Africa, but now consist only of remnants reduced to a low level of culture. These people differ from the neighboring Bantus in being lighter in color and having tufted hair in small separate patches over their heads. The Bushmen are wanderers, living by the chase, while the Hottentots possess herds. They thus became the envy of the Dutch settlers when they began to trek north into the interior from the Cape. Contrary to the earlier opinion, it is now believed that the Bushmen are the older stock from which the Hottentots branched off. The Dutch in many cases did not hesitate to mate with Hottentot women, thus producing a mixed people, the Bastards, and adding to the racial complexity of the African scene.

In order the better to understand the racial issues with which our study deals we need to make another distinction. It is that between those parts of the Sudan and Bantuland where Europeans are relatively few in number and those in which they form a considerable part of the population and have come to make a permanent home. In the former, Europeans consist of government officials, traders, managers, and missionaries. The climate is so unfavorable that white men have not, and will not, come in large numbers—it must ever remain the country of black men. The situation in those sections is in sharp contrast with others where climatic conditions are far different and where white men with their families have come in large numbers as permanent residents. The Kenya Colony in east central Africa and the Union of South Africa are the chief sections where these conditions prevail, though the Tanganyika highlands, Angola, and Northern Rhodesia also have their quota of permanent European settlers. The presence of white men in large numbers who are there to stay has created a problem unknown elsewhere in the world. Here the white man is a minority group, very vigorous and self-assertive, in the midst of an overwhelming majority of black men. It is quite different from the situation in the United States, where the whites form the basic population and the Negroes are and will doubtless remain a minority group.

The situation is so different that it becomes necessary to consider the problem of the relation of the races under these divergent conditions separately. For the most part the sections of the continent where white men are relatively few in number are parts of the colonial empires of European nations; while white man's land is mostly in the Union of South Africa, which is one of the independent, self-ruled commonwealths of the British Empire. The principal exception is Kenya, a crown colony of Great Britain, though there are other and smaller permanent white settlements, as already mentioned, which are not within the Union of South Africa. At any rate the problems of racial relations in the Union and in Kenya are so different from those in the colonial areas that we must consider them separately.

Colonial Africa

It is impossible as well as unnecessary in a study of racial relations to attempt to deal with many other problems of colonial life and administration. Some of these will be touched upon in a later chapter dealing with racism and world order. We must recognize, however, that the issues of race are so intimately related to economic, political, and religious problems that it is not possible to deal with one, even in a brief sketch, without running over into the field of the others. But we shall keep the emphasis on race and deal with other features only incidentally.

In the parts of the continent of Africa with which we are dealing, four European powers are represented by their colonies: Portugal, Belguim, France, and Great Britain. The Portuguese colonies are Angola in West Africa, south of the mouth of the Congo, and Portuguese East Africa (Mozambique) on the opposite side of the continent. "Unstable home government, lack of consistent planning, inferior personnel, and inefficient administration have combined to make of the Portuguese possessions the most

149

backward of all, with the sole exception of the Spanish" [7]—which are not located in black Africa and so do not come within our survey. Singularly enough, but in conformity with the Portuguese pattern in the homeland and in Brazil, race prejudice is less evident in these colonies than in those of other European nations. Interbreeding both within and outside the marriage bond is fairly frequent, with the result that discrimination is less strictly enforced and the relations between the races are more free and easygoing. With the general Portuguese policy of assimulation of cultures, racial amalgamation has proceeded farther here than in other parts of Africa.

The Belgian Congo has had a strange and contradictory history. A recent official government brochure on Belgian colonial policy completely evades the notoriously corrupt administration when the so-called Congo Free State was the personal property of King Leopold II of Belgium.[8] The "Congo Atrocities" at the end of the nineteenth century became a stench in the nostrils of decent men the world over. Against this background, since the colony was taken over by the Belgian government, there has been remarkable improvement. The ideal is now stated ·in these words, "Colonization is a work, a great work in the service and interest of the primitive populations of which the colonizer has taken charge." [9] With a new ideal has come more enlightened practice, especially in social services, though much is left to be desired. So far as race is concerned the lines are far more strictly drawn than in the Portuguese colonies. This means not only social segregation, but strict concentration of the central administration in Belgian hands and with little promise of improvement. Education is almost entirely agricultural and technical. Little or no thought is given to the training of the native peoples to assume responsibility in colonial administration and government.

[7] Raymond Kennedy, "The Colonial Crisis and the Future," *The Science of Man in the World Crisis,* ed. Ralph Linton, p. 334.

[8] Albert de Vleeschauwer, *Belgian Colonial Policy* (1943), p. 48.

[9] *Ibid.,* p. 4.

France possesses the largest colonial area in Africa. Most of it, however, is outside the scope of this study, but Senegal, Ivory Coast, Dahomey, and French Equatorial Africa are in black man's Africa. The policy has consistently been one of assimilation, and in this it has diverged from both the Dutch and British. Her purpose has been to make the colonies a part of the French nation, one and indivisible, whether found in France, Africa, or French Indo-China. To accomplish this it has been a very definite part of the plan to raise the "elite" in the colonies to a position of equality with the European and make them feel that they are first of all Frenchmen rather than Negro Africans. The most notable illustration of the success of this policy was the late Felix Eboué, who when he died in 1944 was governor-general of French Equatorial Africa. He had been honored as a member of the Empire Council and "Compagnon de l'Ordre de la Liberation." He was a Negro born in French Guiana, whose ability was recognized as he was raised step by step to a position of commanding influence. To him the gratitude of the Allied Nations is due because of his courage (in 1940) in turning against the Vichy government and throwing in his lot with Free France. This was at a time when Germany controlled the Mediterranean, and the route through central Africa, where he was in control, was the only means of communication and transport of supplies from the Atlantic seaboard to Egypt and the Mediterranean.[10]

The case of Felix Eboué is thus singled out, not because he is the only Negro who deserves mention, but because he became more prominent politically than any other and also because he has been very influential in the making of the newer policies which will undoubtedly govern French administration and attitudes in the colonies. He stood solidly for the policy of assimilation, which to him meant "that the evolution of the colonies must never tend to a separation from the mother country, but it must be aimed at strengthening the bonds which tie all colonial territories together

[10] See "French Colonial Policy in Africa," *Free France*, special issue No. 2; also Walter White, *A Rising Wind*, pp. 103-22.

with metropolitan France, with a view to forming one single national entity, one and indivisible." [11] Eboué also believed in the already-existing policy of raising "the status of the 'notables évalués' in French Equatorial Africa." [12] What share the masses of the people are to have is not made clear despite the enlarged plans for their better education, which "will be directed towards this progressive accession to public office," [13] an accession which on paper at least, is broad and impartial. One of the weaknesses of the French administration has been just at this point, that is, in the disproportionate emphasis placed on the elite as contrasted with the uneducated common people. They are helped less than in British colonies, but in spite of this the very fact that some native Africans could and were lifted to the status of European Frenchmen indicates that the color bar is to a certain extent let down and Negroes and whites tend to become equal. "The subject peoples of France are recognized as potential equals; they can look forward to full French Citizenship when properly qualified." [14] An important conference held at Brazzaville, on the Congo, in the early weeks of 1944 took an enlightened stand on colonial policy, which gives hope that the laxity in administration in the African colonies will be changed as the new France emerges and is able to make good her promises.[15]

The chief British colonies in Africa are Sierra Leone, Gold Coast Colony, Nigeria, Kenya, and Northern and Southern Rhodesia. The population of these colonies is the largest of any colonial power on the continent, but they are very uneven in population and in the relation of the races in them. Kenya and the two Rhodesias resemble the Union of South Africa in the nature of their racial tensions, in that white men and their families have

[11] *Free France*, special issue No. 2, p. 6.

[12] *Ibid.*, p. 9.

[13] *Ibid.*

[14] Raymond Kennedy, *op. cit.*, p. 330.

[15] Since the death of Felix Eboué his widow has been elected a member of the French Constituent Assembly from the island of Guadeloupe, the first Negro woman to be thus honored.

settled permanently in the highlands away from the malarial low-lands and are insisting on their dominance over the black men.

In the colonies on the west coast the combination of intelligent administration and adherence to the strictest code of segregation between the races creates a situation different from that in the colonies of other powers. British success as a colonizing nation is to be accounted for by the highminded integrity of colonial officials, both in the colonial office in London and in the various colonies. "Natives often express a grudging admiration for the moral rectitude, financial incorruptibility, and legalistic fairness of Britishers, especially government officials, in the colonies"—grudging because "bonds of mutual friendship and affection are lacking." [16] The roll of eminent and highly respected British colonial officials is large. Among them none can be placed higher than Lord Frederick D. Lugard, governor-general of Nigeria 1914-19, and Sir Gordon Guggisberg, the founder of Achimota College in the Gold Coast Colony. As high-sounding as are the declarations of colonial policy by other powers, none have equaled the British in performance. They have done more to provide social services and education, from the lowest grades to the university level, than any other nation. The ideal has of course not been reached, but the purpose exists and points forward to "the development of political institutions and political power until the day arrives when the people can become effectively self governing." [17] This comes directly from the colonial office in London, 1941, as the report of the Advisory Committee on Education in the Colonies. In June, 1945, a "Report of the Commission on Higher Education in West Africa" advocating the establishment of a full-fledged university was presented to Parliament.

As a result of this policy little unrest has been found in the native population. In West Africa the native people were heartily with the British in prosecuting the war against the Fascist powers. They are in better condition and have more advantages than they

[16] Raymond Kennedy, *op. cit.*, p. 320.
[17] *Mass Education in African Society*, p. 4.

have ever known before. Why then is their admiration of the British official "grudging"? Why should it not be? With all the good will and administrative efficiency it exhibits, "The British Colonial code draws the most rigid color line of all. Paradoxically, the greatest colonizers in the world are the most provincial people in their attitudes towards strange groups and cultures." [18] The color line is a bar not only against association with the masses of the people; it is just as strict against the "elite," the influential and intelligent leaders. Here is a confession from a well-known British publicist: "And have we yet left behind us what Condorcet called 'our bloodstained contempt for men of another colour and another creed?' Do Africans even now find in many of the Europeans they encounter brothers, whose 'friends and pupils' they are eager to become?" [19] How unfortunate that men in government service, who are faithfully wearing themselves out in utter devotion to those over whom they have been placed are not, and cannot be, appreciated at their true worth for the simple reason that they are caught up in a system which makes the one other thing which is essential impossible, a system based on the outmoded theory that the white race is inherently superior to the black so that true fellowship is excluded.

The attitude in Kenya—and Northern and Southern Rhodesia —is based on the same racist assumption but has a different manifestation. The fundamental question is that of land. Whereas in the other colonies native interests have been safeguarded, in Kenya the allotment of land as between the 20,000 Europeans and the 3,-000,000 Africans is most unjust. On the surface it would seem that the native Africans are being fairly well treated. The Europeans have been allocated 16,700 square miles, while the natives have in their reserves 43,000 square miles. But in Kenya the areas where the soil is good and the rainfall abundant are limited. One half of this good land has been given to 1,600 landholding Europeans and their families, with about 120,000 African employees, while the

[18] Raymond Kennedy, *op. cit.*, p. 320.

[19] H. N. Brailsford, "Socialists and the Empire," *Fabian Colonial Essays,* p. 20.

other half must support 3,000,000 Africans. The situation is even worse than these figures would indicate. Of the 16,700 square miles allotted to Europeans "only about two-thirds have in fact been taken up, and of these two-thirds the greater part is not being properly worked," [20] yet the Africans cannot make use of any of these areas. Where the Africans are compelled to occupy the land and cultivate it, the climate is unfavorable to health—to that of the Africans as well as of the Europeans. Much the same can be said of the situation in Northern Rhodesia. Southern Rhodesia has done somewhat better by the African natives. In both we find injustice with respect to land and other restrictions galling to the natives. But there are no such legal disabilities as the Jim Crow laws in the United States. The natives have certain political rights, but so slight is their influence that they feel they are oppressed and set aside at every turn.[21] Other aspects of racial tension in Kenya are so much like those in the Union of South Africa that they need not be considered separately.

Union of South Africa

The racial problem in South Africa was created by the coming of two groups of Europeans, the Dutch or Boers, and the British. The first navigators who reached the Cape of Good Hope were Portuguese, but they did not permanently settle in that region. They were superseded by the Dutch, who with the English became masters of the sea route to India and the Indies. But even the Dutch for a long time looked upon the Cape as only "a freshment station for the ships of the Dutch East India Company *en route* to the Spice Islands." [22] But by the end of the eighteenth century a permanent settlement had been established, and of course in a short time contact had been made with the natives, the backward Bushmen and Hottentots. Slaves to do farm work had already been

[20] C. W. W. Greenidge, "Land Hunger in the Colonies," *Fabian Colonial Essays*, pp. 192-94.

[21] See Jomo Henyatta, *Kenya: the Land of Conflict*, for the side of the native African.

[22] *Encyclopedia of World History*, p. 859.

introduced from West Africa and Asia. The small Dutch population was early increased by the arrival of refugee Huguenots, fleeing from religious persecution in France. These immigrants were in the course of time completely amalgamated with the Dutch. Then came the British, who were quite as intent as the Dutch to maintain a supply depot on the route to India. Difficulties which led to armed conflict naturally arose. The Cape passed back and forth several times between the two nations, but finally by the Treaty of Paris in 1814 the British were given complete possession. Since 1910 the whole of South Africa has become one of the commonwealth of nations in the British Empire.

Though for over a hundred years Great Britain exercised sovereignty over the land, now the Union of South Africa is an independent dominion in direct control of all its internal affairs. This is an important distinction and must ever be held in mind. But while the Dutch Boer and the British have been united under one government, they are yet far from being at one on many questions. One of the chief causes of difficulty in the early days was the difference in attitude toward the native population. In 1807 the slave trade was abolished in the British Empire. This immediately created a labor problem at the Cape. The question was at once asked, if they could no longer have slaves from elsewhere, why should not the Hottentots near at hand be drafted for service? In 1809 by legal enactment the Hottentots were restricted in their movements so as to force them to work for the whites. This was really a form of slavery, and it could exist because, while the slave trade was gone, slavery itself was not abolished in the British Empire until 1834. Soon after the final British occupation of the Cape, English missionaries began to arrive. They worked not only for the conversion of the natives but also for an improvement of their helpless condition. This meant trouble. The Dutch farmers raised strong objection to every move which tended to prevent unrestricted use of the natives. As yet the British were not present in sufficient numbers to be a part of the problem, but after 1820 many

156

began to come in as colonists who took up land for permanent occupany.

The most serious breach occurred after the complete abolition of slavery in the Empire in 1834. Thirty-five thousand slaves were freed in South Africa, compensation being given for their loss.[23] The Dutch, however, claimed that they were unfairly treated in these payments and were deeply disgruntled. In addition, Kaffirs, Zulus, and other Bantu tribes more vigorous than the Hottentots and Bushmen, rose in revolt because of the steadily advancing encroachment of the Dutch into their ancestral landholdings. These and other difficulties, rankling in the breasts of the sturdy but exceedingly conservative Dutch, led to the Great Trek in 1835-37. About 10,000 Boers, cattlemen and farmers, moved north, passed beyond the Vaal River, and settled in the country known later as the Transvaal, or the South African Republic. Here they thought they would be beyond the irritating restrictions imposed by the British. They could have slaves, or, if not, could treat the native population as they believed the blacks should be treated without the exasperating opposition of the idealistic English missionaries.

But difficulties did not cease. The vision and ambition of Cecil Rhodes only brought to a head the restless advance of the British northward into the heart of southern Africa.[24] The culmination came with the South African war, which lasted from 1899 to 1902. The Boers, splendid marksmen and hardened campaigners though they were, could not hold back the disciplined pressure of the British army and finally capitulated. A few years later a constitutional convention was held which agreed on a form of government for the Union of South Africa. This constitution was approved by the British Parliament in 1910. The total population in the Union of almost 10,000,000 is unevenly divided into some 2,-000,000 whites and 8,000,000 blacks. The Boers outnumber the British by a few thousand and look upon themselves as forming a

---

[23] *Ibid.,* p. 861.

[24] See Stuart Cloete, *Against These Three,* for a vivid portrayal of Paul Kruger, Cecil Rhodes, and Lobengula.

different people though belonging to the same nation. The language difficulty is hard to surmount, both the Boers and the British holding tenaciously to their native tongues. The chief things which bind them together at the present time are their opposition to the native population and their purpose to keep the natives in perpetual subordination.

The natives suffer under serious disabilities. "In Africa nothing is of greater importance than the right to occupy land." [25] The same author summarizes the situation thus, "Africans have been deprived of land which used to belong to them; in some territories what is left is insufficient for their needs; and they are not always secure even in the possession of what they still hold." [26] The situation is a little difficult to understand, in view of the vast size of Africa and the smallness of the population, until it is realized that there are vast areas that are uninhabitable and incapable of cultivation. In the Union of South Africa it has long been recognized that the "amount of land available for African use is grossly inadequate," [27] but very little change for the better has been made.

It is only fair to state another side. When the Dutch became settlers in South Africa, they came into contact with the Bushmen and Hottentots. But there were migratory movements among Bantu tribes who lived northeast of the Cape, so that as the Boers and the British moved north and east, they collided with incoming Kaffirs armed and conquering as they came. Violent warfare for rights of possession followed, and the European with better arms won. So the Bantus were not exactly driven out of their ancestral home; they were intruders themselves and were made to submit to the Europeans. In addition, the Europeans frequently defend their presence by the claim that the Africans do not know how to cultivate the soil but only misuse it. Why then should not they, the superior Europeans, be given what they can more profit-

---

[25] G. W. Broomfield, *Colour Conflict: Race Relations in Africa*, p. 18.

[26] *Ibid.*, p. 19.

[27] *Ibid.*, p. 29.

ably use? But when these considerations are seen against the background of deep race prejudice, which cares little or nothing for the good of the natives, they lose much of their force. No matter how skillful the natives may be as farmers, they are inferior and can claim no rights as against the Europeans.[28]

Taxation weighs heavily on the Africans. In many sections the direct tax is so heavy that they cannot make the required payments. This has resulted in the migration of the people away from the countryside to the towns, cities, and mining centers where they can earn cash. In many cases where a whole family does not move, the father feels compelled to go to these centers and be absent for long periods of time, thus breaking up family and village life with resulting demoralization, both moral and social. Says Gerald Broomfield, "It is also beyond question that the great bulk of migration—whatever its immediate causes—is a result of the coming of the white man, and its effects on the African are the same."[29] All of course, both Africans and Europeans, bear the burden of taxation; but the Europeans are in a favorable position, while the Africans are driven to the wall.

To those not living in South Africa the pass-laws are a strange phenomenon. They are not entirely unreasonable, but their existence and the rigidity with which they are applied are deeply resented by the native population. There are differences in the regulations in the different states, but the same general principle holds good. To cite an example, "In the Transvaal and Orange Free State Africans must take out passes to enter or travel anywhere within the two provinces except the small areas scheduled as native areas."[30] Outside of the Union of South Africa, the colonies of Southern Rhodesia and Kenya have similar systems but somewhat "simpler and less exacting."[31] These passes must be shown on de-

---

[28] H. S. Scott, "The Christian Churches and the Colour Bar," *International Review of Missions,* July, 1942, pp. 301 ff.

[29] *Op. cit.,* p. 37.

[30] *Ibid.,* p. 45.

[31] *Ibid.*

mand, and arrest follows if they cannot be produced. This beomes a hardship for a native traveling in the rain without sufficient protection for his own person or the fragile paper pass. There are suggestions from various quarters that the system be abolished, but as yet they have come to nothing. The natives must be controlled —that is the conviction everywhere expressed in the European community—and this is one good way to keep them within bounds. *The Bantu World,* a native publication, has made some very pertinent and devastating comments on the system.

The "pass" system, so far from helping to control the natives, has been the means of increasing resentment and the commitment of more crimes, has encouraged forgery and created enmity between the police and the African people. Even the diplomatic and tactful enforcement of the law is resented. The "pass" is looked upon as a badge of slavery and a mark of inferiority. The natives are convinced that these laws were enacted not as a means of identification, but in order to facilitate the exploitation of their labor. To continue these laws results in the embitterment of race relations, and makes co-operation between Whites and Blacks increasingly difficult if not impossible. To abolish these laws would go a long way toward creating an atmosphere of friendliness and winning the African's confidence in the justice of the white man's rule. It is encouraging to note that the demand for their abolition is growing.[32]

As galling as are the pass-laws they do not approach in importance the conditions under which South Africans are compelled to work. Slavery is gone, but at certain times and places a forced-labor policy has been used which has compelled the native to work against his will for foreign masters. This was condemned by the Geneva Convention in 1930, which described and proscribed such labor as "work or service which is exacted from any person under the menace of penalty, and for which such person has not offered himself voluntarily."[33] As a result of this stand forced la-

---

[32] Blaine E. Kirkpatrick, paper based on *South African Outlook,* Aug. 1, 1941, p. 150.

[33] As quoted in Broomfield, *op. cit.,* p. 53.

bor is being abolished, but the history of its use helps us to realize the attitude of the Europeans toward the natives as subordinates who should be made to serve even if they do not willingly offer their services.

A real and very serious problem of the present day is the inequality of wages as between European and African workmen. Even though improvement is to be noted in recent years, the discrepancy is appalling. And behind this is the color bar, which effectively shuts out the natives from many forms of skilled labor.

The Union of South Africa maintains what is called the "civilized labour policy" and there is legislation designed to prevent the natives from entering the higher grades of skilled employment.[34]

Lord Hailey brings out a further disadvantage which comes to the natives from this legislation:

At the moment it operates as a restriction only on a small proportion of the native labour force which is qualified for entry into skilled employment; but it has a wider influence in depriving natives of the incentive to qualify themselves as "skilled" workmen and in maintaining the system under which native labour is as a whole renumerated at "unskilled" rates.[35]

What is the motive lying back of the restriction? It is very clear.

There is no secret about it. It is because the white man demands protection from competition. If the African were allowed to do skilled or responsible work there would be fewer jobs for the European—so it is argued.[36]

It must become apparent that back of all the measures of repression and the superior attitude toward the natives there is a deep-lying

[34] *Ibid.*, p. 64.

[35] *Report of the Commission Appointed to Enquire into the Disturbances in the Copper Belt, Northern Rhodesia*, July, 1940, as quoted in Broomfield, *op. cit.*, p. 658.

[36] Broomfield, *op. cit.*, p. 66.

and all-consuming fear on the part of the white men as they look around and see a huge native population which, with all of its backwardness, is becoming unified in its desire and purpose to achieve self-respect and win a more honorable place in the life of the country.

What is the actual wage scale? In the mines of South Africa the Europeans receive on the average seven times more than the natives. No one would say that with living conditions as they are the Africans should at the present time receive as much as the Europeans, but that is scarcely the point. The desire which seems to possess the mind of the Europeans is to keep their own wages on a level at which they can live much better than they should naturally expect to live, and this at the expense of the natives whom they look down upon as inferiors who have no right to ask for more. While conditions are serious within the Union, they are worse in the northern territories. In Southern Rhodesia the disparity between African and European wages reaches the ratio of one to sixteen.[37] It is profitable to keep the wages of the natives low, for there are stockholders at home clamoring for large returns on their investments. As late as 1937 the copper mines in Rhodesia were paying dividends ranging from 20 to 80 per cent.

To the disabilities already enumerated we must add, so far as the Union of South Africa is concerned, political impotence and social segregation. Black Africans have no political power, either the right of the ballot or the privilege of holding positions of even lesser authority in the government. By the sheer physical fact that they are outnumbered the white men are frightened by the prospect of being engulfed by black supremacy—it has been spoken of as the nightmare constantly facing the Europeans in Africa. And of course the black men are kept in social ostracism from the white. Where the two races come into contact, it is in the master-servant and employer-workman relations. Intermarriage is banned as completely as in many of the states in our country.

What is the official attitude toward the relation of the races in

[37] *Ibid.,* p. 68.

South Africa? We may take the words of General Jan Christian Smuts, prime minister of the Union of South Africa. His words are the more remarkable in that he is himself an Afrikander, once an enemy of the British when he was a Boer officer in the South African War. He stated in 1921:

The whole basis of our particular system rests on inequality. We started as a small white colony in a black continent. In the Union the vast majority of our citizens are black, probably the majority of them are in a semibarbarous state still, and we have never in our laws recognized any system of equality. It is the bed rock of our constitution. That is the fundamental position from which we start. That is the colour question.

There is little change in a statement made in 1933:

I cannot forget that civilization has been built up in this country by the white race, that we are the guardians of liberty, justice and all the elements of progress in South Africa. The franchise is the last argument, more powerful than the sword or rifle; and the day we give away this final protection we possess we shall have to consider very carefully what we are doing.[38]

But again after another decade Smuts gave himself to a new principle, which "implied that the trustee regarded the rights of his ward as sacred rights. . . . We want to take a holiday from old ideas which have brought nothing but bitterness and strife to our country, and try to the best of our ability to fashion a variegated but harmonious race pattern in South Africa." [39]

This is about the best that the statesman has been able to do. General Smuts has a conscience; he stands for liberty and freedom; but he feels the backward pull of his people, especially the Boers, who charge that their leader has forsaken them by allowing himself to advance beyond the customary and agelong practices

[38] S. G. Millins, *General Smuts,* as quoted in paper by F. Marion Smith. (Unpublished.)
[39] *The London Times,* report of speech made on January 21, 1942, as quoted in Broomfield, *op. cit.,* p. 10.

of inequality, a distinction based upon the most unequivocal acceptance of the doctrine of innate, racial inequality.

The picture presented by the relations of the races in South Africa is not a happy one. In fact it is one of the sorest spots in racial tension to be found anywhere in the world and one which might become an open conflict at any time. Light breaks through, however, at a number of points. One of these is the attitude of the Christian Council of South Africa. This body has taken a most enlightened stand on the color question—so advanced that its very liberality has been an apple of discord. All the Protestant communions within the Union took part in the forming of this council. The largest church is the Dutch Reformed, to which the Boer has traditionally given his tenacious allegiance. It seemed a wonderful thing that this ultraconservative church, a church reactionary not only biblically and theologically but socially, politically, and in every other way, would become a part of such a council. The church is quite unlike the churches of the same order in Holland and in the United States. It reflects the long isolation of the Afrikanders from the people and the life of the mother country. What little connection they have had during the centuries has not prevented the development of a type of stubborn conservatism which is almost unique. Unfortunately as time passed, difficulties arose in the council of churches. The bilingual character of the council was embarrassing, but that could have been overcome. The real problem was that created by radically different attitudes concerning the relation of the races. The breach widened until separation took place, and now in additon to the original Christian Council we have the Federal Mission Council of the Dutch Reformed Churches.

A revealing statement was made by one of their leaders who attempted to justify the action of his church:

The last reason for the failure was the deepest of all: our conflicting views on the right relations between White and Black. The English speaking missionary, especially one born overseas, wishes to see as little difference as possible between the white man and the native. He does not hesitate to welcome the civilized native to his dining table.[40]

He then goes on to mention other practices of the English missionary which, to the Dutch churchmen, are "revolting." Then he closes his statement with these amazing words:

Our case suffers harm because we do not continually hold the principles of Christian race segregation and of sympathetic guardianship before those who think otherwise. If we do this with wisdom and patience in a way that they can understand, it must find acceptance in the long run, eradicate the unhealthy equalizing, and give the native a clear impression of Christian harmony.[41]

Here is a church which has nailed the banner of inherent racial superiority and inferiority to its masthead and believes that all the churches will follow it in the battle line. Its members are deeply religious people, loyal to their church, reading their old Dutch Bibles faithfully. They seem never to have caught the meaning of Paul's words, "God hath made of one blood all nations of men," [42] but have persevered in their interpretation of the curse of Canaan, who shall be a "servant of servants unto his brethren," [43] wrongly equating the Canaanites with the black men among whom they live. Naturally it has not been difficult to make use of a rigid doctrine of God's election and his predestined will for men to strengthen their purpose to keep the black man where God placed him.

In 1860 Indians were invited to come to South Africa because of the scarcity of native African labor. They have been there since that time and now number 250,000. Most of them are found in the Transvaal, where there are 30,000, and in Natal, in which they

---

[40] As quoted in "The Christian Council of South Africa," *International Review of Missions,* XXXIII, No. 131 (July, 1944), 261.

[41] *Ibid.,* p. 262.

[42] Acts 17:26.

[43] Gen. 9:25.

number 200,000. The situation which they face is much like that of the Bantu population of South Africa. During the early decades of their presence in their new home they were more or less contented, being considered desirable citizens, but latterly they have chafed under all sorts of discrimination. It was here that Mr. Gandhi began his career as a lawyer and initiated the practice of nonviolent passive resistance as far back as 1911.

And now the whole matter has assumed even more sinister proportions by the passage of the Asiatic Land Tenure and Indian Representation Act in 1946. An Indian South African writes thus: "This law means the complete segregation of our community and takes away from us our right to free ownership and occupation of landed property except in certain limited and segregated areas." [44] Recently four hundred Indians where thrust into jail at hard labor for camping on a site in Durban which had been forbidden to Indians.

This act is defended by those who are eager to preserve white priority, but it is condemned by Gandhi, Nehru, and the Indian people in general. This opposition is also voiced by many white people in South Africa who realize the seriousness of the new situation created by this last act of discrimination and segregation. What the end will be no one can forsee.

[44] Ashwin Choudree, "South Africa Turns Against Its Indians," *Asia and the Americas*, September, 1946, p. 394.

Chapter IX

Brazil: The Fading Out of the Color Line

Why is there a Portuguese-speaking as well as a Spanish-speaking Latin America? Strange to say the die was cast before anyone in Europe knew that Brazil or the continent of South America existed. Within one year after Christopher Columbus discovered America, Pope Alexander VI, a Spaniard, drew the famous Line of Demarcation north and south in the Atlantic Ocean "one hundred leagues to the west and south from any of the islands commonly known as the Azores and Cape Verde."[1] All newly discovered lands east of this line were to go to Portugal and everything west to Spain. This did not please Portugal; so within another year—that is, in 1494—the Treaty of Tordesillas, which moved the line to three hundred and seventy leagues west of the Cape Verde Islands, was signed between the two countries. When this line is drawn on a map of South America, it cuts across Brazil from the mouth of the Amazon to almost the southern extremity of the country, thus giving to Portugal the most populous and most important part of what is now Brazil. Later its boundaries were moved far to the west, but that has nothing to do with the matter at hand. These transactions took place before the continent of South America had been discovered, but nevertheless are responsible for the situation we face today.

Portugal showed concern for the exploration of the Atlantic and the coast of Africa before Spain. This interest during the fifteenth century centered in the person of Prince Henry the Navigator, who for many years sent his captains farther and farther to the south. The impulse continued long after Prince Henry's death in 1460, so

---

[1] As quoted in Mary W. Williams, *The Peoples and Politics of Latin America*, p. 107.

that in 1488 Dias doubled the Cape of Good Hope (Cape of Storms as it was first called) and in 1498 Vasco da Gama reached the little port of Calicut on the southwest coast of India, thus opening up the sea route from Europe to India and the East. In the year 1500 the Portuguese commander Cabral actually claimed Brazil, which he sighted on his way to the Orient, for King Emanuel of Portugal, and thus re-enforced the provision of the Treaty of Tordesillas. But for years even after a footing had been secured in Brazil, the Portuguese looked upon it as little more than a stopping place on the way to the Indies. The attitude was changed when Portugal began to realize that other colonizing powers, notably France, were casting envious eyes on the land, and that it would be seized if she did not take its colonization seriously.

When, however, the Portuguese were firmly established, the relations of the colony and the mother country were quite different from those between the Spanish colonies and Spain. Portugal did not attempt to exercise the same strict control. There was a viceroy in Rio de Janeiro representing the king, but there was "a strong tendency to exercise local autonomy." [2] One evidence and outcome of this policy was the rise in South Brazil of a body of frontiersmen, a mixture of Indian and Iberian blood, called Bandeirantes (also called Paulistas and later Cearenses). They had courage, energy, and restless aggressiveness and "felt that it was their manifest destiny to occupy if they could and hold for their government the entire continent into which they pushed their energetic way. . . . It was through Paulista enterprise that most of the Amazon basin was occupied and settled, thus bringing to the Brazilian nation an area double that to which Portugal was entitled by the unexecuted treaty of Tordesillas." [3]

As was the case with Spanish America, Brazil felt the thrill of the American Revolution and won her independence at about the same time with the other states in South America. But the

[2] *Ibid.*, p. 247.
[3] *Ibid.*, p. 252.

development took a direction all its own. In the case of the Spanish colonies the example of the United States was followed, and the different commonwealths which were founded became republics. Not so in Brazil. Many of the same grievances which led to the revolt of the Spanish colonies were felt. A spirit of independence had existed under cover for many years, but the end of the Portuguese rule came in a unique fashion. The separation was intimately connected with Napoleon's invasion of the Iberian Peninsula. The royal family of Portugal was in danger of being captured; so in order to escape such a catastrophe the Portuguese fleet, protected by British warships, sailed off to Brazil with the royal family, the court, and many others—altogether about fifteen thousand persons. Brazil naturally entered into an entirely new relation with the mother country, and a decree in 1815 made Brazil co-ordinate with Portugal in a United Kingdom. The king remained in Brazil until 1821, when he returned to Portugal with his court to quiet the troubles which were harassing the country. He left his son Pedro in Brazil. Discontent against Portugal again began to brew, and within a year the break came. Pedro entered into the spirit of the insurrectionists, became their leader, and finally in 1822 tore the Portuguese colors from his uniform and declared Brazil independent of Portugal. In the same year he was proclaimed emperor of Brazil. So Brazil "began its independent career as a monarchy instead of as a republic." [4]

Brazil had only two emperors. Pedro I reigned until 1831, when he abdicated in favor of his son, who was so young that a committee of regents was appointed to take temporary charge of the government. In a short time the young man was crowned emperor as Dom Pedro II and reigned until 1889, when the monarchy was dissolved and Pedro sailed for Portugal. He died in Paris in 1891. He had a long and remarkable reign, a period of "almost complete internal peace," with great prosperity and more freedom than in any other Latin American country.[5]

[4] *Ibid.,* p. 323.
[5] *Ibid.,* p. 731.

A change, however, was clearly necessary. It is interesting and significant from the standpoint of our discussion that "it was the slavery question . . . which knocked out the last props supporting the Empire." [6] For a long period slavery had become less and less binding. Manumission was very frequent, and several of the states had passed laws of emancipation. The movement was brought to a head by the vigorous action of the Princess Isabella, who during her father's absence in Europe had been acting as regent. She took a pronounced stand against slavery. As a result of her insistence a bill of emancipation was introduced in the Chamber of Deputies and finally, after prolonged debate, was passed. On May 13, 1888, all the slaves in Brazil were freed. They numbered at that time about 700,000. This move was hailed with great jubilation on the part of all except those who had lost their slaves. These turned against the government which had failed them. The passing of this law brought an end to the monarchy as well as to slavery; that is, it gave an opportunity to those who were dissatisfied with all sorts of governmental abuses to unite. The result was that the republic was proclaimed on November 15, 1889. Since then, with many ups and downs, the republic has continued to exist with no serious danger that it will be overturned.

The population of Brazil, as of all other parts of Latin America, was originally Indian. For many centuries—it may be milleniums—before the coming of the white man the Indian had penetrated every part of the continent. Some of them, as we shall see in dealing with Spanish-speaking Latin America, had developed a remarkable degree of culture, but the Brazilian Indians were not in that class. Ruins in western Brazil indicate that some had risen to a higher culture, but for the most part they represented about as backward and uncultured a group of tribes as could be found from Bering Strait to Tierra del Fuego. No one knows what their numbers were. Estimates vary from 200,000 to over 1,000,000. Their story is a sad one. "He [the Indian] had

[6] *Ibid.*, p. 739.

experienced four centuries of cultural disintegration, confusion, and in some instances, extermination." [7] Possibly most of the Brazilian Indians were living along the more desirable coast lands when the Portuguese arrived. They were hunters and rude agriculturists. From the start their contact with the white man was demoralizing. The Europeans were adventurers who wanted material wealth and had no consideration for the aborigines.

One of the earliest results of the contact of the two races was miscegenation. The early Portuguese in Brazil were mostly men, and they began at once to form irregular unions with Indian women and in some cases to marry them—it made very little difference which. Be it said that the Portuguese brought with them their families to a greater extent than the Spaniards. The terrible statement is made that the white men "possessed themselves of the Indian women and the Indian men were either exterminated in battle or driven into the friendly wilderness of the hinterland." [8] As with the Bandeirantes already mentioned, so in western and northern Brazil, the second generation were *mestiços,* a mixture of European and native Indian blood. Driven back into the western wilderness where they still live precariously, the pure-blooded Indians before long ceased to be an important part of the population. The Portuguese tried to enslave the Indians, but they did not thrive as slaves. This has been true of the Indians in both continents. They were restive and felt themselves free men, not to be possessed by another. So they fought back and died if necessary; or, if possible, they escaped the bondage of slavery by retreating farther and farther into the wilderness away from the cruelty of the white men.

This means that in Brazil the Indians as a separate people ceased to exist in the parts of the country where the white men settled. In dwindling numbers they lived in their old haunts but did not, and could not, continue their old free life. The increasing scarcity of Indians and their resistance to compulsory labor were

[7] Harold E. Burkard, "The Indian in Brazil." (Unpublished.)
[8] *Ibid.*

the reasons for the importation of Negroes from Africa. The one thing that the Portuguese would not do was to work with their hands—they must have labor, if not the Indians, then the Negroes. It is sufficient to say here that, when the Negroes were brought into Brazil, they too mated with Indian women and added another to the racial types in the land.

The Indians then lost their identity in the coastal areas, but their influence remains. So universally did the early Portuguese mingle their blood with that of the Indians that a permanent and indelible mark was left on the Brazilian ethnic type. The *mestiços* in Brazil form a most important part of the population, and through them the Indian strain continues to make its contribution to Brazilian life. In recent years the lore of the Indian has become a subject of interest and investigation on the part of Brazilians. They have begun to realize that there are worth-while values in this factor of their racial and cultural heritage and that they should give it credit for many good things in their life. To be specific, certain features in the simple agriculture of the Indians, such as the technique of preparing manioc flour, have been taken over, as have folk music, the dance, handicraft and artistic designs which the Indians created. "A less purely individualistic attitude toward life" seems to be an Indian trait, community solidarity being inevitably associated with tribal life. A healthy desire to understand and utilize aspects of this heritage means that the Indians are not being so completely ignored as was the case during most of Brazilian history. It must also be made clear that no aspersions are cast on a Brazilian because Indian blood runs in his veins. That would affect so large a part of the population and so many of the finest families that it would almost place a people in the impossible role of condemning itself to an inferior status.

The Negroes were soon brought into the picture, but even before coming to Brazil the Portuguese had owned and used Africans as slaves. They learned the meaning of slaveholding from the Moslem Moors, who for seven hundred years and more had been present in the Iberian Peninsula. With the culture

172

the Moors brought with them—and it had many splendid features —came the use of slave labor. The Portuguese were apt imitators, and when in the fifteenth century their intrepid adventurers brought back Negroes from the west coast of Africa, they promptly put them to work on Portuguese estates. They were slaves to be sure, but their bondage was not very strictly enforced, and in many cases they were manumitted, married Portuguese women, settled down, and became recognized members of the community. "The Portuguese allowed their Negro slaves to earn and save money; purchase freedom; and rise as ability and opportunity offered. Slaves were treated as virtual members of the household." [9] All the peoples of southern Europe are more liberal than those of northern Europe with respect to intermarriage with other races. None of them mingle their blood, however, more freely than do the Portuguese. They seem to be "color blind." This characteristic they naturally carried with them into Brazil.

The first Negro slaves reached Bahia about 1538. They were brought in, as has been said, because the Portuguese demanded labor and the Indians were a failure. They continued to come until 1850—over three hundred years—when the slave trade was prohibited by law. In 1781 fifty vessels were engaged in the trade. The highest number of slaves brought in any one year was 60,000 in 1848, and this was only two years before the trading came to an end. Let us Americans keep in mind that most of the slaves were brought in on ships flying the Stars and Stripes. It is estimated that 4,830,000 Africans were imported into Brazil. The greatly increased production of coffee in the south increased the demand for labor. All the horrors of the "middle passage" across the Atlantic were enacted in the crowded little ships in which they came. Thousands died at sea; and some, as might be expected, fell into the hands of cruel masters in Brazil; but that was not true of the large majority. One writer gives this summary, "In spite of abuses of slaves by their masters, the relations between the two elements were generally characterized by kind-

[9] Don Ebright, "Racial Roots in Portugal," p. 5. (Unpublished.)

ness and consideration, and for this reason the lot of the Negroes in Brazil was envied by their brothers in slavery in other countries." [10]

Let it not be supposed that all the Negroes were barbarians when they reached Brazil. Many of them were from the more cultivated tribes of the Sudan, and among them were skilled craftsmen. They knew how to work in metals and had some mechanical training. Many never left the coast cities in their new country; and there, under the forms of slavery, they worked as porters, engaged in small shopkeeping, and became mechanics of all sorts. They had their own houses, to a certain extent planned their own lives, and were fairly independent. A striking statement is made by the noted Brazilian writer Gilberto Freyre:

> Some of the millions of Negroes imported to Brazilian plantations were obtained from areas of the most advanced Negro culture. This explains why there were African slaves in Brazil—men of Mohammedan faith and intellectual training—who were culturally superior to some of their European, white, Catholic masters.[11]

With all that, of course, they were still at the lowest rung of the social ladder. The most significant thing was that the Portuguese gave themselves freely to illicit relations with Negro women and even intermarried. These relations were not frowned upon but were actually encouraged. Nowhere has there been so thoroughgoing a mixture of black and white as in Brazil. It was not universal. Voices were raised against it. The church officially opposed irregular unions, and there were some Portuguese who regarded all mingling with the Negroes as debasing. But it continued on a large scale and had its effect in altering the Brazilian type and developing a different man from any other in the world.

It is held that the infusion of Negro blood was beneficial. To quote:

[10] Ira G. McCormack, "Brazil: The Importation of Negroes." (Unpublished.)
[11] *Brazil: An Interpretation*, p. 95.

The early Portuguese colonists were frank, sturdy, simple people. They lacked gaiety; they found it difficult to express feelings of pleasure. In this respect they were not unlike the Indians. By contrast the Negroes exhibited perpetual good humor, childish joy, delight in the smallest interests and incidents of life. They loved bright clothing; they loved to sing and dance. They were kind, helpful, and affectionate. This infusion of Negro blood helped greatly to soften the coldness and harshness of the Portuguese temperament.[12]

The census of 1890 was the last in which racial classification was made. Then 44 per cent were whites, 14.6 per cent Negroes, 32.4 per cent mixed bloods, and 9 per cent Indians. It is extremely doubtful if all the 44 per cent classified as whites were without Indian or Negro strains or both. The census results in Brazil since 1890 make no distinction between the races in the population—they are all Brazilians. "What more is there to know?" they ask.

As might easily be conjectured from the facts which have been presented, there is no color bar in Brazil—the color line is fading out. This has been a progressive development, a process continuing through the entire history of Brazil since the coming of the Portuguese, and still operating. So different is the situation from that in the United States that, whereas in the northern republic "a drop of black blood" in a person makes him a Negro, in Brazil a slight amount of white blood in a person makes him a white. Even as far back as 1731 the king of Portugal decreed that no one should be barred from public office because of his color. Dom Pedro II conferred several decorations and titles of nobility on Brazilians of African descent.

A study of the extent of the mixture discloses significant differences in racial texture in various parts of the country. The *mestiços* approximate one half of the population. Many unmixed Portuguese, Indians, and Negroes are to be found, but so pervasive is the tendency to mingle that there are those who question whether there will not be almost complete assimilation within

[12] Ira G. McCormack, *op. cit.*

175

five or six generations. As long ago as 1912 as acute an observer as James Bryce declared, "As touching the future, it seems certain as anything in human affairs can be that the races now inhabiting South America, aboriginal, European and African, will be ultimately fused. . . . Brazil will be Ibero-American-African." [13] He is somewhat apprehensive as to the quality of the emergent type, but he is sure that there will be a new type. A later and closer student of the problem states an opinion decidedly favorable to miscegenation:

It is commonly thought in Brazil that. the Brazilian mixed-blood is superior in vitality to both ancestral stocks. The mulatto, being a "native plant," is popularly considered to have been better acclimated than either the European or the African. The Indian-white mixed-blood . . . is superior to both the white and the native Indian. [14]

In the northeast of Brazil, it is quite possible that every Negro, so called, has white or Indian blood or both. In the far south, however, the color becomes lighter and Negro blood is far less prevalent.

Nonrecognition of the color bar extends deeply into public life. In the army, Negroes, Indians, and *mestiços* are found in the same regiments. People of mixed blood share in titles and honors equal to those held by the pure whites. The *mestiços* furnish doctors, lawyers, professors, directors of all kinds of institutions (libraries, museums, and others), as well as merchants and lesser officeholders. The following quotation paints an interesting picture:

On every trolley car, every excursion boat, no matter whether one sits opposite a white, a Negro or a mulatto, one meets with the same unembarrassed friendliness. Amongst those dozens of colors and types one never discovers any tendency for one of them to isolate himself from the others, either among grownups or the children. . . . Never

---

[13] *South America: Observations and Impressions,* pp. 482 f.

[14] Donald Pierson, *Negroes in Brazil,* pp. 123 f.

is there any restriction or even private boycott. Whether in the army, in business, in the markets, shops or factories, the individual never considers separating himself from others on account of color or background. They all work in peace and friendliness together.[15]

The result is that in Brazil assimilation has been, and is still, creating a life and an atmosphere different from that in any other nation.[16] Even within the past decade or two a new unity is felt among the people. It has been called a "triumph of amalgamation."

Education is a splendid index of racial relations. As in the southern states in our country before the Civil War, so in Brazil, slavery almost made inevitable an aristocracy of learning. Education was more ornamental than useful. Schools were private or in the hands of the church. The inevitable result of the contempt of manual labor by cultivated people was that literary studies filled the curriculum to the exclusion of anything practical or mechanical. Not until the establishment of the empire in 1822 was any beginning made in free public education. Even now there are two parallel systems: the public-school system and the private schools, mostly conducted by churches, Roman Catholic and Protestant. One result has been that literacy was raised from one sixth of the population in 1889 to one fourth in 1925. Another outcome was that vocational studies came to occupy an important place in the various curricula. But with all that is being done popular education lags. The majority of those of school age and older are still illiterate.

The schools shed much light on racial relations and the ideals which are presented. The law of 1889, which forbids the races to be distinguished in the national census, also applies to education. The fact that some of the blanks to be filled in by students in secondary schools make place for a declaration of color does not lead to differentiation or any form of segregation. All schools

[15] Robert Ledbetter, "Race Relationships in Modern Brazil." (Unpublished.)
[16] Donald Pierson, op. cit., p. 119 and passim.

177

are open to boys and girls of any shade, and no distinctions are made. The same is true of the teaching positions. A man of very dark skin, indicating a preponderance of Negro blood, may be found teaching in a school composed mostly of white children. The Vargas regime just closing, with its notes of centralization and promotion of Brazilian patriotism and solidarity, has been deeply concerned with the content of education. Textbooks have been censored and made to conform to national idealism. With this in view the unity of the Brazilian people has been stressed, and pride in the existence of a Brazilian race has been fostered.

The romantic triad of the homesick Portuguese adventurer, the hardworking African Negro with his exuberant gaiety, and the proud and unconquerable Indian runs through primary school instruction and even appears in scientific textbooks. The tendency is thus to view in a romantic light the varied strains of Brazil's racial heritage, dwelling lovingly on the contributions of each to the state and people as a whole.[17]

Of the Negroes, Brazilians ordinarily say there is no Negro problem, because the Negroes are in process of absorption, and eventually will be completely incorporated. To individuals from all classes of the population this eventual amalgamation and assimilation of diverse ethnic units is a matter of pride and self-commendation.[18]

This is one side of the picture, but there is another. While there is no color discrimination it is noticeable that the higher the academic grade the fewer are the students of dark or very dark skin. There is no formal barrier, but it still remains true that the nearer one approaches the pure-blooded Negro, the lower in the economic and social scale he is found. Again there is a marked difference between students in the vocational schools and in those which lay emphasis on literary and classical studies. Girls with dark skins, coming from the lower strata of society, are likely

[17] J. W. Shepherd, "Educational Reconstruction in Brazil." (Unpublished M.A. thesis, University of Chicago.)
[18] Donald Pierson, op. cit., p. 344.

to choose schools with a practical emphasis to fit them for employment, while girls of pure white blood choose the other schools. Thus does the pernicious distinction continue to obtain between manual labor and leisure. The problem is clearly one of caste, or social and economic standing, and not of race, but it is just as evident that it has racial roots.

A series of letters from Americans living in Brazil gives evidence of the same class problem and of its racial foundations. The letters are from the far south; they would doubtless have been somewhat different had they come from Bahia or even from Rio de Janeiro. One letter states the general situation:

As a whole the Negroes are at the bottom of the economic ladder in Brazil. At the top of this ladder stands a more pure Caucasian group. There is no legal reason and very few taboos to keep the Negroes from reaching the highest rungs of the ladder, but it must be said that not sufficient social or economic help has been given to enable them to do so. The few people of African blood who have reached the top because of superior ability have been recognized without any stigma based on racial origin.[19]

In certain private schools class feeling exists to the extent that "attendance by members of the African and Asiatic races is not encouraged." [20] One does not have to go far in investigating the schools and colleges of the United States to discover an almost identical situation. Of the students in a private school in Brazil it is said, "The student body is predominantly white—much whiter than in many public schools. I have heard children say they prefer this school because its constituency is largely white.... The children in this school are predominantly from rich families." [21] Another letter states that "in boarding school there have occasionally been pupils who have refused to room with persons having distinctive characteristics of the Negro race, and white

[19] A. E. Barnett, "As Missionaries See Race Relations in Brazil," p. 1. (Unpublished.)
[20] Ibid., p. 2.
[21] Ibid.

servants who resented having to sit at the table with colored servants." [22] Another somewhat different letter comes from a teacher in a school in Rio de Janeiro: "I never knew of any feeling or prejudice on the part of the students regarding the Negro ancestry of other students. Occasionally a remark about a person's hair could be heard, but I do not believe such remarks expressed prejudice. Several of our students were definitely Negro." [23]

Likewise in social circles one shade or color naturally predominates. In these circles a fair white girl would not become the wife of a very dark mulatto; but, be it remembered, this would be due not to color or racial background but to social and economic standing.

It is the impression of competent residents well acquainted with the social structure of Bahia that marriages cross race lines more often than class lines; that is, that marriages between individuals from different occupational and income levels within each racial group are less frequent than marriages between members of the different racial groups in the same class! [24]

The fact is that the Brazilians who are called white have in so many cases Negro or Indian blood in varying amounts that invidious racial distinctions are not indulged in. Intermingling is taking place very frequently but with this differentiation, that a white person is more apt to marry a mulatto than to marry a full-blooded Negro, while a mulatto does not hesitate to wed one who is very dark—but again this distinction is based on social standing and not on the fact of color. Is there any wonder that this unique situation in Brazil may be spoken of as the "most daring and voluntary acceptance of racial amalgamation in human history?"

The church, as might be expected, has been influenced by the racial situation in Brazil. The Roman Catholic Church has more or less consistently opposed illicit unions whether between persons of the same race or of different races. With reference to inter-

---

[22] *Ibid.*
[23] *Ibid.*
[24] Donald Pierson, *op. cit.*, p. 147.

marriage between the races, a practice which goes back to the earliest pioneering days and which continues to the present time, the church added its blessing and thus became party to such unions. It is hard to see how it could have done otherwise. The same attitude has been taken perforce by Protestants. One very unfortunate condition is that among the lower classes, living in poverty and frequently far removed from the ministrations of the church, men and women merely took up with each other and reared their families, unsanctioned by the church. The result was a brood of technically illegitimate children, but that was so often the case that little attention was paid to it. The Roman Catholic Church, in varying degrees in different places, must bear a great share of the blame for this condition in that it requires for the performance of the marriage rite financial payment frequently in excess of what the poor people can pay. The only racial discrimination practiced by this church was that for a very long period none except men of European stock were admitted to the priesthood. That of course has been changed. In former days it was a matter of pride for a family to have a son in the priesthood, for that was convincing proof of the purity of its blood.

In the Protestant churches native ministers were ordained just as soon as Brazilians could be found with the necessary consecration and ability and could be trained for their task. The color line was not drawn. How could it be in Brazil? But, notwithstanding, the same attitudes showed themselves in the church as already described in the schools. Where a man of dark color was acceptable as a leader in school and in public life, he could rise to any position in the church; where the feeling was different, as in the south, it would scarcely do to place a man of dark color as the pastor of a predominantly white church. Very significantly, and also unfortunately, where the presence of Negroes or dark mulattoes as members of a church would decrease its prestige, they were not sought after or encouraged to join its membership. There is no insuperable bar to their joining as in most white churches in the United States, but it would prove embarrassing—and that is a real

181

bar when men and women meet intimately as they do in a Protestant church.

One is likely to say at the conclusion of such a presentation, "Well, human nature is just about the same the world over." And the correct rejoinder is, "Yes and No." Yes, human nature is the same, and prejudice and a proud sense of superiority over others are likely to crop up anywhere. They do in Brazil. But human nature is also the same in another respect; it can be directed and educated into channels which cause its attitudes to be far different from those which might other wise be displayed. This is what we find in Brazil. Brazilians are a part of our humanity, but with a different background, exposed to a different social attitude, and definitely educated to think of races as equal, not innately inferior or superior. These people have shown that human nature can react very differently to the fundamental problem of racial intermingling. Increasingly we must study the problem from their angle and learn the values which they find in practices far different from our own. Gilberto Freyre declares, "Even Brazilians with a family or individual past that has nothing to do with Africa, biologically or ethnically, join negroid Brazilians in a feeling, now general though not universal, that nothing is honest or sincerely Brazilian that denies or hides the influence of the Amerindian and the Negro." [25]

It is to be noted that the population problem of Brazil has become more complex in recent years by rapid immigration from Europe, other Latin American countries, and Japan. Only two groups have introduced new phases of racial tension. In 1939 President Vargas acted contrary to the existing law and admitted 3,000 German Catholics of Jewish ancestry. He did this on the appeal of the pope, who desired to find a refuge for some of those who were suffering persecution in Europe.

The situation with respect to the Japanese is quite different. They have been entering Brazil since 1907. By 1924 they were said to number 50,000, and by 1928 about 1,000 were arriving each year.

[25] *Op. cit.*, p. 122.

A Japanese corporation, called the South American Development Company, formed the grandiose plan to settle 400,000 Japanese in the one state of Para, but their plans did not materialize as expected, and in 1932 only 120,000 Japanese were to be found in the whole country. When after that immigration of Japanese increased the government limited their number. The Brazilian Senate went farther and canceled a previous concession of 2,400,-000 acres made by the state of Amazonas to the Japanese government for Japanese settlement. Again in 1937 the number of Oriental immigrants was reduced and placed on a low quota basis. What we may gather from the experience of Brazil with Japanese immigration is that it is not likely to become an important feature in Brazilian life, nor has it created tension between the races. It is not likely that it will alter in even a slight degree the composition of the Brazilian people.[26]

[26] See A. Curtis Wilgus, *The Development of Hispanic America*, for discussion and references.

Chapter X

Race Patterns in Spanish America

Spanish America consists of those parts of the two American continents where the Spanish language is spoken. This means the entire span of territory from the Rio Grande, which divides Mexico from the United States, to the extreme tip of Chile at Cape Horn. It does not include Brazil, where Portuguese is spoken, nor the three Guianas—British, Dutch, and French. In the West Indies, Cuba and Puerto Rico are included, but not Haiti, where the language is French, and many other islands which belong to European powers or to the United States. Spanish America comprises Mexico and the small Central American countries, Guatemala, Honduras, Salvador, Nicaragua, Costa Rica, and Panama, and the larger South American republics, Venezuela, Colombia, Ecuador, Peru, Chile, Paraguay, Uruguay, and Argentina.

The orginal inhabitants of this vast territory were Indians. The anthropologists have appropriately called them Amerinds. When Columbus discovered America, he thought he was on his way to Asia, but on the way bumped into islands which he had never heard of but which he imagined must be the fabled Indies, so he naturally called them by that name and their inhabitants the Indians. When the mistake was discovered, it was too late to change; so we must always be sure to distinguish the West Indies from the East Indies and the American or Red Indians, the Amerinds, from the true Indians of India and the islands off southeastern Asia.

As will be recalled from the discussion of the races of the world and their distribution, all the early inhabitants of the Americas had their origin in Asia. They belonged racially to the Mongoloids, a branch of the yellow-brown race, and reached their new home in all probability by crossing the narrow waterway between Asia and North America in the region of Bering Strait. There is the possibility that some came across the Pacific. At any rate they must have come in small bands over a very long period and remained separate and distinct for ages; otherwise there is no way of accounting for differences in customs and even greater differences in language. The immigrants may have come to America already widely diverse. It is clear that they all belong to one racial stock, but significant differences separate various groups and add much of interest to the study of their life and characteristics.

There are tribes which are very low in the cultural scale. Such were the Indians of Brazil already considered. So also are the poor people in Tierra del Fuego and other tribes. On the other hand various groups both in North and South America exhibited a vigor and intelligence which made it most difficult for the Europeans to overcome their resistance. Among them were the Auracanians in south central Chile who claim that they were never conquered by the Spaniards and live a life of more or less freedom to the present day. There were people, however, who did not show prowess in warfare but who nevertheless developed a culture which is a marvel to the historian and the archaeologist. These groups lived on or near the backbone of the continents from the southwest United States to the southern boundaries of Peru. In order to understand the Indian and his possibilities we are bound to look into this advanced culture. It will serve to show the meaning of the devastating blows dealt by the conquistadors upon remarkable peoples and their civilization many aspects of whose culture might well have been preserved.

Within very recent years archaeologists have brought to light buildings and other remains of a civilization in Guatemala and the Yucatan peninsula in Mexico which had passed away by the time Cortez conquered the country. The Mayas are believed to be the earliest group which began to advance beyond surrounding people, but it is supposed that another culture, the Teotihuacan, arose about the same time and was comparable with that of the Mayas.

185

By the seventh century of our era the Mayas had built splendid cities and produced an advanced culture in Yucatan and Guatemala. They were followed by the Toltecs, who overthrew the Mayas, but continued the cultural tradition, though not on quite the same high level. The Toltecs were in turn displaced by other tribes, the most noted of whom were the Aztecs. They were more warlike and originated the human sacrifices which rightly horrified the European invaders. Their center was what we know as Mexico City. It was they who were barbarously overthrown and whose organization was completely destroyed by the Spanish conquest. We have been made acquainted in recent years with the vast architectural remains of the Mayas and their successors—palaces, temples, and pyramids—and the strange hieroglyphic writing carved in stone, which has been only partly deciphered. All this and much else had interest to only a very few of the invading force. For the most part the Spaniard was an adventurer and wanted gold—all else was as nothing to him—and above all did not these people have an abominable religion? The Roman Catholic priests thought so, and in fact their religion was the least attractive aspect of Aztec culure. So it all went overboard as if it were the product of backward, depraved, and inferior people.

South of Panama another civilization was developed, in many ways as remarkable as that in Mexico but seemingly having no connection with it. In Colombia the Chibchas built up a culture far in advance of the surrounding tribes. This was destroyed by the Spaniards as they went south. But the most advanced culture in South America was that of the Incas with their capital in what we know as Peru. Various tribes seem to have been united under the leadership of an energetic people called the Incas. On the high plateau of Ecuador, Peru, and Bolivia, there was built up a powerful kingdom which displayed not only organizing ability but superb skill in architecture, agriculture, and other directions. This kingdom was at its height when the illiterate and wily Pizarro, with audacity to be matched only by unscrupulousness, destroyed the whole structure by murdering Atahualpa, the pathetic and helpless Inca ruler. Other leaders attempted to recover themselves but failed completely, and the old empire was wrecked. Among the Indians of Peru today many features of the old culture have been preserved but the state as a state was destroyed. So ended the history of the last of the surprising civilizations which the Indian had built up in surroundings altogether inimical to such a development and which demonstrate his remarkable capacities. All that they found was utterly despised by the conquistadors, who set up their rule on Spanish lines and never seemed to realize that they had destroyed something admirable with many features worthy of emulation.

The coming of the Spaniards provides an illustration of racism in various forms. They despised the Indians and treated them with disdain. Opposition was put down ruthlessly. The Indians had no chance when he faced the firearms of the Europeans. In this way many perished, while the majority who submitted were enslaved and put to hard tasks. In some places the natives were driven to work in the mines and were exterminated. The Indians were proud and resisted enslavement and forced labor. At times this resulted in further brutal treatment. As a result in a very few years the natives disappeared in the islands of the Caribbean. They were, it is true, not on the same cultural level with the Indians of the mainland, but the blindness and cruelty of their masters were entirely inexcusable. Some of the Roman Catholic missionaries, who accompanied every expedition, uttered their protest against these abuses. The most prominent was the able and devoted Dominican Las Casas, who made several trips to Spain to present the plight of the Indians before the king and queen. But with all that he and others could do the Indians were so harshly treated that in a short time the island Indians disappeared. In his anguish over the condition of the hapless aborigines Las Casas was led to suggest that African Negroes be imported to save the Indians. This counsel of despair did not succeed in its primary intention, and besides it laid the shackles of slavery upon another race, so

187

that Las Casas with all his good impulses realized,[1] when it was too late, that he had succeeded only in exchanging one huge injustice for another. What might have been his state of mind had he realized the centuries of cruel servitude which lay ahead of millions of the colored race on both continents and the problems in the relationships of white and black which his ill-conceived suggestion foreshadowed!

On the mainland the Indians have survived and are to be found in large numbers. They became attached to the large landed estates which were a part of the economy in every part of Latin America. The wealth of the land was concentrated to a great extent in encomiendas or repartimientos over which the Spaniard landowners ruled like feudal lords with the natives bound to the land as peons or serfs. It was not slavery in name, and yet slaves had as much freedom as was granted the serfs on the encomiendas. Unfortunately very much the same system exists in many sections today, where the Indians are virtually attached to the soil and go with it when it is transferred by sale from one owner to another.

Like the Portuguese adventurers in Brazil, the Spanish conquistadors came to America unaccompanied by women. The most natural thing was to mate with native Indian women. Sometimes the relation was legalized by marriage. The result was the mestizo, who is to be found in every Spanish American country. The Spaniards might despise the Indians, but they did not hesitate to beget a hybrid race. Much of the discussion which follows will be taken up with the relation of white men, Indians, and mestizos. That is the field where race and class tension shows itself in Spanish America. The patterns vary from country to country, but the problem is always the same.

According to W. Thompson, "The origin of the mestizo goes back to the very deliberate amalgamation with the Indian which may be considered the ideal of the original Spanish Colonist." [2]

[1] Mary W. Williams, *The People and Politics of Latin America* (new ed.), chaps. II and IV.

[2] *The Mexican Mind*, p. 27, as quoted in C. S. Braden, "Racism in Latin America," p. 10. (Unpublished.)

Only 10 per cent of the Spanish residents were women as late as 1803, three hundred years after the conquest. Indian women were the more ready to enter into these unions since their children thus begotten were not subject to the forced labor on the repartimientos. On the other hand many Indians refused to bring children into the world because of the fate which awaited them. If a Spaniard did not bring a wife with him from Spain, he was urged to take an Indian wife "in order to promote a measure of domestic morality." So the bringing of mestizo children into their society became a part of the recognized colonial policy and was accepted as a regular procedure both by the state and the church. In the beginning the mestizo child was disliked both by the white and the Indian, but ultimately he became an accepted member of society, though with a standing lower than that of the pure Castilian white.

The Spaniards set up local governments in every part of the land. Interesting to say, the lines of division between the various separate viceroyalties and their subdivisions are the boundary lines of the Latin American republics of the present day. A Council of the Indies in Spain was in charge of the entire domain and ruled with an iron hand. There were many obviously arbitrary and unreasonable regulations which caused deep unrest. What this would have led to had it not been for the American Revolution it is hard to say. What we know is that, when the United States separated itself from the mother country, the leaders in Latin America were incited to do likewise. Napoleon's invasion of Spain destroyed the hold of that country on its colonies. The liberation took place in the early twenties of the nineteenth cenury under the inspiring leadership of Miranda, Bolivar, and San Martin. Republics were set up in each country, and they continue today at all stages of development, from the most backward dictatorships to the more mature democracies. This affects our discussion only so far as the problem of race relations in each of the countries is affected by the form of government and the peculiar racial pattern with which it must deal.

It would be as impossible as it is unnecessary to attempt to discuss the relations of the races in each of the countries. Rather it seems advisable to concentrate attention on the situation in those countries where a peculiar pattern can be studied to the best advantage and thus pass in review all the significant phases of racism in Spanish America.

Cuba

Cuba furnishes a unique and very significant situation. There the Indians early disappeared, and their place was taken by the Negroes. This resulted in the total absence of a mixed white-Indian group. The native Indians seem to have disappeared as early as 1550. By the year 1880, when slavery was abolished on the islands, it is estimated that a million Negroes had been brought into Cuba. Mulattoes began at once to appear. Long before the emancipation of the slaves mulatto children of the Spanish planters occupied a position of privilege in Cuban society. And when the slaves were emancipated, the mulattoes, privileged before, now formed the core of a middle class and came to have an important position in Cuban life.

Figures are confusing when dealing with the racial composition of the populations in these countries. The Cuban census of 1931 gives a total population of 4,200,000, and lists 27 per cent Negroes, 4 per cent aliens, 16 per cent Spanish, and 53 per cent Creoles, persons descended from those who came from Spain in an early day. There are those who would say that only about one half the population is composed of unmixed whites.

Since the entire population of Cuba, black and mixed as well as white, played its part in the liberation movements in their history, there has been a large degree of mutual respect. This does not , mean that the condition of the Negroes in Cuba is one to be envied. The land is under the domination of a sugar economy, and the fluctuations in the price of Cuban sugar in the United States cause serious dislocations in the lives of the plantation workers. They may not be slaves, but their condition on the huge sugar estates is very much like serfdom in other countries. They are not in any real sense free men.

The pure Negroes are at the bottom of the social and economic ladder. On the other hand the mulattoes are far better off. They have successfully entered the professions, have become prominent in the lower ranks of the civil service, and have found their way to a limited degree into the legislative and other branches of the government. There is, however, a real line of cleavage between the mulattoes and the pure Spanish element, which maintains its own cultured traditions and institutions and seems not to look with favor on intermarriage with the mixed group. Even so it is questionable whether racism as such is an important factor in Cuban life. Poverty, misery, illiteracy, and a general lack of culture are the real causes of discrimination, not the mere fact of belonging to a different race. Negroes and mulattoes covet a white skin, for that means added respect and the possibility of advancement. Yet when a person of mixed blood is classed as white, as is the case when his skin is sufficiently white, the meaning can only be that the presence of Negro blood is not in itself a bar to social advantage. But when a man is darker in color, it usually means that he is too near the line of economic insufficiency to be held in high regard. Very unfortunately the incoming of people from the United States has in recent decades increased the tension between whites and Negroes. Their insistence on the color bar as it exists in their homeland is the cause of the difficulty.

There are no legal disabilities which the Negroes must face. They are not discriminated against in schools, theaters, the university, restaurants; on trains; in railroad stations; or in cemeteries or churches. This is a plane much higher than the Negroes occupy in the United States. The Cuban Negroes still feel the weight of social segregation but not in an oppressive and even insulting fashion as do the American Negroes. The law is with the man of color in Cuba. It recognizes no special privileges due the white man on the basis of race. The Cuban Constituent Assembly has made the following declaration of fundamental rights: "All

Cubans are equal before the law. The Republic recognizes no privileges. All discrimination because of sex, race, color, or class, or other affront to human dignity, is declared illegal and punishable." [3]

Puerto Rico

In the neighboring island of Puerto Rico the population has a very different composition. Three fourths of the people are descendants of Spanish immigrants, and only one fourth are descendants of Negroes and mulattoes, though it must be said that among those recognized as whites there are many grays. Among the lower classes and where the two races come into close contact, the Negroes are rapidly merging with the whites. This, however, is taking place almost solely along the coast. In the interior the people are almost entirely white. So the race problem, though existing, is not the cause of the gravest concern to those who are solicitous for conditions in Puerto Rico. That solicitude is caused by the appalling poverty which prevails among whites, Negroes, and mulattoes, with all its attendant evils. The poverty is closely connected with the overcrowding of the island. The population in turn is increasing with great rapidity, with little or no hope of retardation. The Roman Catholic Church, which is exceedingly strong, puts the ban on birth control and makes relief from that angle impossible.

The number of inhabitants in 1899, when the island was taken over by the United States, was 953,243, and by 1935 it had grown to 1,723,584. Consequently the density of population per square mile had grown from 280.3 to 506.8. This makes Puerto Rico the most densely populated region on earth with the exception of the island of Java. When the density of population in Puerto Rico is compared with that in the United States, which has 41 per square mile, the disparity is overwhelming. But in addition to overpopulation, there are other causes of the desperate condition of America's island dependency. Among them is the high tariff on

[3] For many of these statements I am indebted to W. E. Westerbery, "Race Relations in Cuba." (Unpublished.)

sugar, which throws much of the responsibility for the poverty of Puerto Rico upon the American Congress and the people themselves who ignorantly or otherwise allow such conditions to exist. How shameful this should be to a patriotic American, especially when he realizes that all Puerto Ricans are citizens of the United States and have the right to expect better things of their fellow citizens. We need say no more. This is an economic problem rather than one of race; yet because they are of Spanish origin and not Anglo-Saxons, it seems the easier to permit them to suffer than treat them as fellow countrymen.

Mexico

On the mainland the conditions in Mexico are entirely different. This country is predominantly the land of the Indians and mestizos. The last census in which the racial groups in the population were distinguished was taken in 1910. Then the enumeration gave 19 per cent white, 43 per cent mestizo, and 38 per cent Indian. There are those who believe that the true picture today would be more nearly as follows: 8 per cent white, 52 per cent mestizo, and 40 per cent Indian.

Naturally the white man was dominant in the early day, but during the seventeenth century the mestizos began to come in to their own and assume a more prominent position. By the nineteenth century they had an assured place and took their part in all the affairs of the country. Mexico won her independence from Spain through the hearty and equal co-operation of the pure Spaniards and the mixed Spanish and Indian. The opportunity to advance even to positions of the highest importance was open to Indians whenever they showed ability and had the necessary training to be trusted with public office. Benito Juárez (1806-72), statesman, soldier, president of the republic, and more than any other man the hero of Mexico, was a full-blooded Indian. General Lázaro Cárdenas, while president of Mexico, declared:

Mexico is not interested in having the Indian races disappear, nor does she encourage the same. The Government of the Revolution does not relieve the population which is purely indigenous of its responsibility as a factor in the growth and progress of the nation, since it considers the Indian capable, though not on as high a level as the mestizo, yet with the same efficiency as any other *rational* class in the world. All that the Indian lacks is the possibility of education for himself and feeding himself as do other people.[4]

It is significant that Cárdenas himself is a mestizo.

Racism then can scarcely be said to exist in Mexico, as can also be seen from a statement by a modern Mexican writer:

We welcome an Indian into our highest society whenever he adopts our manner and culture; an Indian can marry the daughter of an upper-class family if he only shows a proper behavior; and, if he is a learned man, the Mexican young men are proud to call him teacher.[5]

The problem in Mexico is not one of race but of class standing, resting on economic status and consequent social position. The Indians unfortunately are in a deplorable state of poverty and illiteracy for the most part. They are peons on great landed estates and under the domination of a church which is satisfied with their servile condition and is doing little to relieve it. The problem simmers down almost entirely to one of landownership. Until the stranglehold of the landowner is broken, there is little chance for the Indians. That is the inner meaning of the Mexican Revolution. Let us remember that real improvement has been made, but much, very much, remains to be done. Not only has the government been doing its part to raise the status of the Indians, but enthusiastic young patriots have in recent years gone out into the Indian settlements and set up schools to give youth the rudiments of an education. Their ardor has not consistently held up, but their

[4] H. B. Parkes, *A History of Mexico,* p. 3, as quoted in I. P. Hauser, "The Indian in Mexico." (Unpublished.)

[5] T. E. Obregon, "Are the Mexican People Capable of Governing Themselves?" *Journal of International Relations,* XI, 176 f., as quoted in C. S. Braden, "Racism in Latin America." (Unpublished.)

desire and their actual achievement give promise of a stirring among the intelligentsia, who realize that their country can never make progress so long as it is weighted down with the poverty, illiteracy, and lack of ambition of so large a part of the population.

The Western Republics

Ecuador, Peru, and Bolivia are separate and distinct as political entities, proud even to the point of defiance of their independence, but they have precisely the same problem in the relation of the races. Here again it is the relation of Spaniards and Indians, but a relation which is striking in its contrasts and its intensity. This is the land of the Inca Empire with all of its wealth and glory, but now the Indians, whose forebears were the proud members of that commonwealth, are a broken, subdued people, dominated by a comparatively small group of educated well-to-do whites who jealously guard their privileges and look upon themselves as the rightful rulers of the land. There is a large mestizo class, holding about the same relations to the whites as in Mexico. Only rarely has a full-blooded Indian been able to rise to a position of prominence.

The Indians are usually tillers of the soil. Some come to the towns as laborers, and a limited number work in the mines, but most of these are seasonal workers and return to the land with their earnings. Those who work the soil are in three classes. Many are peons, or land serfs, who for many generations have been attached to the haciendas, the huge estates owned by wealthy white landowners. Such a peon receives a small patch of land with a miserable little hut and in return is bound to work a stipulated number of days each week for his landlord, who also has the right to make use of his wife and children as laborers with no extra compensation. Some receive wages in addition to their patch of land, and some do not.

Another group consists of those who belong to the "communidades," who own and cultivate their land together as groups. They are more fortunate than their fellow Indians on the haciendas.

They are a kind of communistic society, buying, raising, and selling their produce in common. More hope for the future of the Indians is to be found in this situation than in any other. It is reported that there are two thousand of these little communities in Peru alone, criticized and hampered by the large landowners and some officials, but encouraged by the government to some extent.

The third class is composed of those who live on "parcialidades," the free and independent small farmers living far back from the coast and even in the Sierras. They are independent farmers in their own right, owning their own farms and living their own free lives. From the viewpoint of more favored lands we would not consider their lot enviable, but they are at the present time in the most advantageous situation of any of the Indians in these countries. Still another group has recently been investigated, the Indians living still farther back in the Sierras, in remote valleys, almost unknown to civilization, where the soil is so poor that their condition is wretched in the extreme. They have been almost completely neglected by both state and church and are destitute, forlorn, and hopeless.

Here we find both race and class distinction in an aggravated and pitiable form. The whites subjugated the Indians and have kept them in an almost servile condition ever since. There are mestizos to be sure, but in these countries pure-blooded Indians compose a majority of the population, and the line of demarcation between the Indians and the dominant whites is clear-cut and wide. What would have taken place if the Indians had been given a chance cannot be known, but the only condition which has obtained in these three countries since the conquest has resulted in a deep, sullen attitude of resentment and suppressed hate of the whites and their superior and dominating attitude. Speaking particularly of the depressed Indians of the high Sierras, Dr. J. Merle Davis has said:

In the centuries of domination by the white man the Indian has not only withdrawn physically, socially, and economically from his

196

exploiters, retreating into physical elevations so great as to separate himself from modern life; he has retreated also into the inner recesses of his soul and has bolted and locked the door. Neither government, educators, economic and social uplifters, nor the church, have yet discovered the key to that door. Behind it the Indian persists, impenetrable, indestructible, self-contained, unchanged and unchanging, preserving his ancient ideology, his gods, his values, his peculiar motivations, and his way of life.[6]

Conditions much like those already described exist in other Latin American countries each with its own pattern different in detail but not in essential features. This statement would include the particular conditions in the Dominican Republic in the Caribbean, the various Central American States, and the South American republics of Venezuela, Colombia, Paraguay and Chile. But it would not rightly include Uruguay and Argentina nor one feature of the situation in Peru. The two southern east coast countries of Uruguay and Argentina are now almost exclusively white. There are few Indians left, and the mestizos are a small minority and do not constitute a special problem. Argentina has 88 per cent white and Uruguay 86 per cent. The problem in these lands is that of minority groups consisting of immigrants who have come from Europe during recent decades. Peru has been faced with another group, the Japanese. And this is likewise true, as we have seen, even to a greater extent in Brazil, while Argentina has 60,-000 Japanese and Mexico has 4,500.

The Japanese

Both Brazil and Argentina have more Japanese than Peru and Mexico but it is in these latter countries that their presence has caused special irritation. The Japanese have formed compact settlements in each country to which they have gone and have remained distinct from their neighbors. In Peru this separation was carried to the extent that at least in one center a Japanese school was con-

---

[6] "The Indians of the High Andes," *In Him We Move* (report of the executive secretary of the Division of Foreign Missions, 1944), p. 231. See also for complete statement *Indians of the High Andes*, ed. W. Stanley Rycroft.

ducted by Japanese using the Japanese language. This school was closed during the war. One journalist records that the boys were taught military tactics and that at the proper age they would be taken to Japan at government expense for military training and then again brought back to Peru ready at any time to take the part of Japan should need arise.[7] How much of these tales is to be taken at full value is somewhat difficult to say. Probably there is much truth in them, as there probably is in the report that the immigration of Japanese was under the direction of the Japanese government and had in mind designs to get a foothold on the American continent. The same sinister motives were attributed to the presence of Japanese in Mexico. The Mexican government became convinced of this purpose and unearthed incriminating facts which indicated that Japanese were surreptitiously obtaining military information and conniving in espionage operations. All this was in the days before the war. What the conditions will be when Japan's relations to other nations are radically changed one can only conjecture, but they will be very different. The Japanese may remain in these countries; they are likely to maintain their aloofness. Beyond that it is not possible to make predictions.

The Jews

The Japanese do not constitute a trouble center in Argentina, but that cannot be said of the Jews. They are located in nearly every part of Latin America, but there are more in Argentina than in all the other countries combined. There they number between 300,000 and 400,000 with 160,000 in Buenos Aires alone. Besides those Jews who were residents before the war, there may be as many as 10,000 refugees who have fled from German persecution. Brazil has the largest group outside Argentina, with 75,000, plus an even larger group of refugees, estimated at 15,000. Most of the Jews are professional and business men, but there are in addition a number of Jewish agricultural colonies, more or less successful, in a number of the republics.

[7] *Free World Magazine,* II, 81-84, 181-84, as cited in S. D. White, "Orientals in Latin America." (Unpublished.)

Anti-Semitism raised its head only after the rise of Hitler in Germany. Its principal centers have been in Argentina, Chile, and Brazil. In Chile the 20,000 German-born "Aryans" were Hitlerites. The refugee-Germans are naturally opposed to Nazism. There is also a large group of Chilean-born Germans whose affiliations are doubtful, but all together the Jews form a bloc of aliens not assimilated into Chilean life. The same may be said of the Germans in southern Brazil. In Argentina in addition to the 60,000 German-born there are from 250,000 to 300,000 Germans who for several generations have made Argentina their home and were imbued with Nazi ideology. Hubert Herring makes the statement:

Almost all German-born are loyal to Hitler; a large minority, perhaps a majority of the older Germans profess allegiance to the new Germany; an over-whelming majority of the young Germans, whether or not they have seen the fatherland are fervid in their support of Nazi doctrine. 50-90% of the German Argentines stand with the Führer. These are guesses of an informant, no one knows.[8]

They have sowed the seeds of racism in Latin America, in Argentina in particular, so that in that country we find the most virulent and pervasive anti-Semitism.

Now that Nazism has been defeated and a complete change of government is taking place in Germany, what these expatriated Germans will do is a serious problem. The dictator Perón has been confirmed in his claims by being elected president in a popular election. When it is realized that his rule has been Fascist in its every move and that he has been working in close harmony with the leader of Nazism in Argentina, the immediate future for democratic government is not bright. With a powerful army to support his acts the people who stand for a different policy have been able to accomplish little or nothing. This means that the Jews are still in a dangerous situation and will continue to be until a radical change is brought about in the government.

---

[8] *Good Neighbors,* p. 67, as quoted in C. 3. Braden, *op. cit.*

Chapter XI

Racial Minorities in the United States

The groups chosen for study are the Indians, Mexicans, Filipinos, Japanese, and Jews. The Negroes, who constitute the largest minority group in the United States, will be treated separately in the following chapter. The groups selected are not the only minority groups in the country—for example, the Chinese, Puerto Ricans, Cubans, Koreans, and others—but these are to be surveyed because they are the object of special discrimination on account of race or caste prejudice, and are the groups around which problems have arisen which affect American national policies and attitudes.

The United States has been called a "crucible," a "melting pot," and other names which call attention to one of the most remarkable facts in the history of our country. From the beginning a varied assortment of people began to come to America as the land of promise, where they might escape poverty, privation, religious persecution, political intolerance, and military conscription. Even the original stock was not strictly homogeneous. They came for the most part from Great Britain—England, Scotland, and Wales—and also from Holland, followed soon by the Scotch-Irish from Ulster, and later by the Irish from the south and west of Ireland. Germans came and were given a friendly welcome by the Pennsylvania Quakers. They went first to Germantown, now a suburb of Philadelphia, then on into southeastern Pennsylvania, where they settled the countryside and became the dominant and in many sections the only group. German customs and German speech still prevail, and the "Pennsylvania Dutch" are famous for prosperous farms as well as for sauerkraut and beer.

All over the land today distinct groups are to be found and in many cases they have preserved their customs and habits and even their foreign language. So we find the Scandinavian and the German especially in Wisconsin, Minnesota, and the adjacent states, the Dutch in Michigan—in addition to the early Dutch settlements in New York and New Jersey—and the Welsh in little groups in widely scattered mining centers. While in many cases these groups are still more or less separated from their neighbors, they create no problem—no racial problem at any rate—because they are all northern Europeans and are a recognized factor of American life. It became another matter when people from southern and southeastern Europe began to make their appearance in American communities. The problem caused by the coming of the Italian, the Pole, and other Slavic peoples made a great change in the American scene. Here were people who were very different from northern Europeans in economic standing, social outlook, habits, customs, and for the most part in religion. They were Roman Catholics, and while members of that church had been in the colonies from an early day, notably in Maryland and in the Irish settlements, the typical American was Teutonic and Protestant. The Immigration Law of 1924 was formulated and passed with the purpose of diminishing the inflow of these newer people, who were looked upon as aliens who were not in sympathy with American institutions and who, if they came in too great numbers, would swamp the country and pervert the principles for which Americans had always stood. So it was said, and the immigration bill became law. The Americans of British or north European descent looked down on these men from the opposite side of Europe, did not give them a hearty welcome, and called them uncomplimentary names. But they came, made America their home, fitted into the scheme of things economically and industrially, and, even if they were not rapidly assimilated, were gradually accepted as American citizens. They might be different and strange, but underneath all else, did they not come of the same basic racial stock?

The groups we are to study, however, were different. They

201

were outsiders, not aliens who would soon lose their foreignness and settle down and become Americans like the rest of us. The racial difference was pronounced and always evident. The Indians and the Mexicans had different backgrounds to be sure, but the Mexicans were mostly, if not entirely, of Indian blood and so they could be put in about the same category with the Indians, though from another nation. Whatever we may say about the Jews and the fact that they belong to the white people of the world, they have kept apart so long and have voluntarily separated themselves from their neighbors so effectively that they are as if they belonged to another race and frequently remain separate and distinct. So far as the Filipinos and the Japanese are concerned, they belong to the yellow-browns and have a historical and racial background entirely different from old-time Americans.[1]

The Indians

The Indians were here when the white men came. They are the only original Americans. At the time of the coming of the white man they were found thinly scattered over the entire present territory of the United States. No one knows how many there were when America was discovered. According to one estimate they numbered 1,000,000 in Canada and the United States in 1780. Clark Wissler believes this number is too high, and estimates them at 750,000.[2] Even with the larger figure in mind one is at once struck with the small number of Indians scattered over so vast an area. A generation ago we were given to understand that they were a "vanishing race," doomed to die out and disappear in the not distant future. Their numbers kept dropping lower and lower until 1900, when a surprising thing happened—they began to increase and have kept it up ever since. The census of 1900 gave them 250,000, while in 1942 the number in continental United States was 368,920. With a remarkably high rate of reproduction it

---

[1] Wallace Stegner, *One Nation*, and Louis Adamic, *A Nation of Nations*, will provide abundant material.

[2] G. E. E. Lindquist, *The Indian in American Life*, p. 9.

is predicted that by 1980 the Indian population will reach 700,000. The Indians, then, are not disappearing as a people. What is vanishing is the full-blooded Indian. A disproportionate increase of mixed bloods is to be contrasted with the slower increase of full bloods. We must keep in mind that any person with one eighth Indian blood is listed in the census as an Indian and is treated as such by the government. Two illustrations will give the situation a little more concretely. In 1935 out of a population of 4,300 at the Blackfoot agency in Montana only 934 were listed as full bloods. In 1934 sixty-seven tribes were represented in the student body in Haskell Institute, Lawrence, Kansas, the largest Indian school conducted by the United States Government. They came from twenty-five states, so that they presented a fairly good cross section of American Indian life. Of the 741 students enrolled, only 204 were full bloods. The others were in different proportions Indian, white, Negro, all the way from seven eights to one eighth Indian.

From the beginning antagonism existed between the Indians and the white men. There were exceptions, like the kindly and fair treatment extended by William Penn and his Quaker followers and the effective work done by missionaries here and there, such as that of John Eliot and the Mayhew family in Massachusetts in the earliest colonial days and that of the Moravians in Ohio and North Carolina somewhat later; but for the most part the record is one of almost unrelieved and brutal warfare. Indians looked upon the whites as intruders—which they were—and very naturally resisted encroachment on their homelands and hunting grounds. Under constant pressure they were driven relentlessly farther and farther west. Bloody massacres took place, followed by even more bloody reprisals, until in the end the Indians were either exterminated or driven out of their heritage and eventually found themselves located on reservations in every part of the country, principally in the arid west. It was not until late in the 1880's that the Indian wars ceased and the subdued race settled down to a grudging acceptance of its subservience to the white conquerors. This long period has been called "The Century of Dishonor" in a book by that name and received its classic expression in the moving story of *Ramona*, both from the pen of Helen Hunt Jackson. Utterly despised, unwanted, and abused, these "wards" of the government had no worthy future in the estimation of most Americans who took the trouble to understand their plight. Pushed off into reservations in sections where successful agriculture was almost impossible, the Indians were reduced to paupers looking to the government to provide their means of subsistence. In many cases—so frequently that it was considered the general rule—the Indian agents were unsympathetic white men who received their appointments as political plums. Lack of understanding, prejudice against all Indians, downright fraud, and glaring incompetence were widely prevalent and resulted in a still further reduction of the Indians to destitution. But ultimately the conscience of America was awakened, and laws which have resulted in general improvement were passed one after another. Hope has taken the place of despair, and the Indians have made considerable progress in taking their place in American life as worthy members of society.

This does not mean that utopia has been reached. Far from it, the problems which have emerged and are still only beginning to be solved are most baffling. The tribal form of organization continues as the general rule and will probably be in existence for a long period. Two stubborn traditions, coming down out of antiquity, are held by all Indians with great tenacity: the belief that land does not belong to the individual but is the common property of the tribe, and the belief that the community is a democracy in which all the men have the right to discuss and help decide matters of concern in their common life. To give the Indians freedom to act according to these inbred convictions and at the same time to bring them into the full current of American life, where different ideas prevail, can be seen to be most difficult. There are other problems which make evident the anomalous conditions which Indians and their well-wishers face. The Indians are legally citizens of the United States, and yet their lives are so hedged in by laws and regulations involved in their wardship that no one seems able to untangle the sorry mess. In some states they are citizens and yet cannot vote; in others they have full suffrage privileges, yet even there the state and the Indians find themselves in a strange dilemma.

In the Dakotas an Indian might vote for members of the state legislature, might, indeed, even himself be elected to that 'lawmaking body, and yet, on returning to his home on the reservation, be without responsibility to obey the law that he himself had helped to make.[3]

But with all their disabiltiies the Indians are coming into their own. The old idea, so often expressed, that "the only good Indian is a dead Indian" is itself dead. Appreciation is being shown of the contribution of the Indians to the life of America, even of the world. It was they who developed and gave us Indian corn, or maize, both the Irish and the sweet potato, the bean and the squash, all of which have traveled far beyond the seas. So has the use of tobacco, which John Smith and other early Virginians found the Indians enjoying. Thousand of place names from ocean to ocean are Indian or adaptations of Indian originals. Racism is being eradicated. To have Indian blood in one's veins is no longer a bar to free mingling at any level of American social life. Charles Curtis, of Kansas, vice-president under Herbert Hoover, was part Indian as was also Will Rogers, the philosopher-humorist. Indians have entered the armed forces of the nation in greater proportion than the white population. Twenty thousand were in the camps and at the front, in addition to twice that number in war industries.

Indians of today understand that they have been stigmatized as recipients of government bounty without adequate return, and there are many who are honorably attempting to erase the stigma. The Navahos, for example, a large and one of the more primitive tribes, "have petitioned that they may hold these lands [extra

[3] *Ibid.*, p. 63.

lands they are purchasing] subject to the taxation of the state. Their equality with other citizens is more valuable to them than the saving that non-payment of taxes would bring." [4] As a final statement, another quotation from Flora Warren furnishes an excellent summary:

> So far as blood content is concerned, Indian assimilation is proceeding constantly, rapidly, inescapably. Moreover, adaptation to American life is going on with equal speed, despite efforts to hold back the advance in order that aspiring antiquarians may be occupied and curiosity-seeking tourists may be titillated. To attempt the restoration of Indian culture is the most futile of endeavors. . . . Any culture that can be arrested and fixed in its mold is dead and no longer the possession of living human beings. [5]

Under the friendly and intelligent guidance of John Collier, commissioner of Indian affairs, and many wise missionaries, the Indians have been helped to raise themselves to a surprising extent. Much value is placed on self-determination and self-government. Indian cultural values and arts are emphasized, and workable plans have been in operation looking to the regeneration of the land and its communal use. Undoubtedly the fading away of racism is to be accounted for largely by what the Indians have been led to do for themselves. Their growing self-respect and hopefulness have led to respect on the part of white men and a new hope for the future of these first Americans.

The Mexicans

Many Mexicans became citizens of the United States not by choice but by annexation. Texas had been a state in the Republic of Mexico, had won its independence in 1836, and had become a part of the United States in 1845. Many Mexicans became citizens in that political change. The war between Mexico and the United States followed within a year, and in 1848 Mexico was compelled

---

[4] Flora Warren, "Indian-White Relations," in Lindquist, *op. cit.*, p. 65.
[5] *Ibid.*

to give up what we now know as California, Utah, Nevada, Arizona, and a considerable part of New Mexico to the United States. With this transfer of territory the Mexican population of course changed their citizenship. The population was small, consisting of people who had more Spanish blood than the typical Mexicans of the south, but it gave a tone to the life of the southwest of our country different from that in other parts of the land. To that original contingent have been added many recent arrivals, so that along the Mexican border Mexicans form an appreciable and important element in the population. The foreign-born Mexicans in the United States numbered 377,432 in the 1940 census.

Not being subject to quota limitations, Mexicans come into the United States with considerable freedom. In fact they come and go, depending on the labor market in the United States and conditions in Mexico. Poverty-stricken as most of them are in their native land, they welcome the opportunity to increase their earnings in this country. In San Antonio, Texas, they form the largest single element in the population, as they do in many communities in the southwest. Trouble exists and is likely to break out into open conflict almost any time between the Mexicans and the Negroes. The source of the difficulty is economic, but of course it has its racial aspect. The Mexicans can undercut the Negroes by working for less pay, a condition which always leads to antagonism. Along the entire border the Mexicans are looked down on by the white men. For the most part they are poor and illiterate, have little or no public spirit, and are content to live just as they have lived for centuries with no ambition to better their condition. This, of course, cannot be said of all Mexican-Americans, some of whom have wealth and refinement and occupy positions of trust and respect in a number of communities. The condition of most of these people is very unfortunate since they are at the bottom of the economic and social ladder. This has become a matter of solicitude on the part of certain of their leaders as well as of philanthropic and Christian agencies concerned with their uplift.

The Mexicans have drifted north along the lines of rail travel, and colonies are to be found in all our cities as far north as Chicago, where approximately 20,000 Mexicans make their homes at the present time. The men work not only on the railroads leading out of the city but in manufacturing plants, and some were employed in war industries during the war. As seasonal workers the Mexicans are appearing in many communities almost up to the Canadian border. They are considered good workers with considerable mechanical ability. Most of them are not American citizens, and this makes it difficult to obtain employment. It is about the only form of discrimination the Mexican meets with in Chicago. The older men and women feel that they are living in an alien environment and look to the day when they can return south with enough saved money earned at the fabulous rate of American wages to live in relative ease when they return to their accustomed habitat. Members of the younger generation do not feel this nostalgia, take on American ways, want to become American citizens, and are frequently out of harmony with the older folks in outlook and ambitions. Many have become citizens, bought war bonds, and are proud that 10,000 of their fellow Mexican-Americans served in the armed forces of their adopted country.

Attention should be called to a forward step which was taken during World War II. Representatives from the United States and Mexico set up minimum standards for Mexican workers coming into our country. This protected them from certain forms of exploitation by providing means of keeping track of them wherever they went. These standards, which among other items touched wages, housing, and hours of work, give promise of a happier situation for the people from our neighbor republic who choose to come into the United States.

The Filipinos

The Filipinos in the United States are in a very different situation. The group is not a large one, consisting of 45,563 members in continental United States according to the census of 1940. They are scattered widely over the country though most of them are in agricultural employment, the majority in California. Most of them came into the country after 1920, their number according to the census of that year being only 5,603. A considerable group came as students and served in all sorts of capacities in college towns and university centers to support themselves. A very disturbing fact is that the ratio of women to men is very small. During the decade from 1920 to 1930 there were 1,395 males to every 100 females, and today the ratio is 14 to 1. As a result 77 per cent of the men have remained unmarried, which is partly due to the legal restrictions against marriages with American white women in some states.

Very unfortunately the Filipinos have had to bear their full share of racial antagonism. It is even said that they have had heaped on them "the accumulated anti-Oriental venom" of many Californians during the agitation of the past few years. They were in many cases induced to come to this country by glowing steamship posters making exaggerated promises of what they would find in America. They often came from backward groups in the Philippines and were easy prey for the vice mongers and gambling joints in the large cities. Having practically no home life and no social centers to provide stability, they found themselves at a great disadvantage, the objects of disdain and discrimination, demoralized outsiders. Filipinos have entered the armed forces of the nation, but even the uniform of the Army or the Navy has not been the protection it should have been. They have suffered disparagement and have been made to feel that they do not really belong to the country of their choice.

The citizenship status of the Filipinos was a strange anomaly until July 4, 1946. An attempt was made in 1928 to stop Filipino immigration, but it failed. The Philippines belonged to the United States; they were under the Stars and Stripes; the people had received an American education; how could they consistently be excluded? But Filipinos could become citizens only by naturalization, and, being Oriental, they could not be naturalized! Charles Beard declared, "The Filipino hangs between two worlds. He is not an alien, not a citizen, nor can he be a citizen." [6] His plight can be realized partly from the following: "They are barred from public works projects, discriminated against as applicants for relief, denied in most states the right to practice the various professions, are not eligible to citizenship, cannot vote or hold public office." [7] Yet they are subject to the draft and have even volunteered for service. No wonder they have been called "legally undesirable heroes"! [8]

Nor was the prospect any better under the Philippine Independence Act of March 24, 1934. Under this act a quota of only fifty imigrants a year was allowed from the Philippines, a country with a population of 16,000,000, for forty years and more under the American flag. When one realizes that this was the smallest number allowed to any group permitted to enter our country at all, the injustice is manifest. Even the little European principality of Monaco, with a poplation of only 23,973 (census, 1939), was given a quota of one hundred immigrants a year. Let it be said that conditions for Filipinos now in the United States have improved since the outbreak of World War II. Sixteen thousand were in the first draft, and the inducement was held out to those who enlisted that they would become eligible for naturalization within three months. Not only so, but opportunities along other lines have increased. Many were engaged in defense projects, and in parts of California they took the place of Japanese in truck gardening.

The coming of independence changed the entire situation. The United States and the Philippines are now related by treaty. According to this agreement Filipinos are now admitted into our country on the quota basis and can become naturalized citizens of the United States. They are taking advantage of these provisions, and already many have become citizens with great rejoicing.

[6] J. B. Rosemurgy, "The Filipino in the United States." (Unpublished.)
[7] Ibid.
[8] Ibid.

The Japanese-Americans

Of the minority groups we are considering in the present chapter the Japanese-Americans have had the roughest treatment, especially after the attack on Pearl Harbor. This applies particularly to those along the Pacific Coast where most of them had their homes. "Of 126,947 Japanese in this country in 1940, 112,353 lived in the three West-Coast states. Nearly 80 per cent were in California." [9] Most of those born in Japan came to this country between the years 1900 and 1910. As truck farmers they raised a large part of the vegetables used in California. Most of them were engaged either in farming itself or in the distribution and sale of the products of the farms. In California their farm properties were valued at $65,781,000. In 1941 they raised produce valued at $30,000,000. Unfortunately they had not been assimilated into the white population but had kept themselves aloof, and many were living in "Little Tokyos" in a number of the cities. Wide cultural differences separated them from their American neighbors.

There was likewise a cleavage among the Japanese themselves, that between the older group which had emigrated from Japan and their children born in this country. The elders were Japanese with Japanese traditions deeply imbedded in their thinking and directing their behavior. Their children were Americans to all intents and purposes. They were citizens because they had been born on American soil, and most of them wanted to be Americans in every way. Despite everything the parents could do the young people grew up disregarding everything peculiarly Japanese in their background. Many could do no more than speak a little Japanese, scarcely enough to converse with their mothers at home. In fact it is very common to meet young Japanese who know no Japanese at all. So between the issei (first generation) and the nisei (second generation) there grew up a barrier which in many cases tended to disrupt the strongest bond which held this com-

---

[9] Carey McWilliams, *What About Our Japanese-Americans?* p. 3. For an almost definitive statement of this whole problem see this author's volume, *Prejudice, the Japanese—Americans; A Symbol of Racial Intolerance.*

munity together, the family tie. Carey McWilliams suggests that the point had been reached when the nisei were just coming of age and would soon have begun a transformation which would have altered the whole situation and brought the Japanese community much closer into contact and harmony with their surrounding fellow Americans when the blow fell.

The attack on Pearl Harbor was made December 7, 1941. The whole direction of world history was changed, but on no one group did the immediate results fall so suddenly as on the 112,-000 Japanese on the Pacific Coast. Without attempting to trace in detail the events which followed one after another in rapid succession, it is necessary to record that "as a matter of military necessity"—a phrase which was never defined—all Japanese were removed early in 1942 from Washington, Oregon, California, and a part of Arizona to evacuation camps and placed under military guard. Without doubt there were those among them whose sympathies were with Japan and some who were ready to aid Japan in the war. The American information service, however, had done its work so well that those of Japanese sympathies and those who might be classed as dangerous were already known and could easily have been apprehended and taken to places where they would have been harmless. Unfortunately racial prejudice was at work and motivated the drastic procedure which was adopted. General J. L. DeWitt, to whom was committed the responsibility of dealing with the question, made this statement: "The Japanese race is an enemy race, and while many second- and third-generation born on United States soil, possessed of United States citizenship, have become 'Americanized,' the racial strains are undiluted. . . ." [10] In his testimony before the House Naval Affairs Subcommittee on April 13, 1943, this officer remarked that the Japanese-Americans "are a dangerous element, whether loyal or not. . . . It makes no difference whether he is an American, theoretically; he is still a Japanese and you can't change him. . . . You

10 Quoted in McWilliams, op. cit., p. 11.

212

can't change him by giving him a piece of paper." [11] As Carey McWilliams says, "Racial distrust was the chief factor prompting mass evacuation." [12]

Was there any proof that the Japanese had been guilty of disloyalty? None whatever. General DeWitt showed the possibility of sabotage and espionage but at the time when the evacuation orders were issued he could point to no acts which would justify the fear. Many arrests of suspicious characters were made in America, but none were Japanese. Knowing that their own countrymen would immediately be suspected in the United States, the Japanese government had not employed them as agents in this country—they made use of non-Japanese. *"No Japanese Americans, either in Hawaii or on the mainland, have been convicted of either sabotage or espionage."* [13] One of the most unfortunate features of the evacuation was the suspicion which was fastened upon the entire Japanese community. Vindictiveness was carried so far that the evacuation itself was used as *proof* of the disloyalty of the Japanese. A Californian, sent to Washington to lobby for the evacuation, blandly declared: "We're charged with wanting to get rid of the Japs for selfish reasons. We might as well be honest. We do. It's a question of whether the white man lives on the Pacific coast or the brown man." [14]

In a short time the evacuees were removed from the assembly centers to ten relocation camps in Utah, Arizona, California, Idaho, Wyoming, Colorado, and Arkansas. Before this was carried out, the War Relocation Authority (W.R.A.) had been created to take charge of the disposition of the Japanese. This was a civilian board—the Army no longer had any connection with the matter. The change was in the right direction though it must be recorded that the Army carried out its orders efficiently and without friction. It should also be said that the Japanese

[11] *Ibid.*

[12] *Ibid.*, p. 11.

[13] *Ibid.*, p. 8. (Italics are McWilliams.')

[14] Quoted in McWilliams, *op. cit.*, p. 11.

co-operated to the fullest extent and showed a spirit beyond re-proach in a move which was disastrous to many of them econom-ically and socially. The new authority sought to deal with the baffling problems with as high respect for the rights of the Jap-anese as it was possible to maintain.

The next step was to remove the Japanese from the relocation camps. This proceeded with remarkable rapidity. The purpose was to abandon all the camps by the end of the war and see all the 111,000 Japanese relocated with the prospect of perma-nent occupation and support. A more permanent camp at Tule Lake, California, had been set aside for those who failed to give satisfactory evidence that they were not pro-Japanese.

This process of relocation has been carried out with consider-able success, but of course with frequent difficulties. Undoubtedly the national government is eager to see these Japanese become a part of American life, but local prejudices both on the part of groups and individuals often stand in the way. Many Japanese desire to return permanently to the Pacific Coast and are doing so. They are being met with both welcome and opposition. It is too early to say what the final outcome will be, especially when jobs will not be as plentiful as they were during the war. But several results which cannot but be permanent can already be foreseen. Little Tokyos are surely a thing of the past. The Jap-anese are scattered over the country in many centers so that the kind of self-imposed segregation which was evident wherever Japanese groups lived can scarcely be repeated. Many Japanese hail this with satisfaction, looking to the future under a changed mode of life as making possible real participation in American life as Americans. That is the only solution of this problem—there must be assimilation, or there will be continued trouble. By as-similation is meant the acceptance of the Japanese who live in any community as if they belonged to the common life. Inter-marriages are already taking place, but that is not the nub of the problem. Just as we have accepted Italians and Poles into American life, we must accept Japanese. Once they pass back and forth in any community without comment and begin to be taken for granted as if they had an accepted place, the essential thing has been done. Only the years will tell whether Japanese blood will be lost in the common American humanity or will remain comparatively unmixed and pure.

In 1944 there were over 8,000 Japanese-Americans in the Army of the United States. They were singled out for special praise for their gallantry in the Italian campaign. More than 40 per cent in the 100th Infantry Battalion were killed—the entire battalion consisted of nisei. No citizens of the United States have shown more courage or demonstrated a more loyal spirit than these Japanese-Americans, and yet prejudice and bitter hatred have been their lot in many places. Why did we treat American citizens of Japanese descent as if they were no better than alien enemies when German-Americans, with whose homeland we were also at war, were unmolested? The different treatment without question is to be accounted for by race prejudice, that strange unpredictable thing which raises its head and turns a perfectly innocent situation into one of ominous import. At every point where we come into contact with racial minorities the basic problem is not with these minorities themselves, but with the white Americans. The question is, Do they really believe in human beings and the democracy which they profess?

The Jews

We come finally to the Jews. At the beginning of the war there were 16,181,328 Jews in the world, of whom 9,394,072 were in Europe. The statement is now made that under the Nazi terror 5,000,000—more or less—of these European Jews were put to death. This would make America the home of more Jews than any other part of the world, the total being 5,018,251 for North America and the West Indies. New York City has the largest Jewish population of any city in the world, with 2,035,000, and Chicago has the second largest, with 363,000.[15] What these figures

---

[15] *American Jewish Year Book*, 1939-40, as quoted in Conrad Hoffman, Jr., *The Jews Today*, p. 74.

mean is that the problem of Jews and Gentiles, of anti-Semitism, is America's problem more than that of any other country. Is there any wonder that Conrad Hoffman should declare, "Therefore, what the church in America does in regard to the Jews in America will probably be decisive humanly speaking in determining the future of world Jewry." [16]

Until recent years the Jews were a minor factor in American life. By 1826 only about 6,000 Jews had come to America. Sixty thousand more had arrived by 1850, mostly from Germany and Central Europe. After the outbreak of anti-Semitism in Russia the numbers increased rapidly. Between 1880 and 1900, 1,000,000 Jews arrived and they continued coming in large numbers until the Immigration Law of 1924 put a stop to the inflow. Since Hitler came to power in 1933 another kind of Jew has come to this country, not the poor denizen of the ghetto but the cultivated German Jew, scholar, musician, scientist, and the literary man, and others from the higher ranks of society.[17] In view of anti-Semitism in Central Europe it is quite likely that the Jews will form a large part of the immigration in the postwar period.

What is the situation? Many of the Jews are looked on as undesirable in American life. The antagonism has every aspect of racism with the strange anomaly—to repeat—that there is no specific Jewish race and that they are members of the same Caucasian or white ethnic group to which most Americans belong. But the Jews are segregated into self-contained communities which socially and religiously have little to do with their neighbors. The fault is not all on one side. Jewish leaders, both Orthodox and Reform, oppose intermarriage with Gentiles. In customs, religious rites, and worship, they are so different from their neighbors that there exists a bar to close intercourse which is very difficult to cross. Intermarriage is taking place with considerable frequency, but it is doubtful if it is making the relations between the groups any easier.

[16] *Op. cit.,* p. 17.
[17] *Ibid.,* p. 29.

As is always the case when understanding is difficult to maintain, charges are made on both sides which are exaggerated or entirely untrue. Even when on careful investigation the charges are proved false, they continue to be repeated and add to the bitterness which already exists. The Jews are not perfect; neither are the Gentiles. Conrad Hoffman says: "Even if the Jews were perfect, anti-Semitism would probably continue. Whereas originally this prejudice was largely rooted in a religious question, today social, economic, national and racial factors are the dominant causes of this anti-Jewish attitude." [18]

Moreover, the Jews are of all classes socially and at every stage economically. Cleavages among these people are so serious that it is impossible to think of the Jews as one group. The Jews who have become established in this country look down upon the newcomers from Poland and Russia, call them "kikes," and wish it to be understood that they are not to be classed with these undesirables. Another line of cleavage is between the synagogue Jews and those who have left religion behind and become completely emancipated. They may go through religious rites when they are at home, but they are not to be counted on as true to the Jewish faith and as bound by its ethical principles. And then there are the Orthodox Jews who attempt to adhere to the old faith with as little modification as modern conditions will allow, and at the other extreme those belonging to the Reform synagogues. These latter cut themselves off from all the ancient rites except those which can today justify themselves at the bar of reason. They do not look for the coming of a personal Messiah, or a separate national state, and desire at every possible point to be identified with all liberal and forward-looking persons whatever their faith and creed. Representing the intellectual elite, this group contains many—though by no means all—of the Jews who take a prominent place in American public life and in the professions.

[18] *Ibid.*

The antagonism against the Jews shows itself in many ways. The serious aspect of the problem is that the opposition is increasing, literally hundreds of agencies, large and small, taking it upon themselves to propagate hatred and antagonism. Jews are excluded from certain hotels; many summer resorts display signs such as "Gentiles Only" or "Christian Establishment"; Jewish students are barred from national fraternities and sororities and are placed on a quota basis in a number of colleges and universities, all with the result that the Jews in self-defense have been compelled to shift for themselves and to form all kinds of organizations to meet their own social needs, thus emphasizing the segregation which already is practically watertight. Practically, the Jews have all the rights of citizens and hold many important offices in state and national governments. Despite this there is discrimination in political circles as well as in educational and occupational fields. Economically they have made their way with remarkable success. In fact it is economic rivalry which causes a considerable part of the prejudice against the Jews. The Jews have the reputation of being not overscrupulous in business transactions, and of edging in at every opportunity to gain an advantage over their Gentile (or Jewish) competitors.

So the tale goes, and even in church circles, where fairness might be expected in judgments of our fellow men, the seeds of anti-Semitism find lodgment and are propagated far and wide. Anti-Semitism has not broken out in this country into pogroms and killings, but no one can tell what will happen now when prejudice against minority groups is likely to grow to ominous proportions. When jobs become scarce and a "scapegoat" psychology has been developed, suspicion is likely to seize upon any shred of evidence, magnify it, and use it as justification of the untoward action which may be attempted.

The gratitude which all Americans should feel toward Jews can scarcely be exaggerated. Benefactors like Julius Rosenwald, the friend of the Negro; public servants like Louis Brandeis, justice of the Supreme Court; moral leaders like Felix Adler, founder of the Society for Ethical Culture; makers of public opinion like Adolph Ochs, the owner of the *New York Times;* religious leaders like Rabbi Stephen Wise, of the Free Synagogue in New York; scientists like Charles Steinmetz, the "Wizard of Schenectady"—these are men who take front rank among America's great and noble men. Few communities can be found in our land where there is a considerable Jewish group in which some names do not stand out as leaders of distinction and genuine worth. They have made a contribution to American life without which we would be far poorer and less worthy of respect.

When a Gentile is willing to break through his initial prejudices and become friendly with Jews, he has a happy surprise. He discovers that there is a significant group of Jews whom he can count on to be his trusted friends, men who have many of the ideals he cherishes and will go the full distance in building up attitudes of understanding and mutual helpfulness. There is no step more needed than this in combating anti-Semitism. We cannot hope for a complete breaking down of the bars as long as religious and social segregation is the rule on both sides, but wonders can be wrought by removing causes of misunderstanding and entering into fellowship just as far as conditions will allow. To do this rests as a heavy duty on the Christian community which more than any other gives direction to American public opinion. The Jews are with us; they are here to stay. Certain barriers seem beyond our present ability to remove. We must learn in spite of real difficulties to live with our Jewish neighbors in peace and mutual regard. This is not a utopian dream: it is a possibility which can become actual. The way is by understanding and friendly concern each for the other, to be exercised in season and out of season, no matter how great the opposition or from what source it comes.

Chapter XII

The Negro in American Life

Negroes are Americans not by choice but by compulsion. They were brought to these shores against their will. The problem which we face by their presence among us is not of their devising; it is one for which the white men are solely responsible, and which had its beginnings very early in our history. According to John Smith's *Generall Historie of Virginia,* there arrived in Jamestown in 1619 "a Dutch man of warre, that sold us twenty negars." [1] This was only twelve years after the first permanent British settlement in the United States and before the landing of the Pilgrim Fathers in Plymouth in 1620. From that beginning the importation of Negroes continued for nearly two centuries, that is, until the slave trade was abolished by Great Britain in 1807 and by the United States in 1808.

Slavery had its opponents in the American colonies as early as the eighteenth century. In various ways the colonies of Pennsylvania, Virginia, South Carolina, and Massachusetts made vigorous attempts to curtail the import of slaves, but their efforts were of no avail because the mother country was profiting greatly by the trade. The cities of Bristol and Liverpool were being made rich by their slavers. "Thus while the mother country prohibited slavery on her home soil she not only encouraged but enforced it in her colonies." [2] Thomas Jefferson was opposed to the institution and wrote a clause for the Declaration of Independence against slave importation, but it was not accepted. He continued his opposition, but slavery was becoming more and more profitable in the South, so that it became a recognized

[1] As quoted in Edwin R. Embree, *American Negroes: A Handbook,* p. **11.**
[2] H. W. Elson, *History of the United States of America,* p. 443.

institution during the early days of the republic. The most important event in this process was the invention of the cotton gin by Eli Whitney in 1793. This device made it possible to separate cotton fibers from the seeds easily and inexpensively. Its introduction at once resulted in an enormous increase of cotton and in the consequent increase in the demand for slave labor in the cotton-producing area. The cleavage between North and South became wider and wider. Slavery decreased in the northern states and soon passed out of existence but in the South the institution became more profitable as the demand for cotton spread and grew by leaps and bounds. Cotton was produced both for consumption in the United States and for export to England, whose mills depended on the cotton supply from this country.

During this period and until the middle of the nineteenth century vigorous voices were being raised against the ownership of human beings by others and against the conditions under which the slaves were compelled to live and work. These protests came from the South as well as the North. There are those who believe that slavery would have ceased to exist without a bitter contest between the two sections had it not been that the problem became involved in a struggle for political power between the slave and the free states. Then the only possible outcome was war—the war which was fought out to a finish in 1861-65 and resulted in the emancipation of the slaves and the saving of the federal union of the states. In the North slavery was not profitable and early ceased to exist; hence the conscience of the growing majority, who believed that slavery was "the sum of all villainies," as it was called by John Wesley, the founder of Methodism, could assert itself and become a dominant motive among the masses of the people. On the other hand the opposition to slavery on moral grounds found it hard to live in the uncongenial soil of the South and was ultimately stifled under the weight of political and economic pressure. While in the North most of the preachers were challenging chattel slavery as contrary to the Bible and Christian teaching, in the South equally sincere ministers of the gospel were proving to their own satisfaction that slavery was encouraged in the Bible and that it was conformable to Christian tradition. They deplored the evils which they knew existed but contended that they were abuses of a system which rightly conducted was best for all, owners and slaves alike.

But the irrepressible conflict came, and the slaves were freed. The Emancipation Proclamation was promulgated by Abraham Lincoln January 1, 1863, and a new era in the life of the Negroes in America was begun. It is true that the proclamation applied only to the slaves in the states which were in revolt against the Union and that slavery as a whole did not cease to exist until December 18, 1865, when the Thirteenth Amendment to the Constitution became a part of the basic law of the land. Yet the act of Lincoln in 1863 ushered in the new day of freedom and may well be considered the red-letter day for Negroes in the United States.

The story of the Negro from that day to this has been one of the most amazing records of progress in the history of mankind. This progress has been accomplished against the most strenuous opposition of those who believed that they belonged to an inherently inferior race and that they should be kept in permanent subservience. The sudden change in status from slavery to freedom did not in itself accomplish what many idealists thought would almost immediately and automatically follow. The weary and discouraging years through which the freedmen had to travel seemed at times to belie the promise of a new and satisfying life which emancipation held out. Yet the Negroes could never have made a start toward the goal so long as they were bound by the shackles of slavery. Abraham Lincoln's act marked the turning point. It was the beginning of a new era without which nothing else could have taken place.

It is only by the strenuous use of imagination that we, more than eighty years after the event, can visualize the conditions which were faced by 4,500,000 people just made free. They had

222

been slaves with no rights which white men were bound to respect. They were bought and sold at the block as livestock. All
too often, especially upon the death of an owner, families would
be torn apart never to be united again. Young Negro girls were
frequently at the disposal of their owners or the sons of the family. As a result the number of mulattoes grew wherever slavery
existed, gradually changing the ethnic type and producing almost a new race. All were classified and treated as Negroes and
slaves no matter how much white blood ran in their veins.
There was no mestizo class of intermediates between white and
black as in Latin America. Naturally a slave psychology developed. They owned nothing; therefore they could feel no
sense of responsibility. They became shiftless and had no ambition and no incentive to work and better their condition. It
is a wonder that any self-respect remained in them at all. But
it did, and restlessness and dissatisfaction were present widely.
The chief dread which filled the breasts of white men and
women in the South was that the slaves would rise in revolt,
turn against their masters, and break down the social structure.
They had reasons for their fears. At least twice the threats took
shape in definite action. "The first was the Denmark Vesey
plot in Charleston in the summer of 1822. The second was the
Nat Turner insurrection in Southampton County, Virginia, in
1831. In addition to these frequent rumors of slave unrest swept
the South at intervals." [3]

This is not the entire story. While cruelty existed—and there
was plenty of it—kindly disposed masters were to be found everywhere. Mistresses were deeply concerned for the welfare of
the slaves and gave themselves to helpful ministrations. The
church was also concerned. It was the rule that slaves might attend church with their masters, sitting in the gallery which was
reserved for them. The story of the self-sacrificing white ministers of the Protestant denominations who gave themselves to
the conversion of the slaves is a notable one. As the result of these

---

[3] Dwight L. Dumond, *A History of the United States*, p. 247.

labors practically all the Negroes came over to Christianity and eventually became members of some church, usually the Baptist or Methodist. A Negro ministry arose, and some preachers became famous, both among their own people and the white people, who would come in large numbers to hear them preach.

With all their laughter and gaiety there has always been an undertone of melancholy and sadness in the Negro which has expressed itself in plaintive verse and song. In the midst of their sad lot religion became their consolation. The deliverance of the children of Israel from their bondage in Egypt became a favorite theme; and the prospect of heaven, a beautiful place of freedom and rest among the blessed around the great white throne, comforted them amid the tribulations through which they were unwillingly made to pass. So there was hope as well as despair on their journey through life. One of the finest gifts of the Negroes to American life is the "spirituals"—those simple, cheerful, yet plaintive songs which all Americans know and cherish.

When freedom came to all the Negroes in the United States, about a half million were already free, some in the South as well as in the North. Manumission was not uncommon; and, even more significantly, many slaves had been permitted by their masters to pay for their freedom, working at times through long years for the precious boon. Thus there was a group which had risen above the level of most of their people and had some preparation for a life of freedom and of responsibility for their own career. This, however, was not true of the vast majority, who had more or less complacently accepted their subservience and had little or no ambition to do anything themselves to better their condition.

With such a background the Negroes were compelled to face a new life at the close of the Civil War in 1865. One of the most regrettable periods in American history is that of reconstruction, when the South was treated as "conquered territory" and the government in the individual states was conducted under the protection of northern armies. Unscrupulous political adventurers from the North, "carpetbaggers," joining with equally vicious white politicians in the South, "scalawags," took advantage of the ignorant Negroes and the poor whites who had the vote, and ran the state governments. The inevitable result was that confusion, corruption, and every form of misgovernment scandalized right-thinking men everywhere. One of the first acts of President Rutherford B. Hayes, when he came to office in 1877, was to recall the Union troops from the southern states. For this he is held in honor by the white south. The state governments could now be taken over by the white population which had been restrained and frustrated during the occupation by the Union troops. There was a tremendous sense of relief, to put it mildly, all over the South.[4]

That is one side of the shield, but there is another, not so frequently mentioned but momentous for the Negroes. They had had a voice in the government during reconstruction days. In the new regime there was a complete rightabout-face. In one way or another the Negroes were thrust back into impotence and lost even the slightest voice in public affairs. True, most of them were ignorant to an appalling degree and had no political competence, but it must also be pointed out that this was equally true of large numbers of white men in the South, "poor whites," but these were given the vote while the Negroes were deprived of it. The factor in the history of the period which should be known is the part played by a group of Negroes who deserve far more credit than they have received. A number of the Negro members of the state legislatures and representatives of the states in the national Congress were men of ability and true worth. J. C. Gibbs, to use one illustration, a graduate of Dartmouth, was secretary of state in Florida and later became state superintendent of schools.

---

[4] For relation of President Hayes to the return of state governments to the white South see H. J. Eckenrode, *Rutherford B. Hayes, Statesman of Reunion,* especially chap. X, pp. 235 ff.

All told, sixteen Negroes served in the Federal Congress during the Reconstruction years. Twelve of these men had been slaves or were born of slave parents; the other four had received a more or less complete college education in the north or abroad.[5]

In fairness to the Negroes the well-considered words of Professor J. G. Randall, of the University of Illinois, deserve attention:

> Another unfair conclusion is to attribute the excesses of the carpetbag period to the Negro. Though the Radicals used Negro voting and office-holding for their own ends, Republican governments in the South were not Negro governments. Even where Negroes served, the governments were under white control. . . . That the first phase of the Negroes' experience of freedom after centuries of slavery should occur under the degrading conditions of these carpetbag years was not the fault of the Negro himself but of the whites who exploited him.[6]

One of the worst features in the violent reaction was the use of cruelty, intimidation, and force to cow the Negroes into docility. The Knights of the Ku Klux Klan rode the countryside; in hooded disguise and with mystic rites they carried out a campaign of merciless terrorism as savage as anything in our history. The object was to subdue the Negroes so that "white supremacy" should be recognized and only "lily white" governments should control the destinies of the states involved. Despite two amendments to the Constitution of the United States which were calculated to give Negroes their rights as citizens, the several states were able to devise laws and adopt regulations which virtually nullified the plain intention of the Constitution. It is quite true that Negroes were handicapped by many disabilities, but southern white men took advantage of their po-

[5] Ina Corinne Brown, *The Story of the American Negro*, p. 90; also see Howard Fast, *Freedom Road*, for a moving story of reconstruction in South Carolina, based on the sources.

[6] *The Civil War and Reconstruction*, p. 854.

sition to retain their supremacy and deprive Negroes of their rights even though they were free.

The number of Negroes who were brought from Africa is unknown. According to the first census, taken in 1790, there were 757,000 in the country. Since that time they have steadily increased and in 1940 they numbered 12,800,000. At the same rate of increase their numbers now must be considerably over 13,000,000. While the Negroes thus continue to comprise a not inconsiderable part of the people, their numbers show a steady decrease in proportion to the total population. In 1790 they made up over 19 per cent of the population while in 1940 the proportion was less than 10 per cent, which means that by natural increase and an amazing immigration the white people have been increasing more rapidly than Negroes in the United States.[7]

Great changes have taken place in the distribution of the Negroes. At the end of the Civil War nearly all the Negroes lived south of the Mason-Dixon line and the Ohio River; now more than one fourth live outside what is known as the Old South. The most remarkable movement in Negro population has been the mass trek since World War I into the cities of the North. In 1940 New York City had a Negro population of 458,000, thus giving Harlem, where most of the New York Negroes find their home, the largest Negro population of any city in any part of the world. Chicago has 278,000 Negroes, and Philadelphia 251,000. These figures would have to be increased by many thousands to include those who have come into these centers since 1940. There are now six cities north of the Potomac and the Ohio rivers which have Negro populations larger than the Negro population in any city in the South. The causes of this movement are chiefly economic. More pay is the lure which has brought most of the people north.

So long as "King Cotton" reigned in southern agriculture and industry, the Negroes, who were the chief cotton cultivators, could find employment and were not greatly tempted to leave

[7] Edwin R. Embree, *op. cit.*, pp. 18 f.

their old homes. But the situation has changed, particularly since the period of World War I. Competition with other countries has gone hard for American cotton. India, Egypt, China, and Brazil have entered the field and are able to undersell the American exporter. In addition, the boll weevil has been a devastating pest in recent decades. The depletion of the soil is increasingly adding to the necessary expense for fertilizers—it is known that cotton takes more out of the soil than most other crops. Erosion in the cotton fields is carrying off millions of tons of the precious soil itself. And to these hampering conditions must be added the antiquated methods of farming which prevail through the entire South. The Negroes are finding it steadily more difficult to keep soul and body together either as independent farmers or as share croppers and are beginning to cast their eyes about for better places to live and rear their families. They have inevitably turned toward the cities of the North. Let it be said that this same difficulty confronts the white tenant farmers and the white share croppers, whose condition is almost as deplorable as that of the Negroes, with the advantage, however, always on the side of the white men. What we face, then, is a most serious economic and social condition affecting the entire South and growing in intensity each year. The invention and use of the mechanical cotton picker, which is being used ever more widely, is sure to throw out of employment hundreds of thousands of Negroes and white men now working in the cotton fields.

When the Negroes were snatched away from their native habitat in Africa, they represented many tribes scattered along four thousand miles of coast. They spoke different languages and dialects and were at different stages of cultural development. By no means were all of them wild savages. In many cases they came from peoples who were skilled workers in metals, knew what settled agricultural life meant, and had arts and skills of no mean order. But they were all herded together and subjected to the horror of the middle passage across the

Atlantic. So severe were these experiences from the time of capture in Africa to arrival at the American port of entry that only one out of five survived and reached the slave market. Differences in language, culture, and former habitat were completely ignored, and the poor creatures were sold indiscriminately to every part of the South. This resulted in such mingling that it soon became impossible to determine the origin of any second-generation Negro. He might be bred of parents and earlier forebears from places far apart in Africa.

Other minglings took place. The Negroes found little difficulty in mating with the Indians. This continued as long as Indians lived in proximity to Negroes, the result being that at least part of the Negro population has some Indian blood. But it is the white men who took advantage of Negro women who are chiefly responsible for the mixed strain in Negro blood. Almost never were the matings on the basis of marriage. The white men from northern Europe spurned such a suggestion. But that did not keep them from illegitimate unions during all the days of slavery—and even since. Thus the white men produced a hybrid race. The result is that we have in the American Negroes today a mixture of the three basic ethnic groups of the world: the whites, the yellow-browns, and the Negroes. So far has this process gone that, according to an estimate by Professor Melville Herskovits, only 20 per cent of the Negroes in this country are of pure African extraction. No wonder Dr. Edwin R. Embree declares that the Negroes in America are a new and distinct ethnic group, which he calls the brown race. The difference in attitude of the Latin-American peoples and the people of the United States toward a person of mixed race is very marked. In Latin America a man is often called white if he has even a modicum of white blood in his veins, while with us in the United States the slightest presence of Negro blood consigns the possessor and his family to the status of a Negro with all the disabilities attached. The color line here is most sharply drawn, and the distinction between a white man and a

Negro with even the slightest trace of Negro blood is as rigidly made as the line between a white man and the blackest of Negroes. Blood relationship counts for absolutely nothing so far as it concerns the right of a man of color, even almost white, to claim relationship with a white man, even though he may be closely related. This fact is fundamental in attempting to understand the position of the Negro in American life.

Negroes are severely handicapped at many points. Distressingly unfavorable living conditions are reflected in sickness and death rates which contrast sharply with the rates for white people more fortunately situated. In 1890 the annual death rate of Negroes was a little less than thirty-five per thousand while that of whites was twenty. By 1940 the conditions had so far improved that the rate for Negroes was reduced to fourteen, while that of whites had come down to a little over ten. The life span for Negroes is even now eleven years below that of the average for all Americans, that of the Negroes being fifty-one as contrasted with sixty-two for the population as a whole. Sickness is much more serious among the Negroes than among the whites, with tuberculosis the chief scourge. This disease is serious even in the South and fastens readily upon the Negroes as they leave the more open life of the Southern farm and come into crowded and unhealthy tenements in Northern cities. The contrast between the two races as regards the incidence of tuberculosis is startling. Studies made in 1938 in forty-six cities disclosed a death rate from this disease of 238 per 100,000 Negroes in contrast with 48 for the same number of whites, a difference of nearly five to one. In some of the cities the disparity was even greater.[8]

Venereal disease has been all too prevalent among Negroes, in one southern county the syphilitics reaching the appalling total of 40 per cent of the people. Poverty, lack of opportunity with consequent lack of ambition, overcrowding, particularly in cities, and general aimlessness are largely responsible for this

[8] *Ibid.*, p. 26.

condition. This can be seen from the fact that the rate was actually reduced from 40 per cent to 10 per cent through an intensive campaign of ten years in one center. With these figures in mind it is significant to record that tests which were made a few years ago indicated that Pullman porters showed very slight taint from veneral disease, even lower than the average in the total population. All of this goes to show that the blight of disease is not inevitable but can be dealt with and reduced to a surprising degree by careful attention and energetic action, provided the will to better the condition of the Negroes is present. This can be said also of the sacrifice of life both of mothers and babies at the time of childbirth. Whenever the antiquated and unclean methods of ignorant midwives are replaced by the scientific methods of modern obstetrical practice, the conditions improve and the death rate falls very markedly.

Negroes have suffered a serious handicap educationally. At the time of emancipation only about 5 per cent of the 4,500,000 Negroes were literate, that is, could even write their own names and read a simple sentence.[9] As a result of heroic efforts both by state agencies and private philanthropy, this scant 5 per cent has now been raised to more than 85 per cent. While this shows notable progress, not too much emphasis must be placed on it. In many cases *little more than sheer literacy* has been achieved. The instruction given in Negro schools, particularly in a number of states, is so inadequate and inferior that the Negroes are not fitted to compete with their white neighbors in dealing with the ordinary affairs of life. Discrimination is glaring in the amounts spent for Negro schools as compared with white. In the United States as a whole an average of $80.26 was spent in 1936 on each pupil in the public schools. When this is contrasted with the amounts spent for education in the southern states in the same year, it is evident that both white people and Negroes are at a distinct disadvantage in that region. In the South as a whole $49.30 was spent for each white child and $17.04

<hr>

[9] *Ibid.*, p. 31.

for each Negro child. These are averages. What of the figures in individual states? In Georgia the figure for a Negro child dropped as low as $8.75; in Mississippi it was $9.30. This means that a Negro child is not given a reasonable chance to take his place in the economic and social life of his community.

One of the finest examples of devoted service in American history was the manner in which church groups in the North entered the field to provide education for the freedman. Looked down on by the southern people and barred from their social circles, these devoted men and women spent their lives in service for the ex-slaves. Many mistakes were made; but, in spite of conditions sufficient to discourage the hardiest optimist, progress was made, and today as the result of their vision many institutions dot the South, some of them attaining high ratings in the records of educational associations. Hampton Institute in Virginia, Atlanta University, Fisk University in Nashville, Howard University in the nation's capital, Tuskeegee Institute in Alabama—founded by a noted Negro, Booker T. Washington—and a number of others have proved themselves worthy members of the family of American colleges and universities. These to be sure stand out as beacon lights in sharp contrast with many institutions for Negroes, but they have proved what Negroes can do educationally when given the opportunity. Many Negroes have found their way into institutions in the North which are almost wholly white. There they are handicapped by poor preliminary training, but a considerable number make good, some showing marked ability and making exceptional records. As many as two hundred have received the Ph. D. degree from white institutions and have become leaders among their people.

At no place have Negroes been limited more seriously than in being deprived of their rights as American citizens. The Constitution declares that "the right of citizens of the United States to vote shall not be denied or abridged . . . on account of race, color, or previous condition of servitude," yet the Negroes have been, and are, denied these rights in many southern states. One of the methods early used was the "grandfather clause," which means that if a person's grandfather had not been able to exercise the franchise, he could not do so either. This prevented Negroes from casting their votes and put the stigma of racial inferiority upon them. Not being allowed to vote in the Democratic primary nominating elections, as was the case in many sections, effectually kept the Negroes from the polls. The poll tax has been retained in a number of states as a prerequisite to voting. It is not a large sum and often—where it is enforced in their case—prevents white men from voting as well as Negroes. The underlying purpose of this tax, however, is to make it impossible for poverty-stricken Negroes to exercise their rights as citizens. Still another method of exclusion is to require all voters to qualify by property or education or "character" tests. White men are either excused from these tests or are readily qualified, while the Negroes are usually declared ineligible by white examiners or judges who understand that part of their job is to make it impossible for the Negroes to qualify.

The white men in many places in the South feel that their supremacy is in jeopardy—and that must be preserved at any cost and by any means. No longer in any state of the Union does the Negro population outnumber the white, though in some counties in the deep South this is still the case. But still the prejudice against Negro participation in politics exists. To the typical white man it is literally unthinkable that an ignorant and despised group should be a power at the polls and that a Negro might be elected to public office. As conditions are today in hundreds of southern communities, the situation is really very difficult. Negroes have been given no opportunity to assume responsibility. But there is more to be said. If the white people did not hold the Negroes in such contempt and were willing to do more to lift them to the place where they could take their rightful share in the life of the community, there would be encouragement and hope; but unfortunately such has not been, and is not, the case in the vast majority of communities. Again, what the intelligent Negroes see, and what many white people know in their hearts, is that there are many "poor whites" who are ignorant and utterly unqualified to vote but yet are not debarred. No, all means must be used to ensure white supremacy, which has become a fetish in most parts of the South. Why not be fair to all? That is what the Negroes ask.

In the North the situation is different. Negroes have the franchise and take great interest in the elections. No longer bound, as they were for so many years, by loyalty to the Republican party, the party of Abraham Lincoln, Negroes now choose the candidates who will stand by them in their struggle for advancement, irrespective of party. They have been able to elect members of the House of Representatives in the United States Congress, and many representatives in state legislatures and municipal councils come from among their people.

Closely connected with political handicaps is the unfortunate criminal record of the Negroes. They are too often looked upon as born criminals. They are said to know nothing of sexual morality, and the common opinion is that Negroes will always steal. Of course this is unjust, but it continues to be repeated. Their crime record is advertised. Always when a Negro commits a crime, it is stated that he belongs to the colored race. About all the news concerning Negroes to be found in some newspapers is the record of their crimes. The statistics are against them. In proportion to the population there are three times as many Negroes behind prison bars as whites, native whites at least.[10] But other facts cast a different light on the situation. Policemen in the South are almost without exception whites. Fortunately, this situation is being changed here and there with surprisingly good results. White policemen come from a class which is likely to harbor the most resentment and indulge in the most bitter hatred against Negroes and can be counted upon to accuse Negroes and to do them injury at the slightest prov-

[10] M. S. Stewart, *The Negro in America*, p. 25.

ocation. Many acts are considered criminal when committed by Negroes which are looked upon quite differently when committed by whites. This is particularly true of the way in which the charge of vagrancy is abused in the case of Negroes. Thus the crime record of Negroes appears worse than it actually is. Not only so, but Negroes have little chance in contrast with white men either to have an impartial hearing or to receive just punishment for their crimes. Their testimony in court is of little weight. They have no prestige in a trial as compared with white men. A judge and jury often start from the assumption that the Negroes are in the wrong and that it does not much matter anyway how they are treated.

Negroes have suffered cruelly from overcrowding, particularly in northern cities. In recent years their coming has been a veritable mass movement largely to improve their economic condition but also to escape social disabilities and discrimination in the South. Their presence has caused consternation among property owners in every community into which they have so suddenly come. Real estate values at once topple, and every such section of a city becomes undesirable to white residents, who move away as soon as possible. To meet the situation hundreds of communities, large and small, have formed organizations to resist the movement by entering into covenants not to rent or sell property to Negroes. Whether these covenants will be legally upheld by the highest courts has not been finally determined; it seems likely that they will have to be liquidated in time. In the meanwhile, however, the Negroes are passing through the experience of paying high rents for inadequate housing, in many cases unsanitary, with its entail of the dreaded tuberculosis and other diseases. Relief projects are already to a slight degree relieving the pressure, but much remains to be done to remove this condition, which exists in almost every city where the Negroes have come to make their home. But undoubtedly they have come to stay, and provision for their shelter simply must be made.

The many forms of social discrimination and injustice are another harassing feature of Negro-white relations. In almost every place where Negroes and whites might meet and have fellowship, the Negroes are refused this relationship. Particularly in the South but in places in the North they must not make use of public parks or playgrounds or libraries. Places of amusement are for Negroes only, if they have such an opportunity at all. In all of the southern states the "Jim Crow" system prevails. They must travel in separate railway coaches, in designated seats on streetcars and busses, and must wait for trains and buy tickets in separate rooms in railway stations. They are supposed to be provided with accommodations equal to those for the whites, but nowhere are the provisions adequate. So, they not only travel in poor cars but are constantly made to suffer from the consciousness of being inferior, not worthy to associate with their superiors, the whites. Hotels, restaurants, and cemeteries are for whites or Negroes as the case may be, with no intrusion on either side. This rule of segregation includes Christian churches. A few Negroes belong to white churches in the North, and in some cases in the South older Negroes are allowed the privilege, coming down from slavery days, of attending white churches. This is so uncommon that it stands in striking contrast to the almost universal rule that white churches are for the whites and Negro churches for the Negroes.

The church situation demands a further word. Not only is segregation the rule in local churches and congregations, but continues to hold its sway in larger denominational and interdenominational assemblies. It is almost impossible to hold such meetings in southern cities. Even where Negroes are allowed to attend, they are set off by themselves separate from white people. In northern cities where segregation does not obtain in the meeting places themselves, Negroes find it difficult if not impossible to secure hotel accommodations with the whites; and even where that is possible, they are denied entrance into public dining halls. Of course the church is not responsible for this situation; it is only another illustration of the handicaps and indignities which Negroes are compelled to bear.

The situation differs in the various Protestant denominations. At one point they all hold to the same practice—Negroes and white people are not members of the same local churches. Several experiments are now being made to include both races in a single congregation, but there is little likelihood that this will be widely practiced, at least in the near future. The Presbyterian and Protestant Episcopal churches scarcely have a serious problem, the number of Negro members and churches being relatively few. But in the South Negroes are not members of the same Presbyteries with white ministers and elders even in the so-called Northern Presbyterian Church (U.S.A.). Since each Baptist and Congregational local church is independent and is not under the authority of a central organization, the question of race relations does not arise as in churches with central legislative bodies which control the individual churches. But even in these cases, particularly among the Baptist, there is a problem. At the present time the more or less influential conventions with which Baptist churches are affiliated are divided on race lines, the white churches having their northern and southern conventions and the Negro churches their national convention.

But recent events among the Methodist churches have brought the whole question of the relation of the races into significant focus, which is being watched with the deepest interest not only among Methodists but widely among other Christian bodies. In 1939 three Methodist bodies became one—the Methodist Church. This union brought 324,769 Negroes into the new church, 7,160 of whom had been members of churches in white conferences and the remainder members of Negro conferences in the former Methodist Episcopal Church. The new church was divided into six jurisdictions, five being geographical and consisting almost entirely of white members and one a Negro jurisdiction extending over a considerable area of continental United States. There were a number of cogent reasons for a jurisdictional system from the standpoint of efficient administration of a large and widely scattered membership, and it is quite likely that time will confirm the wisdom of the church in adopting the present plan. But there is another factor which is causing serious thought in the minds of many members of the church. A separate Negro jurisdiction means segregation—segregation on the grounds of race, no matter what other grounds may justify it. Without doubt the unification of the churches could have been accomplished on no other plan. The Negro leaders realized that and gave their consent to the arrangement. They too believed it was for the best interests of the church. But now that unification has been accomplished, many among both the white and the Negro members of the church are very uneasy and are wondering if an injury has not been done to the church by such discrimnation between its Negro and white members.

Among the resolutions passed by the General Conference of the Methodist Church in 1944 the one on race is significant. It opens with a general statement:

We believe that all men are children of God and brothers one of another. "No group is inherently superior or inferior to any other, and none is above any other beloved of God." [11]

This resolution is followed by certain "proposals for action." Among them is the following:

We look to the ultimate elimination of racial discrimination within The Methodist Church. Accordingly we ask the Council of Bishops to create forthwith a commission to consider afresh the relations of all races included in the membership of The Methodist Church and to report to the General Conference of 1948.[12]

As early as 1943 the Women's Division of Christian Service adopted this statement:

[11] *Discipline of the Methodist Church,* 1944, p. 569.
[12] *Ibid.,* p. 570.

It is deadening to the effort to achieve brotherhood to assume that we have it when it has not been achieved. The jurisdictional organization of our church tacitly accepts the principle of segregation. Methodist women have an obligation to stimulate within the Church an increasing awareness of the contradiction between our Christian ideals and our plan of organization.[13]

This statement was reaffirmed in 1945 and was then adopted by the Board of Missions and Church Extension.

In general much good will exists between Negro churches and white churches and there is an increasing number of white church members who deplore existing conditions and are seeking to mitigate the resentment which the Negro community increasingly feels. Most American Negroes have been and are, devoted Christians, but in recent years a small but growing number of the Negro intelligentsia, particularly the sophisticated among them, have turned away from the church, believing that it has little to offer as the Negroes long for, and move toward complete emancipation.

Social taboos are frequently annoying, exasperating, and humiliating. In the South the unwritten rule has been never to address a Negro as "Mr." or "Mrs." A Negro's first name is to be used or such a designation as "boy," "uncle," or "aunty." When a Negro has done well and has begun to make a name for himself, it is a great relief for the white community if he can be addressed as "Professor" or "Dr." These are professional titles and do not carry with them the social recognition implied by the use of "Mr." and "Mrs." This is a sore spot in the mind of the southern people with regard to Negroes. The Negroes must be kept in their place and that "place" means a recognition that the Negroes are to be completely excluded from all that even hints at social fellowship between the two races. What is always in the background is the fear that the slightest breach in the tight wall of racial caste might lead to intermarriage. So

[13] *Journal of the Sixth Annual Meeting of the Board of Missions and Church Extension of the Methodist Church*, 1945, p. 294.

sensitive are most southerners on this point that at the first suggestion of a more liberal attitude the red herring of miscegenation is dragged across the trail. The almost inevitable question, "Would you want your daughter to marry a nigger?" immediately clouds the issue and makes logical discussion impossible. The fear of intermarriage has found expression in legal enactments in twenty-six states—more than half of the forty-eight—forbidding marriage between the races. And yet with all this, in thousands of cases white men and women all over the South have great confidence in and even affection for individual Negroes and would do anything for them. But—and this is the point of importance —the Negro must not aspire to any but a secondary place and must never expect to be given the slightest social recognition.

In spite of all disabilities Negroes have been forging ahead and are filled with ambition and hope of occupying a worthy place in American life. Most of them are still attached to the soil in southern states, and their condition hangs as a dead weight on the small but determined group who have come into a new world and are making real progress. Poverty and ignorance still stand in the way of more widespread achievement. Realizing the conditions with which they started so few years ago, we can only wonder at what the Negroes have accomplished. One hundred and seventy-five thousand are reported as owning their own farms,[14] and they conduct countless stores and little businesses wherever they live. Even in the realm of large business they have shown a splendid beginning, the promise of much more in the future. Such an institution as the North Carolina Mutual Life Insurance Company, with headquarters at Durham, is an illustration of a wisely managed concern reaching out through its agents to every part of the South. All this is hopeful and is to be emphasized, but the fact must ever be kept in mind that the Negroes are always at the lowest rung of the social ladder and are in a very unhappy state. Much of this they share with the "poor whites" who as share croppers are held in the same state of semi-peonage as the Negroes.

[14] Edwin R. Embree, *op. cit.,* p. 40.

In the North and in the South Negroes have found openings in the heavy industries, in steel mills, in manufacturing plants, in automobile factories, and in slaughtering and meat-packing industries. Here they come into contact with the powerful labor unions, some of which admit them to membership while most do not. The C.I.O. has taken the step of making Negroes feel that they really belong to the American labor movement. A very successful Negro union is that of the Brotherhood of Sleeping Car Porters, which is a Negro monopoly. Its success is due not only to that fact but to wise leadership and the high type of Negroes who are porters.

The chief white-collar job of Negroes is teaching. Of course they teach Negro children only, that is, with a few exceptions in northern cities where white and Negro children frequently are assigned to the same room on the edge of the Negro districts. But here again Negro teachers work against a tremendous handicap. The Negro school building and equipment are usually very inferior, and the teaching load much heavier than that of white teachers and the salary less. At best the average salary is small in the South.

Closely associated with the teacher is the preacher. He is more than any other the leader of his community, spiritually and otherwise. Unfortunately his training in most cases is all too meager, and often his moral ideas are not high. This might be expected. What is far more important is that there is a growing number of well-trained, able, and exceedingly alert preachers who understand the situation of their people and are proving themselves the leaders needed in the new day. One of the most unfortunate features in the racial situation is that fellowship between these men and their white brothers is not more constant and effective. There is loss on both sides from this failure. As in the case of the teacher the stipend of the preacher is very inadequate, so that all too frequently he must eke out his salary by doing something else as a necessary side line to keep soul and body together. But there is an increasing number with churches worthy to be compared with good white churches.

Negroes have entered the medical and the legal professions. Four thousand Negro physicians were listed in the census in 1940. Aspiring students find it exceedingly difficult to gain entrance to white medical schools. They may, however, receive their training at one of the two first-rate schools of their own race. The field is almost limitless despite the many disabilities in hospital and other training facilities. Very unfortunately Negro physicians are debarred from most hospitals. That they are capable and are rising to wide recognition as physicians has been proved a number of times. Recently at Fort Huachuca, Arizona, where a large Negro army camp was located, a remarkable situation developed. The hospital there was recognized as one of the most efficient army hospitals in the country. It was manned entirely by Negro doctors and nurses, but this did not prevent white officers in the area from choosing this hospital for themselves over white hospitals which they might have patronized.[15]

Negro lawyers are not having an easy time. In addition to the handicaps faced by all young Negroes in securing professional training young lawyers who hang out their shingles are apt to discover that most of their own people would prefer to go to white lawyers. They have learned that a lawyer of their own race is not acceptable in a courtroom—nearly all of course have white judges and other officials. This has discouraged most young Negroes from entering the law, and as a consequence there were in 1930 only 1,200 Negro lawyers in the whole country, and two thirds of these were in other than southern states.[16] Yet there have been many distinguished Negro lawyers, some rising to the bench as judges known and honored widely.

In several other fields the Negroes have made a remarkable showing. As athletes they have carried off the honors in a number of events. Jesse Owen has never been surpassed as a sprinter, and

---

[15] M. H. Bickham, "An Illinois Code of Race Relations," p. 10. (Unpublished.)
[16] M. H. Stewart, *op. cit.*, p. 14.

Joe Lewis, the "Brown Bomber," is still the undefeated champion of the heavyweight ring. Until very recently the major baseball leagues were exclusively white, but in the autumn of 1945 a Negro was signed up as a member of the Montreal team, a "farm" of the Brooklyn Dodgers. An even more prominent place has been taken by Negroes in the field of entertainment as actors and singers. One need only be reminded of Marian Anderson and Paul Robeson to realize how far they have traveled. But even beyond this Negroes have been well-known poets and writers. Paul Laurence Dunbar ranks high among American poets, and today W. E. B. DuBois is a recognized authority on certain aspects of sociological research. These are but significant illustrations to which many other names might be added. But even so short a sketch must not fail to list the names of Booker T. Washington, the founder of Tuskegee Institute, and George Washington Carver, professor in that institution, famed as a scientist and benefactor of his race through his researches. Only one conclusion can be reached—that a race which has produced such men and women can scarcely be inherently inferior and, if given the opportunity, will come to its own and make its contribution even more widely to the life of the world.

The Negroes are putting up a successful fight; they are forging ahead slowly but surely. As in every other such case advance depends more upon them than upon any who may come to their assistance. Many Negro organizations have been created to further their interests. Several of them have come to such maturity that they have wide influence, being in several cases national organizations with branches and offices in every section where there is a sizable Negro community. Backed up by a vigorous Negro press they are quick to seize on every case of injustice and discrimination and push the claims of their people. What the immediate future has in store no one can say. Increasing tension may be expected now that Negroes from the armed services are returning to their homes. They have fared well—with many injustices to be sure—in the armed forces of the nation. Equality with white soldiers in pay, food, and clothing is of course the rule. They have borne their share of hardship and have freely suffered and died for their country—a country which has given them grudging recognition. They have had a splendid record on a number of fronts. Have they not the right to expect better treatment than in the old days before they were drafted or enlisted? Much depends on the answer to that question; it is for the white man to make the response.[17]

What do the Negroes want and what are they striving for? The word "opportunity" covers the essential meaning better than any other. Professor Gunnar Myrdal presents a most significant analysis of the aims which intelligent Negroes have set before themselves and their race. Strangely enough it is in almost the exact opposite order from what the southern white man believes the Negroes want. According to the white man's diagnosis the discriminations against the Negro rank in the following order:

1. The ban on intermarriage and sex relations involving white women and colored men;
2. The established etiquette governing personal relations between individuals of the two races;
3. Segregation in the schools and churches;
4. Segregation in hotels, restaurants and theatres;
5. Segregation in trains, street cars and busses;
6. Discrimination in public service;
7. Inequality in political rights;
8. Inequality before the law;
9. Inequality in jobs and relief.[18]

The Negroes themselves would rank them in quite different order. What they want first is equality of opportunity in securing jobs and relief when it is needed, and so on from point to point in the

---

[17] See Walter White, *A Rising Wind*, for a statement by a witness of the relations between the races in the armed forces in Europe and Africa.

[18] Gunnar Myrdal, *An American Dilemma*, I, 60 f. This two-volume work is the most important ever published on the American Negro problem.

reverse direction from the white man's order of importance. This certainly should make it easier to work out a basis of understanding. At every turn the Negroes want opportunity—merely a fair chance in the elemental items of labor, pay, housing, and schooling. So far as intermarriage is concerned, only theoretical extremists would harp on that, and they would receive as little hearing from self-respecting Negroes as from whites.

One of the most interesting and significant developments in the whole situation is the change taking place in the hearts and minds of white people themselves. This is true in the South as well as in the North. In many cases they are not willing to acknowledge the change and want to think of present conditions as permanent, but there are many signs that not only young people but enlarging groups of adults realize that they are living in a new age and that the so-called old solutions are no longer applicable.[19] They cannot but be impressed by the inescapable fact that the Negroes are an integral part of American life and that by keeping the Negroes down they are depressing the whole level of the nation's life. The underlying truth in Abraham Lincoln's famous dictum is more and more being accepted—that our country cannot continue to exist half slave and half free.

The Negroes are not now slaves, but the same principle holds good. In present-day dress what Lincoln said might be phrased: Our nation cannot continue to exist part oppressed and part free, a part of the people living under the stigma of perpetual inferiority and another part considering themselves inherently superior, part grinding under the yoke of arbitrary discrimination and part enjoying the full fruitage of unlimited opportunity and privilege. So it comes about that in essence the problem of the Negroes in American life is the problem of the whites. Whether our nation shall become just and fair and truly democratic and be known for

---

[19] Attention should be called to the vigorous stand taken by Mr. Virginius Dabney, the Richmond editor, against the segregation and Jim Crow regulations in Virginia streetcars and busses; also by Governor Ellis Arnall, of Georgia, who is urging his fellow citizens to give the Negro fair treatment economically.

these virtues depends upon the white people far more than upon the Negroes.[20]

Gunnar Myrdal calls his work *An American Dilemma.* What creates the dilemma? Just this, that we Americans, all of us, have sworn wholehearted allegiance to the American creed that "all men were created free and equal" and should have equal rights and opportunities; *and we do not live up to it.* We simply will not surrender our fundamental conviction, as found in the Declaration of Independence and the Constitution, particularly in the Bill of Rights; but we stumble and hesitate at carrying out these doctrines with reference to the Negroes. We are thrown into a dilemma. There is only one way out, and today is our day of opportunity. We can prove to the world, which is watching us with both eyes wide open, that we are sincere and mean what we say when we lose no occasion to publish abroad our belief in man as man and in his essential dignity as one created by the one God who is over all, black as well as white. This is the greatest American issue—we must be true to what we profess or lose our own self-respect as well as that of mankind.

[20] We can look upon the defeat of the Fair Employment Practices Corporation in the United States Senate as only a temporary defeat. But we can also look upon it as an act of despair that recourse must be had to the filibuster as a means of defeating a resolution which would otherwise have become law.

Chapter XIII

Racism and World Order

"World order" is the phrase used to designate the way in which the affairs of the world are conducted and the way 'in which its varied component parts are related. The aim of all right-minded people is to create a world order which will be truly orderly, a system of international relationships which will bring freedom from disturbance and secure tranquility and peace. The main thesis of the present discussion is that racism does not do this, but always creates, or tends to create, chaos by disrupting harmonious human relations.

We have discovered how diverse the points of racial contact have been and yet how unified the problem of racism always is. The same fundamental attitudes and the same motivations have ever been present. Racism is based on the belief that the particular group to which one belongs is superior to others and that this superiority is inherent in the biological and cultural constitution of the group itself and cannot be aleniated as long as the group keeps intact and does not debase itself by mingling with others. The attitudes toward those belonging to other groups may range all the way from benevolent pity to bitter hatred, but they always assume a superiority which cannot, or should not, be questioned. We have seen in a dozen or more different lands how this attitude works out in practice. Having made this survey, we must consider the problem as a whole and realize how the order of the world is affected in its wider reaches. Racism cannot be isolated. Like the Spanish influenza of a generation ago, it leaps national boundaries and runs the danger of affecting the world and engulfing all peoples with its devastating influence. The ramifications of local racial disturbances affect far wider areas and in some cases en-

247

danger the peace of the entire world. A lynching in the United States becomes headline news in Moscow and Chungking; a flare-up between whites and blacks in Kenya or South Africa arouses the ire of the American Negro press. We live in one world, as Wendell Willkie reminded us, and what affects vital human relations anywhere becomes an issue between men everywhere. Often the racial factor is obscured by its entanglement with other issues or by the angle from which any particular question is being viewed, but it takes only the slightest probing to come into contact with the racial animosity or fear which lies close under the surface.

At the conference on "Christian Bases of World Order" held in Delaware, Ohio, March 8-12, 1943, the first of the factors in world order which was presented was that of race. But, in addition, economic freedom, the relation of land and human welfare, politics, health, the workers of the world, and human character were all discussed from the standpoint of their relation to world order. All of these factors are related to the race problem and frequently receive their form and reveal a peculiar intensity by their racial connection. By no means should one go to the extent of saying that all the other issues are aspects of the race problem, but it is difficult to escape the conclusion that of all the ills to which humanity finds itself heir today there is none more virulent and none which has so many facets, involves so many human beings, and affects so many world issues as that of race. After our emergence from World War II with all of its loss and devastation, the longing for peace possesses the minds and hearts of men in every land. Not only are church bodies and other organizations giving themselves to the promotion of peace, but the nations themselves provide the clearest evidence of a determined purpose to prevent another world war. Examples are the conferences at Dumbarton Oaks, Bretton Woods, and at San Francisco, where representatives of fifty nations met and constructed the Charter of the United Nations, whose preamble begins with the words, "We the peoples of the United Nations, determined to save succeeding generations

248

from the scourge of war, which twice in our lifetime has brought untold sorrow to mankind. ...." Our concern here is to make plain the supreme importance of achieving harmonious race relations if there is to be any assurance that these hopes will be realized.

One of the most striking and long-continued conflicts is that between the Jews and the Arabs, especially when the question of a homeland for the Jews in Palestine is broached. Many Jews and their well-wishers are convinced that it is only a matter of fundamental justice that they should be granted a permanent home somewhere. And what location is more appropriate than the land where they lived for so many centuries, where their religion came to its fulfillment; the land of David and Solomon, of Isaiah and Jeremiah; the land which furnished the background and gave local color to their most priceless possession, the holy Torah, the Old Testament of the Christian Bible. Certainly a strong case can be made out for a permanent center for refugee Jews from Europe. And this can be said irrespective of the pros and cons of the setting up of an independent Jewish nationality in the Holy Land.

But the Arabs do not see it that way. Palestine is a Holy Land for them too. Did not their Prophet Mohammed ascend to paradise on a memorable night in his early career, and was it not from the very dome of the rock in the old temple enclosure that he made his ascent? Not only so, but Jerusalem and Palestine were conquered by Omar in the earliest days of Islamic expansion, and for only a short century during the early period of the Crusades was Palestine taken away from them. The political ascendancy of the Turks in the Near East did not alter the situation essentially, for they too were Moslems and were just as jealous of Palestine as the Holy Land of their common faith as were the Arabs.

According to the Balfour Agreement which was issued during World War I, Jews were allowed to settle in Palestine. Many of them came. They were remarkably successful along many lines. Tel Aviv, a city on the coast of the Mediterranean, has been a model of municipal order. Irrigation projects and scientific farming have set the type for the entire Near East. The very success of the enterprise has, however, been a red flag to the Arabs, who have increasingly voiced their envious opposition. Ibn-Saud, king of Saudi Arabia, has declared that he would use armed force to drive the Jews out, should the peace conference decide to grant them a permanent abode in Palestine. The entire Arab world, particularly the states in the Near East, Iraq, Saudi Arabia, and Egypt, is at one in violent opposition to the plan.

Our concern is to indicate the sources of the opposition. It has a long history. For a short time after Mohammed went to Medina from Mecca in A.D. 622, both he and the Jewish tribes in the vicinity of Medina believed that there might be a close union between the two peoples. Had not the Prophet declared that he came to restore the pure religion of Abraham? But both were doomed to disappointment. Mohammed was sure that the Jews would recognize him as an authentic representative of the old Jewish prophetic line, while the Jews thought that Mohammed would come over and embrace Judaism. The result was not only estrangement but persecution and warfare, the Moslems having the advantage and driving the Jews out of Arabia. And now again after these many centuries the old feud has broken out again with new virulence.

Originally Jews and Arabs were probably different branches of the Semitic stock with their origin in the Arabian penninsula, but the Jews today are a mixture of many racial groups while the Arabs have remained more purely Semitic. In Palestine at the present time economic jealousy adds to the racial antagonism. The Jews have again fulfilled the Old Testament prophecy that "the desert shall rejoice and blossom as the rose." [1] Thus again racism is combined with other factors. Here the factor is economic, but underneath the jealousy aroused by prosperity lies buried—not very deeply—religious and racial alienation so intertwined that they cannot be successfully disentangled. The net result of the whole complicated issue is a combination of bitterness and envious pride which provides another tension point in international relations which disturbs the equilibrium of world order.

[1] Isa. 35:1.

This is but one illustration. We have surveyed others, one of which is the presence of the European settler in East and South Africa. After what was presented in a former chapter, it is not necessary to survey the facts again. They may be summarized in a few sentences. It was impossible for the newcomers to do as the English colonists did in America—either exterminate the natives or drive them permanently out of the land. What they have done is to seize the power, render the natives helpless, and rule the country to their own advantage. Arnold Toynbee analyzes the situation as follows:

First, the White people have established an ascendancy over the people of other races with whom they have come to share their new homes. Secondly, these white masters have almost everywhere abused their power in some way and in some degree. Thirdly, they are haunted by a perpetual fear that some day the positions may be reversed, that by weight of superior numbers or by a more successful adaptation to the local climate or by ability to survive on a lower level of subsistence or by readiness to do harder physical or intellectual work, the man of Color may eventually bring the White Man's ascendancy to an end and perhaps even establish an ascendancy of his own over the White Man.[2]

The new aspect of the situation is that the relation of black man and white man in Africa is echoing around the world and making the tensions between races more difficult of solution because of the attitude of implacable hostility displayed by the whites toward their black neighbors in Africa.

Our own racial attitudes in the United States are entering into a new phase, one scarcely dreamed of a few years ago by anyone, and one whose ominous significance is not yet appreciated by a vast majority of our people. In the discussion concerning the location of the capital of the United Nations organization, racial attitudes played a significant part. The southern states of our country were ruled out because of Jim Crow discriminations. The

---

[2] Arnold Toynbee, *A Study of History*, I, 210.

question was even raised as to the suitability of any American city in view of our general attitude, in the North as well as in the South. An editorial in the highly influential English journal the *Manchester Guardian Weekly* states: "The decision in favor of the establishing of the headquarters of the United Nations Organization in the United States is to be deplored." The chief reason for this contention was that Europe was likely to be a storm center of international complications for years to come and that the capital of the new organization should be closer at hand than across the ocean in the United States. But among several other reasons was included "the delicate matter of race and colour prejudice."[3]

Many of our people might learn a wholesome lesson from a recent decision of the Supreme Court of the Province of Ontario in Canada, which disallowed the legality of covenants between citizens to prevent the lease or sale of property to people of another race or ethnic group. As significant as the decision itself was the reason given for it. The court stated that in view of the fact that Canada had adopted the Charter of the United Nations it was clearly bound by its provisions, one of which was "to encourage respect for human rights and for fundamental freedoms for all without distinction as to race, sex, language, or religion. . . ."[4] The United States has also adopted the same charter. Are we to be consistent as Ontario in accepting the provisions of the charter in guiding our own national affairs? But let us, at least, understand that this is what is involved in our action if we mean to take it seriously. What is becoming clearer and clearer is that our race problem is not ours alone but involves the whole issue of international relations in the new world into which we are emerging.

In his recent volume of lectures delivered in the United States, the eminent Brazilian writer Gilberto Freyre sheds light from another quarter on the question we are discussing. He declares:

[3] "The Eclipse of Europe" (editorial), Oct. 12, 1945.

[4] See "Anti-Semitic Land-Sale Clause Declared Illegal," *The Globe and Mail* (Toronto), Nov. 1, 1945.

The Soviet Union and Brazil, though fundamentally different in their conceptions of social and economic organization, will probably join in the near future as leaders in a movement toward making of racial equality an international issue similar to the one that united such different communities as China and Japan in 1919.[5]

The reference is of course to the plea that a declaration of racial equality be placed in the Charter of the League of Nations. The declaration was not allowed because:

"Wilson, who was presiding, ruled that it was not effective because the vote was not unanimous." Whatever Wilson's motives, Japan blamed him and grew bitter against the United States. In Brazil, the decision had little repercussion at the time and hardly affected Wilson's enormous popularity. But Brazil is becoming increasingly conscious of the fact that its mixed population gives its people a feeling of unusual solidarity with Asiatic, African, and Indo-Hispanic nations.[6]

The same author drives his thought home in this further statement:

From a purely social point of view, such have been the changes for the better in the relations between the two countries that today even a coloured man, if sent as emissary from Brazil to the United States, would probably find a decent (if not warm) reception in this country, at least among the best-educated Americans. The point is important: a changed attitude towards men of colored races seems to some students of inter-American relations essential to the development of Pan-Americanism if the latter is to mean reciprocity and effective mutual respect.[7]

Colonies

One of the most important phases of the relations of more advanced and retarded peoples is that of colonies. It is a problem as old as recorded history. When have ambitious nations been without their outposts among strange and more or less distant

[5] *Brazil: An Interpretation*, p. 127.
[6] *Ibid.*, pp. 127 f.
[7] *Ibid.*, p. 146.

peoples? Egypt controlled Nubia along the upper reaches of the Nile and looked upon its inhabitants as inferior blacks. The Greeks had their colonies to the north on the shores of the Black Sea and to the west in Sicily and southern Italy, which still retain evidences of contact with the Greeks. The Phoenician cities of Tyre and Sidon were famous colonizers, sending their merchants westward in the Mediterranean and through the Pillars of Hercules into the Atlantic as far as Britain. They established settlements of importance in Spain, but their great success was the city of Carthage, which for decades dominated the West and rivaled the rising city of Rome. In the modern era the colonizing ardor of Portugal and Spain opened up and occupied great sections of the newly discovered world. They were followed by the English and the Dutch, deadly enemies of the Portuguese and Spaniards. They fought between themselves for the mastery of the East. The French played their part both in North America and in Asia. They carved out an ambitious empire, but lost it on both continents. Britain came into possession of almost every land which the French had occupied, and at the beginning of World War II the French had in Asia only Syria, Indo-China, and a few little toe holds along the coast of India. But in Africa, France has a huge realm extending from Algeria south as far as the Congo. They also have possession of the island of Madagascar. Thus almost all of Africa, together with great tracts of Asia (India, Ceylon, Burma, Indo-China) and the island world to the southeast of Asia, is occupied by Europeans as overlords.

On what basis if any can such domination be justified? In the early history of colonization and almost to our own time no formal justification was deemed necessary. An ambitious and energetic nation took it for granted that, if it had the military power, all it had to do was to march in and take possession with no questions asked as to the rights of the subject peoples. Might made right— it was the accepted rule. What became of the native races did not particularly matter. They might be driven out, or they might be enslaved and compelled to serve their masters. The land and the people were exploited for the sole benefit of the homeland. The Spaniard carried this idea of forced labor so far that the poor natives in the island world of the Caribbean soon died off and African Negroes were brought in to take their place. In the modern world, from the age of discovery in the fifteenth century until the nineteenth century, the exploitation of native peoples has been the accepted practice. The purpose of colonization was to enrich and give prestige to the colonizing power. Financial returns were more than adequate. Frequently they soared to unbelievable percentages on the original investment. Thus did Europe become rich and powerful at the expense of the soil and the peoples of her far-flung colonies.

As true as the statements just made are, the subject is so large, complicated, and varied that a further analysis of the situation must be made. At once we find ourselves face to face with the twin problems of colonies and imperialism. While they cannot be separated, either theoretically or practically, the emphasis in each case is different. The colonial problem is primarily economic; that of imperialism is political. Imperialism is always involved whenever colonies exist, but an empire must not necessarily possess colonies—the self-governing dominions of the British Empire are not colonies, and the empire would continue to exist without any colonies at all. But nevertheless at the present time every empire is a colonial empire, and the same questions emerge in every case. From the viewpoint of the studies in this book, that of racism, the colonial and imperialistic problems are bound together by the fact that distinctions of race lie at the bottom as the most fundamental feature of the colonial imperialistic system. To quote:

The first of the universal traits of colonialism is the color line. In every dependent territory a true caste division exists, with the resident white population separated from the native masses by a social barrier that is virtually impassable. The color line, indeed, is the foundation of the entire colonial system, for on it is built the whole social, economic, and political structure. All the relationships between the racial groups are those of superordination and subordination, of superiority and inferiority.[8]

The same author states, "About one third of the land area of the earth is colonial territory; and of the two billion population of the world approximately 700,000,000 fall in the category of subject peoples." [9] Of these, 500,000,000 are subject to Great Britain, India of course accounting for 350,000,000 of this huge total. France and the Netherlands come next with approximately 70,000,000 each; then comes Japan, which counted 30,000,000 in her colonial empire; when World War II began the United States and Belgium followed with about 15,000,000 each; and finally Portugal with about 10,000,000 in her African possessions.[10] We have already considered the conditions in the African colonies and discovered how different they are. What now is the attitude of the home governments and of interested groups toward colonials and the whole colonial problem?

The crudest possible attitudes were expressed by German writers when Germany was glorying in her new colonial empire. Friederich Naumann puts it thus:

History teaches that the general progress of civilization can be realized only by breaking the national liberty of small peoples. . . . History decrees that there should be leader nations and others that must be led, and we ought not to wish to be more liberal than history itself.[11]

Another German writer, Dr. Paul Rohrbach, expressed himself even more bluntly:

Rights of natives, which can be recognized only at the cost of holding back the evolution of the white race at any point, simply do not exist. The idea that the Bantu, Negroes and Hottentots in Africa have a

[8] Raymond Kennedy, "The Colonial Crisis and the Future," *The Science of Man in the World Crisis,* ed. Ralph Linton, p. 308.
[9] *Ibid.,* p. 307.
[10] *Ibid.,* pp. 307 f.
[11] As quoted in J. H. Oldham, *Christianity and the Race Problem,* p. 95.

right to live and die after their own fashion, even if multitudes of human beings among the civilized peoples of Europe are in consequence forced to live in cramped proletariat conditions, instead of rising to a higher level through the full exploitation of the productive capacity of our colonies while at the same time the whole cause of human and natural well-being, whether in Africa or in Europe is thereby helped forward—such an idea is absurd.[12]

These men were Germans writing a generation ago. What they propounded were Nazi doctrines before the rise of Hitler and Nazism. We need not wonder at the brutality of the German troops in southwest Africa in slaughtering the Herero, who had risen in revolt against their conquering masters. Let us not think that such sentiments and actions have been confined to the Germans. The British have taken their share in the suppression of native peoples in more than one colony. The lowest point however was reached in the treatment of the natives of the Congo when that huge land, rich in rubber and other products needed in Europe, was in the hands of Leopold II, king of Belgium. That there is a better side we shall proceed to show, but we must be reminded that the background of cruelty and unrelieved exploitation has in most cases been present and has helped to color the resentment of the native peoples even when better conditions have come to prevail.

At best the problem is a most difficult one. If there is to be colonization at all, is it possible to provide for the welfare of both the European colonial powers and of the native peoples? We have not done very well in the past. Mr. Graham Wallace states the historical situation in very plain language:

On the practical point . . . whether the stronger race should base its plans of extension on the extermination of the weaker race, or on an attempt within the limits of racial possibility to improve it, Christians have, during the nineteenth century, been infinitely more ruthless than Mohammedans, though their ruthlessness has often been disguised by more or less conscious hypocrisy.[13]

[12] *Ibid.*
[13] *Ibid.*, p. 96.

257

We rightly shrink from thinking that what-so-called "Christian" nations have done should be attributed to Christians, but the fact remians that Christian sentiment in Eurpean countries has not sufficiently asserted itself to restrain the evil doings of their fellow-countrymen in colonial areas.

That conditions have improved there can be no doubt. The very attempt to justify colonies and the principle of colonization indicates that conscience has come alive. The rights of the native races have become the concern of all those who in any capacity must deal with the practical problems involved. What are they? The Western world is in need of the products of Asia, Africa, and the island world. The mere mention of rubber and oil brings the problem home to every automobile owner in the United States and in Europe, not to mention a hundred other articles and raw products which are essential in Western life and industry. There will probably be complete unanimity in the thought that some way must be found to make available what all the world needs. The problem is, Can this be done without infringing on the rights of native peoples? Or, to take a further step, can it be done and at the same time advance their interests and make them sharers of the prosperity which comes to the people across the seas who benefit by their labor and the richness and productivity of their land?

These questions can be rightly approached only by putting ourselves in the place of the native peoples themselves. The European has always thought of them as inferior, inherently inferior with no hope of significant change in their status. We have presented good grounds for the conclusion that there are no inferior races, that if given the opportunity—education, improvement in hygiene, economic possibilities, a new philosophy of life—every race might rise to heights now undreamed of and take its place as a worthy member of the community of mankind. What we must recognize, however, is that these peoples are backward or retarded, and that they have a long distance to travel before they can take the political reins into their own hands and be able to maintain themselves in the competitive life of modern times. One of the arguments used to justify colonies is that so long as native peoples remain in their present condition of backwardness and cannot fend for themselves, some kind of protection or wardship must be imposed by more advanced peoples.

The clash of these two principles is always present in colonization. The desire for gain and the need of the civilized world for the products of the tropics on one hand and the rights of backward peoples and their own develpoment on the other—these two interests like the scales of a balance are almost always in a state of unequal equilibrium. The man of business hears the insistent call of the stockholder at home for larger returns; the government official must maintain the prestige of his nation; but the conscience of the nation at home, fed by the humanitarian on the field—very frequently a missionary—who is in close contact with the thought and life of the natives, sounds its call for justice and the well-being and advancement of the backward peoples. Undoubtedly much improvement has been made. One of the finest and most remarkable factors has been the intelligent and hearty co-operation of numbers of colonial governors and other officers, who have taken to heart the welfare of the native peoples and have done all in their power to remedy abuses, check the rapacity of the conscienceless trader, and provide for the protection of the peoples under their care. Many have come to see that the dignity and prestige of their native land would be promoted more by a policy of justice and defense of the rights of native peoples than by sheer, callous exploitation. Still it remains true that at best the whole idea of colonization is so closely connected with that of exploitation that many despair of real advance, especially in very backward regions, unless a drastic change is made.

This has been recognized by enlightened persons in a number of the colonial powers. At least on paper very noble sentiments have been expressed not only by individuals and interested groups but by the governing powers themselves; for example, the conference held in Brazzaville, French Equatorial Africa, which was opened on Monday, January 31, 1944, to consider the entire problem of colonial policy. Under the presidency of M. Pleven, commissioner of colonies, and the inspiring leadership of Felix Eboué, this conference took an advanced stand on all questions affecting the welfare of the native. The conference, as might be expected, considered everything in the traditional twofold frame of French colonial policy—the ultimate complete assimilation in the circle of French culture and the giving of special attention and privileges to the elite.[14] Within this framework the economic, physical, educational, and social welfare of the natives was made predominant. Free France at least intends to initiate reforms which will give hope to her colonials. While the way may be long and the performance may not for years match the adopted policy, there is splendid promise of a better future.

The situation in the Netherlands Indies is different both from that in the French and the British colonies. Raymond Kennedy, an authority on the East Indies, writes:

> The color line is quite apparent in the Indies, but it is not nearly so rigid here as in the British possessions. The Dutch suffer less from preconceptions of racial superiority and inferiority than most Western peoples, and are unusually liberal in their attitude toward deviations from the colonial code of caste. ... The allegation of innate inferiority of the darker peoples, so often heard in British dependencies, is rarely encountered in the East Indies.[15]

The Netherlands East India Company for a long period held the authority in these islands; but, even after the Dutch government became directly responsible, "Holland took no interest in native welfare or internal affairs except as these related to the flow of profits from the colony." [16] Not until the beginning of the present century, when an "ethical policy" was adopted, was there any recognition of a "civilizing mission." What this meant was that "the interests and welfare of the Indonesians would in future take

[14] See "French Colonial Policy in Africa," *Free France,* special issue No. 2.
[15] *Op. cit., pp.* 324 f.
[16] *Ibid.,* p. 325.

precedence over all other considerations in the administration of the Indies." [17] But while this did register a wholesome change, the actual task of the application of this new policy has proceeded exceedingly slowly. To quote again:

The 68,000,000 Indonesians are an economically inert mass occupying the lowest levels of income and occupation. . . . Those who work for wages are hired almost exclusively as coolies, servants, and other menial employees. And so, for all the lack of pure racial prejudice as exhibited in British colonies, a rich native, or a native with a really good job, is almost as rare in the Indies as in the British dependencies. [18]

An account has already been given of the conditions in British colonial Africa. What has been accomplished there—as well as in other British possessions—has been partly at least initiated and constantly backed up by humanitarian groups in the homeland which have been insistent on recognition of the rights of native peoples as far as British rule extends. Such an organization as the Anti-Slavery and Aborigines Protection Society has had an honorable record in defending the rights of natives, and so have other organizations, among which the missionary societies have had a conspicuous place. Recently, however, a remarkable change has taken place in the political situation in Great Britain which will affect colonial policy profoundly. Reference of course is made to the sweeping victory of the Labor party as a result of the parliamentary election held in May, 1945. That party is now in power and stands for a policy quite different from that of the Tory party of Mr. Winston Churchill, which for so long had been in power in Parliament. For a number of years the Fabian Society in Great Britain has been devoting a part of its energy to studying the problem of colonial policy and administration. When it is understood that this society has for many years been intimately connected with the development of the Labor party and has provided a notable part of its intellectual leadership, the significance of recent events

[17] *Ibid.*
[18] *Ibid.*

can be clearly seen. What has been produced by the Fabian Society and partly embodied in a volume entitled *Fabian Colonial Essays* is likely to be incorporated in the colonial policies of the Labor government.

What do we find there? A frank recognition that great changes are imperative if the rights of man as man, which the Labor party stands for, are to be adequately recognized. One of the greatest needs is economic rehabilitation. Poverty stares one in the face immediately on setting foot anywhere in the Dark Continent. Why should this be when there is fabulous wealth in minerals and almost limitless productivity in soil and forests and animal life? The simple but adequate answer is that so much of the profits of industry and agriculture has been drained off and taken to the homelands that little is left for the African. Speaking of the gold-mining industry, a well-known publicist writes: "None of the profits go back to the West African village: they are spent in Kensington or on the Riviera. If any workers are benefited, they have white skins. This is the nature of empire. It means conquest and exploitation by an absentee overlord." [19] Has this writer forgotten the excellent system of native farming and industry in Nigeria? Probably not, but the system as a system has been set to the tempo of exploitation. One need only read Rita Hinden's article with the suggestive title "The Challenge of African Poverty" to be convinced of the reality of the need. One quotation from this essay will suffice. An impressive survey of good things which Britain has provided is followed by these words:

We may have done all this and much more, but it has brought no real happiness and satisfaction. Why? Because, reducing the answer to the simplest terms, our coming has upset whatever balance there was in African life. We have brought new ideas, new standards of living, new wants and new visions, yet we have prevented the Africans from taking their full share of all these desirable things which we have held

[19] H. N. Brailsford, "Socialists and the Empire," *Fabian Colonial Essays*, p. 32.

before them. We have upset the old while withholding the new—or at least any but the most shoddy fraction of the new.[20]

The colonials are thus exploited for the benefit of stockholders at home, but that is not the end of their plight. The administration in each dependency must be self-supporting. This means taxation, which adds to the burden of the native taxpayers. To make his accounts balance each year the administrator finds himself in a tight place. He may be a man of most generous impulses with a sincere desire to give the natives advantages which they do not possess, but his funds are limited. This explains why the natives are so poorly provided with educational opportunities, health services, and other welfare agencies—there is simply not money enough left for these purposes· It is the fault of a system which is geared to the old abominable policy of exploiting the natives for the benefit of the stockholders at home.

Is there any wonder that the question of colonies and their administration should have been one of the most important issues at the San Francisco Conference? What we have in the Charter of the United Nations is most significant. One of the chapters of the Charter deals with an international trusteeship system, which is to be set up under the authority of the United Nations.

The basic objectives of the trusteeship system . . . shall be:

a. to further international peace and security;

b. to promote the political, economic, social, and educational advancement of the inhabitants of the trust territories, and their progressive development towards self-government or independence as may be appropriate to the particular circumstances of each territory and its peoples and the freely expressed wishes of the peoples concerned, and as may be provided by the terms of each trusteeship agreement;

c. to encourage respect for human rights and for fundamental freedoms for all without distinction as to race, sex, language or religion, and to encourage recognition of the interdependence of the peoples of the world; and

[20] *Fabian Colonial Essays,* p. 54.

d. to ensure equal treatment in social, economic, and commercial matters for all members of the United Nations and their nationals, and also equal treatment for the latter in the administration of justice, without prejudice to the attainment of the foregoing objectives. . . .[21]

The scope of this trusteeship system is clearly defined. It shall apply to such territories in the following categories as may be placed thereunder by means of trusteeship agreements:

a. territories now held under mandate (dating back to the Treaty of Versailles of 1919);

b. territories which may be detached from enemy states as a result of the Second World War; and

c. territories voluntarily placed under the system by states responsible for their administration.[22]

To "assist the General Assembly [of the United Nations] in carrying out these functions, there is to be set up The Trusteeship Council."[23]

It will be seen that this trusteeship system will in no sense administer the existing colonies of the various powers. Each will proceed according to the decisions of its own governing authority. But it should also be equally evident that such a system once in operation will likely set the type for all colonial administration and thus bring in a new era for the native peoples in the possessions of the colonial empires. A very high standard has been set. It will require time and much patience to realize the objects proposed, yet this system does express what the people of good will really feel with reference to the rights of human beings. It is a great step in advance when high idealism, in addition to being expressed by interested onlookers, is voiced with official sanction as the solemn purpose of the nations in their relations with the retarded peoples of the world.

[21] *Charter of the United Nations,* Article 76.
[22] *Ibid.,* Article 77.
[23] *Ibid.,* chap. XIII.

Imperialism

Colonial policy is closely connected with imperialism. In the course of recorded history empires have existed almost from the beginning. The Egyptian, Babylonian, and Assyrian empires take us back milleniums before the time of Christ. They rose, had their day, and ceased to be. The greatest of all the empires of antiquity, the one whose influence on history lasts down to our own time, was the Roman Empire. It embraced almost all the then known world. With a genius for organization and with a deep understanding of the psychological principles on which diverse peoples could be held together, Rome exercised her sway with remarkable tolerance, giving to the national groups incorporated under her regime religious and cultural rights which kept them at least fairly satisfied with her domination. Of course the essential element of every empire was present, the absolute requirement of obedience and submission to the paramount power.

We have empires today—some small and insignificant, scarcely worthy to be called by the name; and others, powerful and wide-ranging, surpassing at least in the case of the British Empire even the fondest dreams of a Roman Caesar. But the French and Dutch also are colonial empires, exercising control over immense populations and vast areas of the world's surface. The empires of Belgium, Spain, and Portugal are greatly attenuated and cannot be ranked with the other three. In the case of the British Empire a clear distinction must be made between the free and independent dominions and the colonies. The Dominion of Canada, the Union of South Africa, Australia, and New Zealand, are equal partners in the British Commonwealth of Nations, each voluntarily entering into a union which binds all of its members in allegiance to the empire but leaves them free to control their own local affairs and to decide their own destiny. According to the Statute of Westminster, which was drawn up in London in 1931,

the British Parliament gave up all claim to make laws for the dominions or to declare void any law that they made. It was recognized that the dominions might choose their own governor-generals, who had hitherto been appointed by the British government to represent the monarch. The word "colony" was no longer to be applied to any of the dominions. "The Crown is the symbol of free association of the members of the British Commonwealth of Nations." The dominions are united by their allegiance to the British sovereign, but are otherwise to all intents and purposes independent nations.[24]

Very different problems are presented by the relations of Holland, France, and Great Britain to their colonies. The fundamental reasons for the differences are racial and cultural. The line between the people of the possessing nations and their colonials is fairly clean-cut. "The colonial areas are those inhabited almost completely by the two darker races, Mongoloid and Negroid; the zone of independence is populated for the most part by the Caucasoid or white race." [25]

We have good reasons for believing that the rights of the natives in the colonies will be given increasing recognition and that they will be accorded opportunities which they have only here and there known in the past. But that is not quite the point. Co-operation with native peoples may take the place of exploitation; unprecedented educational and economic opportunities may be opened up and yet the sorest point in the whole realm of colonial empire may remain untouched. What colonials are now beginning to envisage is self-government and in some cases more than self-government within the colonial system—complete independence. This rapidly growing and passionate desire strikes at the foundations of the very idea of empire. With all the splendid plans for bettering conditions in colonial areas no imperial power has, until the present day, shown willingness to consider a severance of relations between itself and a dependency.

But do what we may and think what we will, the spirit of nationalism with all its good and evil is abroad in the world. It

[24] J. H. Robinson, *Medieval and Modern Times* (2d rev. ed.), p. 813.
[25] Raymond Kennedy, *op. cit.*, p. 306.

is an authentic note of the new world order. We Americans ought to be the first to sympathize with any such movement in view of our own history, especially when the provocation is so much greater than that which led our forefathers to give voice to the Declaration of Independence and achieve their freedom.

The movement is now coming to maturity because of the processes set in motion by the Western nations themselves. Education is a hallmark of Western culture, and the white man has taken it with him in his colonial ventures. Sometimes the boon has been very sparingly given; often it has not been given by the rulers themselves as a part of their official task. But the schoolteachers, in most cases missionaries, soon began their work in every field; and, once the work was begun, the ultimate result was inevitable. Backward peoples began to realize that there was a world of opportunity and new life they had not dreamed of, and that it was for them. English literature, exhaling at times almost unconsciously the very life breath of freedom, the knowledge of democratic institutions, the rights of the common man, and above all the Bible with its conception of the infinite value of the individual, created a new outlook and a new spirit in the man of the East. Not only so, but a newly found regard for their own literature and the noble things in their tradition, frequently brought first to their attention by the European himself, has given the people of Asia a sense of their own worth and significance. Why should they be under the dominance of an alien power? Why should they not be free and independent like those who exercise rule over them and who, frequently unintentionally, have made them realize the possibilities of their own manhood as a member of the human family?

The tinderbox of slowly accumulated conviction and desire was touched into flame by the victory of Japan over Russia in 1904-5. This little Eastern nation greatly surprised the world, both East and West, by defeating Russia. Japan had learned one of the lessons the West had to teach and learned it all too well. Unfortunately she had laid her hand on the material rather than the spiritual aspects of Western civilization and had become strong as a military and naval power. Armed with Western implements of war, Japan turned the tables and, following the example of the West in the East, became an imperialistic power. So the first objective of the peoples of Asia in World War II was to break the hold of their own neighbor; but, now that the Japanese have been driven back within the bounds of their own island home, the desire for emancipation is again turning against the original European aggressors whose example Japan so successfully followed. In India, where the people have not experienced the immediate presence of the Japanese conqueror, the tension has produced a continuous current of increasing opposition during the years of the war. What form the end will take and when it will occur no one can say. What we do know is that the movement is like the steady advance of a glacier which cannot be resisted.

The uprising in French Indo-China, the open revolt in the Netherlands Indies, especially in Java, the restlessness in Burma, as well as the demand of India for independence, are daily reminding us that the European empires in Asia are being challenged at the basic point of the right of one people to hold authority over another against its will. A century ago the suppression of revolting native peoples was taken almost as a matter of course. Chaos would have resulted if peace and order were not restored. But now the situation is very different. In each case just mentioned an educated leadership which cannot be pushed aside —more efficient in some places than in others—has arisen. The leaders are intelligent serious-minded men who know what they are doing and who base their attitude on the fundamental principle that no people should be held under the domination of any power against their own reasoned judgment.

We must not allow ourselves to forget that the imperial powers face real problems most difficult of solution. There may be justification of domination by a colonial power when native peoples are still in a primitive state and cannot stand alone commercially or politically in the world in which we live. Some kind of colonial administration or trusteeship by an international organization like the United Nations is necessary. The time is not ripe for independent nationality in many areas of the world. For years these people must be directed by those more advanced, that is, until they shall be ready for self-government and even independence. But just here, as we have already seen, is one of the causes of complaint.

Adequate plans for the coming of the day of true self-government—not to speak of independence—are not being made in most areas. Fortunately the Charter of the United Nations has placed at least the first of these ideals before the dependencies of the world. Instead of subsiding, the demand for more of the substance of government and freedom to direct their own destinies will become an ever more insistent note of colonial peoples. A crisis is certain to arrive now here and now there, whenever it becomes evident that the only way in which a colonial empire can maintain its position is by compulsion. Increasingly the moral sense of the world will revolt at the continuance of such a policy, and thus empires as we know them today must gradually disappear. A member of the British House of Commons frankly states that "European domination of other continents" and "European monopoly of industrial activity and development" are things which "belong to the past. . . . Any empire based on the idea of racial superiority—and despite all rhetorical declarations to the contrary the British Empire has been and still is so based—cannot survive unless it is prepared to maintain itself by the Hitler method of brute force." [26]

The problem of empire presses more sorely in India at the present day than in any other colonial dependency. India has been called the "Crown Jewel" of the British Empire. Mr. Churchill declared in 1930 that "the loss of India would be final and fatal to us. It would not fail to be a part of a process that

[26] J. F. Harrabin, "Geography and the British Empire," *Fabian Colonial Essays,* p. 47.

would reduce us to a minor power." [27] He made it clear while he was prime minister that he did not propose to be present at the dissolution of the British Empire. The only real justification for England's presence in India was that England had made a valuable contribution to India's life and that great disorder and possible catastrophe might be India's fate should the paramount power be withdrawn. Many Indian leaders denied this and claimed that the evils which their country suffered come solely because of exploitation and maladministration on the part of the British.

So the strife of words went on for year after year, becoming more bitter as the war came to a close. The British themselves began to change. A commission headed by Sir Stafford Cripps went to India in 1943 and made an offer which went beyond any previous proposal. Its rejection by the Indian Congress leaders was based almost entirely on its failure to include the right to complete independence should the Indians themselves so desire. This omission was a source of dissatisfaction to many, even in Great Britain. H. N. Brailsford declared: "There our duty is plainly to hasten the grant of unqualified self-government, which means, if Indians insist upon it, independence." [28]

One of the most remarkable events in the history of East and West took place in the spring and summer of 1946. Another commission was sent to India, and this time the offer included the right to complete self-determination, even to the extent of deciding whether India should remain a member of the British Commonwealth of Nations or be completely independent. Never in human history had such an offer been made by an imperialistic power to one of its dependencies. It was accepted by the Indian leaders, and the land is now being governed under the interim leadership of Jawaharlal Nehru. As soon as possible a constituent assembly will be convened to adopt a permanent constitution.

The significance of what is taking place should not be missed by having attention diverted to such a difficulty as the refusal of

[27] An address Dec. 12, 1930, as quoted in Louis Fischer, *Empire*, p. 66.
[28] *Op. cit.*, p. 24.

Mr. Jinnah, now apparently ended, to accept the offer of the British government and come in to form a united India. Ominous and uncertain as the immediate future of India may be, nothing that may happen can dim the luster of the enlightened action of the labor government in London in making good its promise to inaugurate a new era not only in internal policy but in relations with colonial dependencies. This is the significant thing for us in our discussion of racism—racism in its relation to imperialism.

That the labor government in Britain is determined to carry such principles into its relations with all British dependencies is clearly revealed in the following statement made in the House of Commons on July 9, 1946, by A. Creech-Jones, undersecretary for the colonies: "We are actively engaged in sacking the contents of the old imperialism, and we are as eager as any other country for the building up of the colonial peoples to freedom and social happiness." He went further and declared that the Colonial Office had established the following principles:

1. Britain will see that discrimination and racial superiority are made to disappear as soon as possible and that the relationship between Britain and her colonies will be one of partnership.

2. Political and economic privilege and domination must go, and the people of the Colonies should go forward to political freedom and responsible self-government.

3. The economic exploitation of natural resources and the peoples of other colonies for the ends of certain groups, whether internal in colonies or externally, must go; it is the responsibility of the government to attack the very essence of economic imperialism.

4. The test of the new British policy should not be British advantage but the happiness, prosperity and freedom of the colonial peoples themselves.[29]

One final consideration demands our attention. We must lift up our eyes and take a steady look into the future. The war through which we have just passed was not a conflict of races. Britain fought Germany, and both are Teutonic. China and Japan

[29] According to report of the *Chicago Sun* London Bureau, issued July 10, 1946.

were in mortal conflict for eight years, and they both belong to the Mongoloids. But will that alignment always obtain? We are bound to take heed of the possibility of a situation quite different. Should we of the West, the white man in Europe and America, persist in our attitude of superiority toward the people of color and treat them with disdain, as inferiors, we can only expect in due time to reap the whirlwind of retaliation and vengeance. God grant that that day may never come, but let us remember that we have good authority for holding that "whatsover a man soweth, that shall he also reap." No power in the world can prevent the colored races, the peoples of Asia and Africa, from uniting because of common grievances against centuries of domination by the white man and ending this domination by the use of means we have taught them so well to use.

Such a terrible outcome is not necessary, nor will it come if we eschew the rights we have exercised and treat the other races with consideration, justice and respect. It will mean that the policy of exclusion on account of race, unfair advantage taken of peoples who are just emerging from their backwardness, and above all exploitation in all its forms must be consigned to the limbo to which we have relegated the rack, the thumbscrew, and burning at the stake. They have no place in a world of free men, each of whom has the right to live his own life freely and without fear. The United States took the right step in giving independence to the Filipinos, but it still has a long way to go in giving justice to the Negroes within its own borders. Our country has also started in the right direction in placing the Chinese on the same quota basis with Europeans with respect to immigration; but, again, we must treat other peoples in Asia similarly. We are now learning to be better neighbors to the Latin American lands, but our dealings with the people in Puerto Rico leave much, very much still to be desired. Australia will be compelled by the good sense of its own people to realize that its White Australia Policy is heaping up enmity against itself which someday will come back on its head. Great Britain's presence in India and Africa, Holland's dominance over the Indies, and the French occupation of vast tracts in Africa and Indo-China are all cases in point. Only a change, and at many points a drastic change, in policy and practice will start the thinking of the colored peoples of the world in another direction, away from bitterness and resentment to reconciliation and good will, in answer to offers of co-operation and understanding on the part of the West.

There is improvement but it is very slow and fitful. The false ideology of the Nazi with his theory of the master race has received only the rebuff of military defeat. It was only a quarter of a century ago that the American Lothrop Stoddard was urging the Nordic to gird himself before it was too late and make himself the dominator of the "lesser breeds," no matter what the cost in life or wealth. It is rapidly becoming too late for that, but it is not too late to turn around and offer the man of color the hand of fellowship and co operation and thus save the world from the conflict which will come by following any other policy, whose end can be only the defeat of the white man by overwhelming numbers and unity of purpose on the part of those he has so long considered his inferiors. This is the ultimate issue of racism and world order. It is full of possibilities, either terrifying or promising hope, depending upon the attitude and practice of the white man in the decades of the immediate future.

Chapter XIV

The Christian Faces the Color Bar

Racism is a malady of the human mind and heart. It is virulent, complicated, and contagious. Sooner or later every man finds himself face to face with men of other races and must assume one attitude or another toward them. Our final task is to ask what Christian men and women and the Christian church should do as they come into contact with other races and groups which are retarded physically, economically, educationally, and socially.

Attention must be called again to the fact that racial tensions rarely if ever exist alone, that economic and religious differences are almost always involved. Those who live on an appreciably lower economic level are likely as a class to have poorer health, to be ignorant and usually illiterate, and therefore to occupy a very low and even despised social position. Religious differences often keep groups apart, so that they do not know and consequently cannot understand each other. The position taken in this book is that differences in race not only are a cause of friction in themselves but add to the difficulties just mentioned and accentuate them to such an extent that the problems involved become far more acute and difficult of solution.

Certain facts—that a pure race cannot be found and that groups, even very different groups, have mingled more or less freely through the centuries—seem to indicate that, had it not been for other factors, we would not have the phenomenon of racism in the world today. Be that as it may, racial tensions do exist, as we have had ample opportunity to see, in the countries which have been passed in review. So important have they become that perspective at times is well-nigh lost and race has been held responsible for a whole brood of ills which upon closer analysis might be assigned to other causes. We are compelled to accept the situation as it is and realize that racism is a fact of most serious import and stands out as an issue without whose solution the peoples of the world are likely to ruin their lives.

What is the Christian to do when he faces these facts? The first duty undoubtedly is to understand the problem and the issues at stake. One of the worst features in the present situation is the presence of "prejudice," which according to its etymology means a "judgment formed beforehand," that is, before the relevant facts are known. This has resulted in distorted views, of which one of the most regrettable forms is the stereotype. To most people a mental picture immediately arises in the mind whenever a Jew or a Negro or some other person is mentioned. Unfortunately it is usually a distortion, a "caricature," which, according to Webster, is a "grotesque or ludicrous exaggeration." Untold harm is being done in our dealings with fellow human beings through ignorance—an ignorance which often persists in the very presence of people who if known in their true light would really be quite different from the stereotype which has deflected our vision.

Is it possible for Christian men and women to come to know the realities of the problem and enter into the attitudes of peoples of other races and nations? Adequate knowledge becomes the indispensable foundation of all effective action. A somewhat startling statement is made by Gunnar Myrdal about the situation in our country: *"The simple fact is that an educational offensive against racial intolerances, going deeper than the reiteration of the 'glittering generalities' in the nation's political creed, has never been seriously attempted in America."* [1]

The situation is better than it was even a decade ago. Leaders in American life and many in the rank and file have been led to realize that we face an ominous issue and that something must be done about it. This is one of the most hopeful aspects of the situation in the United States. The great task of education lies

---

[1] *An American Dilemma*, I, 49. (Italics are Myrdal's.)

ahead, but increasing numbers are becoming informed and are considering the problem seriously and with intelligence. The startling fact is that there are so many white people in our country who live in close proximity to people of other races and groups, Mexicans, Japanese, Jews, and Negroes, and do not truly know what they are like. How often white people have been heard to say, "We know the Negro," when only a few minutes' conversation will bring out the facts that what they are familiar with is a stereotype and that the Negro as he really is today is as if he did not exist. The Negro in America is changing rapidly, and only those who are willing to take the time to become informed can justifiably claim to know him as he is.

Among the groups which are attempting to understand the meaning of the issues of race are those in the churches. This is as it should be, for the obligation resting on them is heavier than that on any others. The situation is exceedingly serious. It is no wonder that many Negroes, despite their tradition of deep religiousness, should be looking askance at the church and even turning away from religion itself. When the plainest implications of brotherhood are repudiated by the vast majority of church members in their racial contacts, what are the Negroes to make of it? In most cases this attitude is not one of ill will; it is racism, the assumption of inherent superiority of white over black. But it does its deadly work even when the attitude is not enmity but pity, even benevolent pity which is willing to reach down and offer help. So long as the help, however, is shot through with condescension it lacks one of the essential ingredients of Christian brotherhood, that of equality as children of a common Father.

Education on a wide scale and by all the methods now used to communicate ideas and inculcate attitudes must take the place of the indifference which so widely prevails. More practical programs such as that which has been so successfully carried out in Springfield, Massachusetts, must be attempted. In every such plan Christian men and women will have their part, but their obligation goes farther and deeper. We can truly understand other human beings only by having personal fellowship with them. The stereotype can be altered or entirely transformed only by closer contacts than most of us have had. We must be educated not only by reading about other people and listening to addresses but by friendship. Then a new world begins to be opened up. We had thought that Jews were—there is our stereotype again, but we discover that there are Jews and Jews, just as there are Gentiles and Gentiles, and that they should be judged, just as we Gentiles would desire to be judged, by the better people among them. The National Conference of Jews, Catholics, and Protestant is doing much through its round tables and other gatherings to dispel prejudice and misunderstanding. It makes a mighty difference when we meet strange people face to face. We recognize that we are kin in spite of the obstacles which have kept us apart.

The situation is different with respect to the Negro. For the most part he is a fellow Christian with ourselves and not a member of another religion as is the Jew. The color bar, however, becomes very real, about as insuperable as religious differences. The obligation to understand each other is imperative; and when the attempt is sincerely made to enter into the mind of the Negro and to allow him to enter into ours, some amazing things happen. We discover that he is fundamentally like ourselves, with feelings as sensitive and aspirations as noble as fill the breasts of white people. Yes, there is a bar which must be broken through. It is based on color, but it is far deeper; it is the bar of suspicion and fear and resentment, which have accumulated through the centuries of oppression and neglect and condescension on the part of the white man. We are probing pretty deep, but it is only at such depths that we strike the reality on which a new life of brotherhood can be founded. As hard as it is for many white people, with their traditional attitudes, to have fellowship with Negroes, it is a Christian duty. What motive is sufficient for effecting this change? May we not put it in the pointed words of a publicist who writes not ostensibly as a religious man but as a statesman? Speaking of turning over a new leaf and giving the African a chance this Britisher H. N. Brailsford says:

> Why should we do that? Because we believe that sound economics point this way? Because we think that in the long run our own interests will be served by these measures? Never. Men who have no hotter fire than that in their bellies will stammer and wilt and yield, as soon as the battle looks doubtful. We shall do all this for the simple peoples of the Empire and do it at some cost to ourselves, only if our motive is brotherly love. Whether we think of them as our fellow-workers, or as our fellowmen, it must be a warm impulse of fraternity that drives us to defend them and to aid them. If we have in us the faith and the love this great adventure demands, we shall succeed. If we lack this principle of action then our plans are a dreary intellectual exercise and nothing more.[2]

The need is not only to understand others but to become acquainted with ourselves. What is the meaning of this strange and perverse tendency in human nature to look down upon and despise another person? From what does it spring in our own inner being? To put it more concretely, What is it that prompts an ignorant white man to blurt out, "I'm better than any nigger," when by every standard which can be suggested—physical strength, intelligence, education, business acumen, social grace, nobility of character, spiritual sensitiveness, and other traits—many Negroes surpass this deplorable white man? Far down in human nature there is always a tendency to pride, ready to spring into activity at any slight provocation. When it becomes aroused, it can find satisfaction only in a feeling of superiority to someone else. The self-esteem of one filled with such pride suffers without that sense of superiority. He must find some other person with whom he can compare himself, favorably of course to his own ego. In the case of the type of white man we have cited it is easy to find one to whom he can feel superior. He makes his exaggerated estimate of himself in contrast with a member of a race tradition-

---

[2] "Socialists and the Empire," *Fabian Colonial Essays*, pp. 33 f.

ally assigned to innate inferiority. The pattern already exists; he fits into it readily.

Why this ruinous tendency should lie embedded in human nature is a part of the profound mystery of evil. Why should the possibility of any evil thought or deed exist in those who are potentially sons of God? The only answer which satisfies at all is that virtue would be an impossibility were not the possibility of evil also present. The Creator has made us for fellowship with himself, but such fellowship is possible only when it is compounded with ethical ideals and moral content. To be real at all, character depends upon freedom of choice and that in turn can be possible only when an open alterative exists. That is, a man must be able to go wrong as well as right, or there is no meaning in the moral struggle. As long as human nature runs true to form we shall doubtless find some who will respect and be brotherly with their fellow men, and there will be those who will act otherwise. The tendency to pride, one facet of which is racial pride, is always present. It is one of the things against which we are all called on to wage constant warfare.

The pride whose danger we have been exploring is removed by a wide gulf from wholesome self-respect. Nothing can be expected of the individual or nation which does not hold up its head and display the elemental self-respect on which everything in character is built. A man or a people must have significance in his own sight or never expect to have the favorable regard of others. One of the saddest, if not the saddest aspect of the life of the depressed classes in India is their cringing servile attitude, their inability to look men of other castes straight in the face as free men confronting free men. Until there is born in their own hearts a sense of having intrinsic worth, these creatures cannot hope to be respected by others. Richard Wright, in his frank and fearless revelation of the experiences of his boyhood as a Negro in the deep South, shows how he maintained almost unconsciously his sense of personal worth. He declares, "It had not occurred to me that I was in any way an inferior being. And no words that I have ever heard fall from the lips of southern white men had ever made me doubt the worth of my own humanity." [3] This attitude is often spoken of as pride, a worthy sense of one's own proper dignity and importance. But there is a wide chasm between what is more properly called self-respect and the pride which injures and demoralizes. Such pride is not only a feeling of one's own importance but the assumption of superiority over others. Self-respect is compatible with humility; pride is not. Herein lies the essential distinction.

Coming into close quarters with his own lurking pride and racial self-esteem, a Christian will begin to realize how subtle and insidious the tendency to racism is. Sometimes it is found in the form of benevolent, condescending pity and may find expression in lofty religious verse. We are familiar with Rudyard Kipling's "Recessional," in which the "God of our fathers" is invoked to curb the pride and pomp which come "with sight of power." The prayer is repeated with deep sincerity:

> Lord God of Hosts, be with us yet,
> Lest we forget, lest we forget.

Kipling does not hesitate to rebuke the white man for having a "heathen heart" when he puts his trust "in reeking tube and iron shard" and gives himself to "frantic boast and foolish word." It is for that repentant spirit which the hymn breathes that it lives and is included in our Christian hymnals. It does so despite the Kiplingese assumption of superiority of the Anglo-Saxon over "lesser breeds without the law." He ardently advocates our taking up the "white man's burden" and fervently believes that it is none other than God himself

> Beneath whose awful hand we hold
> Dominion over palm and pine.

---

[3] Richard Wright, *Black Boy*, p. 227.

Kipling was only one of many in the Western world who are exponents of the policy of benevolent paternalism over the peoples of Africa and the East who are thus consigned to remain in a subject state.

At other times racism justifies itself under the plea of self-defense and self-preservation and thus answers to a fundamental right recognized by society everywhere. It becomes a virtue in the minds of those who are on the defensive. One of the most striking expressions of this attitude was that of Sir Thomas Watt who years ago in speaking of racial tension between white and black in South Africa, declared:

> This matter is to us in South Africa such a vital and fundamental matter that no ethical consideration, such as the rights of man and equal opportunities for all non-Europeans, will be allowed to stand in the way. It is a question of self-preservation with us.[4]

A fatal hardness overtakes men when self-interest becomes the only or even the primary motives of their lives.

Racism of the most cruel kind can hide behind Bible precedent. The strict Bible-reading Puritans could bring themselves to believe that their antagonism toward the Indians of New England even to the point of extermination was in accord with the injunction which came to the ancient Israelites to wipe out the Canaanites who were living in Palestine when they made their conquest. A biblical writer long after the event declared that their bloody assaults were based on a divine command.[5] The more pious Puritans, whose consciences must at least have been troubled, were more than ready to find some way of rationalizing their conduct. Racism, the simon-pure article, seen by itself for just what it is, runs counter not only to ordinary humanity but to any religion which believes in the welfare of all men and is seeking to bring peace and harmony to the whole world. But

[4] As quoted in Edward Grubb, *Christianity as Life*, p. 270.
[5] Deut. 20:17.

when other demands arise and become imperious, racism can change its color and seem to be a worthy attitude. And yet it continues to do its deadly work both on the sufferers and on those who have turned against their fellows. The defense of slavery was thundered from a hundred southern pulpits before and during the Civil War—yes, and from northern pulpits as well. The texts were of course from the Old Testament but in the days before the idea of progressive revelation was dreamed of they could be used as authoritatively as texts from the New Testament.

An even more subtle form of justification of racism comes out of the record of the covenant relation between Jehovah and the people of Israel. In this sacred relation an agreement was entered into between God and Israel to the effect that God would be in a special way their protector if they would obey his commandments and worship him alone. Thereby they became the chosen people, separate and distinct from the neighboring nations. What we today believe to have been the purpose of God in thus singling out one people and making them his own in a peculiar sense was that they might "be a blessing" to all the world and thus justify God in his method and acquit him of the charge of playing favorites. But the actual outcome was a form of racism which has carried through to our own time in the intense nationalism and exclusiveness of Orthodox Judaism. Did God have this in his purpose when he established the covenant with this one people? If so, racism has high justification. The only way in which we can find peace of mind with reference to God's dealings with the world is to believe that his ultimate plan was for the whole race, and the choice of Israel was to fit a people for the high task of conveying the message of his purpose to all nations everywhere. This we believe as Christians was the inner meaning of Messiahship, as discerned by the evangelist of the Exile [6] and fulfilled by Jesus Christ, who came as the Saviour of the world.

But unfortunately the Jewish people as a people did not thus

[6] Isa. 40–45.

read God's dealings with them. They wrapped the cloak of smug satisfaction ever the more closely about themselves and took on the typical attitude of racism, looking upon themselves as superior to other nations in view of God's choice. After the return from the Babylonian exile this conviction led to a drastic act of the utmost severity. Under the leadership of Ezra all those who had taken wives from peoples other than Jews were commanded to give them up.[7] It may have been necessary, as many biblical scholars hold, for the leaders to take such a stand. They were convinced that it was the only way to preserve their people from the contamination that would have made impossible the carrying out of God's ultimate purpose. But the fact is that it buried the Jewish people deeper in the morass of unsympathetic racism and engendered a pride which became insufferable. So far did this extend that we are told that in Jesus' day Jews had "no dealings with Samaritans." These poor Samaritans were halfbreeds, a mixture of Jews and Assyrian colonists brought into the country after the fall of Samaria in 722 B.C. They were utterly despised by the Jews as mongrels. No race antagonism today is more bitter. When a Jew of Galilee made his journey to Jerusalem for one of the religious festivals, the natural thing for him to do would be to travel directly south through Samaria; but no, that would result in defilement. So he would cross the Jordan just south of the Sea of Galilee, journey south on the eastern side, then cross the Jordan again near the ancient site of Jericho, and climb the long, steep ascent to the city of his desire—all because of his racial antipathy toward the people who had mixed blood and who, therefore, would defile him.

Even today it is at times a little difficult to discover which is the more powerful motive in the life of the Jew, the desire to preserve the purity of his blood or the passion for his religious heritage. The two are very close together and seem to depend one on the other. Especially among the orthodox the old racism still retains its hold. In fact it is an essential part of their outlook

[7] Ezra 10.

RACISM: A WORLD ISSUE

into the future, when all people will accept the God of Israel and be united in the coming Messianic Kingdom. In the Kingdom-to-be the choice of Israel is still to hold good. All the world shall worship the one true God, but the Jew shall be in the place of pre-eminence. The priesthood is his and his forever and cannot be transferred to anyone not of his people. The Gentile must always remain subordinate to the Jew—such is the meaning to an orthodox Jew of the ancient covenant relation between God and Israel. Be it said that these views and this attitude are disavowed by leaders in Reform Judaism.[8]

It has been necessary to tell the story of this particular form of racism because there is no better illustration of its strength and subtlety. Racism is exceedingly paradoxical. It may emanate from the basest and most self-centered of human motives; on the other hand it may rise out of the deepest conviction of profoundly sincere religious men and women. And yet it always runs true to form; it is always the assumption of inherent superiority over others who are inferior only because they belong to another race or group. Are we to conclude that racism is wrong in some cases and right in others? Can self-preservation or religious conviction condone what, if it springs from other motives, is an unmitigated evil? The answer must of course be no. The determining factor in answering such a question is to determine what racism is and does in the mind and heart of the one who cherishes it. It always raises one above his fellows and necessarily involves an attitude of pity, disdain, or contempt, as one goes down the scale from more elevated to baser feelings on the part of the "superior" person. It is even possible to assume the mock-heroic and travesty both Alfred Tennyson and Sir Galahad by the raucous shout, "My strength is as the strength of ten because my race is pure." [9]

In other words this attitude destroys, or tends to destroy, the fundamental basis of democracy, that "all men are created free

[8] Ferdinand M. Isserman, *This Is Judaism*, pp. 134-39.
[9] A. J. Toynbee, *A Study of History*, I, 219.

and equal," and arbitrarily places one section of humanity in a position apart and separate from all the rest. It is the most char. acteristic expression of pride in ourselves, our own worth and achievements, which could be exhibited. However it may be justified, and whatever relations it may have to movements which are far more noble than itself, racism springs ultimately from exaggerated self-esteem, and against this attitude all wholesome religions rise in protest.

Rationalization has had a large part to play in soothing the consciences of those who are at least uneasy because of the treatment of backward peoples. Raymond Kennedy makes the statement that "every institution of human society is supported by a code of rationalism." [10] He then recounts the characteristics of the colonial system and shows that each unfortunate attitude is rationalized and made to appear justifiable. The color bar is justified by the doctrine of the inherent superiority and inferiority of races. It is not true, but it is believed and it thus serves as an excuse for what might otherwise be rather a strong dose to swallow. So of the political subjugation of native peoples: they cannot rule themselves; so they must be ruled by a stronger people. The chief flaw in that rationalization is that no adequate measures have been taken to prepare the people for self-government. And so from one point to another the merry game of self-justification goes on.[11] The warning of the ancient prophet Jeremiah, "The heart is deceitful above all things, and it is exceedingly corrupt; who can know it?" [12] finds exact fulfillment in the wily way in which racism seeks to escape self-accusation.

No single group in modern times has exemplified the ideals of brotherhood more than Christian missionaries who have gone to the most abject and degraded tribes in Africa and the South Seas and in spite of misery and dirt and brutality have believed

---

[10] "The Colonial Crisis and the Future," *Science of Man in the World Crisis,* ed. Ralph Linton, p. 311.

[11] *Ibid.,* pp. 311-18.

[12] Jer. 17:9 (A.S.V.).

that these creatures, spurned by most Eurpoeans as worthless, were also men and women for whom Christ died. Their faith has been rewarded in countless cases, and whole villages and communities have been reborn into a condition worthy of Christian fellowship and capable of entering into a common life on high levels of brotherhood. While this is true—and the brief words used to describe it have been all too inadequate—complete freedom from racism has not always been achieved even in this group. There have been missionaries who have devoted their lives to the uplift of the people whom they love and yet have carried abroad some vestiges of class distinction and of race prejudice. This is mentioned to illustrate the thesis that no attitude harbored in the heart of man is so difficult to dislodge as the feeling of being innately superior to those who evidently are in a backward condition. This is more easily understood in the case of debased savages who in their native state are often repulsive, but it is inexplicable when Europeans or Americans carry the class feeling which exists in their own countries to the mission field and make the Chinese, Indians, and others feel that even in the Christian church there is failure at the point of full democracy and fellowship.

In India caste distinctions which have bound the lives of Hindus for three milleniums have to be resisted with the utmost strenuousness. Very rarely in Protestantism but usually in Roman Catholicism, certain of the caste regulations have been carried over and have been tolerated even in partaking of the Holy Communion. The Roman Catholics have taken the position that this inconsistency would be sloughed off in time as the Christian community matured and entered more fully into the meaning of fellowship in the church. An onlooker can only conclude that this expectation has not been fulfilled and that more drastic measures are needed. The Protestants during the past hundred years have acted on the conviction that so dreadful a plague should be met at the outset by a firm refusal to sanction it in any particular, and they have their reward in a united community.

When the late Bishop Chitambar, whose "father was an orthodox Maharattha Brahman," [13] proved that Christian grace could drive out his age-old prejudice, it was just one more, though withal a notable, illustration of the triumph of the love of Jesus Christ.

The most difficult problem, however, is with the thousands and tens of thousands of members of the Christan church in the United States and South Africa and in other countries who fail to live up to their profession of belief in Christan fellowship and give themselves to the most vigorous defense of racial discrimination. Many in this number really have a spirit of benevolent pity toward their more unfortunate brethren but have not allowed that kindly attitude to control their relations with them. In their case the adage that actions speak louder than words finds perfect illustration. They may sympathize with, pity, and even have a sentimental love for all God's children, but it does not control their conduct. It is well to look this fact straight in the face when we are dealing with the solution of racial antagonisms, for somehow Christian profession which should have resulted in a cure has not been effective. Undoubtedly there has been in varying degrees a mitigation of the severity of their attitude, but in many cases church members are as rigorous in applying the customary regulations demanded by the white people as those who make no pretensions to adhere to Christian principle.

A remarkable illustration of this form of myopia is the case of the well-known hymn writer John Newton. In *The Methodist Hymnal* seven numbers come from his pen. Among them are the well-known hymns beginning, "How sweet the name of Jesus sounds in a believer's ears" and "Glorious things of thee are spoken, Zion, city of our God." No one can doubt the presence of both lyrical power and genuine religious emotion in what he has contributed, but we are almost stunned to learn about his experience. Percy Dearmer says of John Newton that he was converted while he was "the servant of a slave-dealer in Africa," that "he began to change after an awful night steering a waterlogged ship in the face of death. He was converted; but went on for six years as the now pious skipper of a slave-ship." [14] A man converted to God and destined to become the author of hymns breathing the highest sentiments of Christian devotion continuing to engage in the hideous slave traffic—what can we make of that? Are we to doubt the genuineness of his conversion or the sincerity of his trust in Jesus Christ as his Saviour? Hardly, but something was wrong, very wrong. There was a blind spot in John Newton's moral and religious vision, so that at least in those early years he could not see the incongruity of being at the same time a slaver and a faithful Christian. His conscience was sadly in need of Christian enlightenment. His blindness at that point prevented him from realizing that what he was doing was completely out of harmony with his Christian profession.

This of course is not an isolated case. Is there any one of us but is guilty of attitudes and practices which do not fit into the pattern of living which we as Christians have taken upon ourselves? It is a universal experience; we are all tarred with the same stick. It may not be our relation with other races; but whatever direction our wrong practice may take, it is an inconsistency which ought to be eradicated. The danger point is reached when it finally dawns upon us that such an utterly incongrous practice or attitude of mind is ours, and we are tempted to temporize with it. If we yield to that temptation, we immediately set in motion the process of disintegration which ultimately can result only in mere formal adhesion to the Christian way or complete atrophy of moral and religious life.

A clear realization of the meaning of racism must precede all else, placing before us the facts of the relations of races and the biological and environmental factors which lie back of present conditions. But when the situation is seen in its full meaning, we find ourselves at a point of crisis. Refusal to face facts is not only an acknowledgement of the weakness of our position but an indication of moral and religious fear—fear that we shall have to

[14] *Songs of Praise Discussed*, p. 3.

take a step which will not be looked upon with favor by our community and may result in at least a certain amount of ostracism, which of course is a terrible prospect for most of us. And yet, when the light has dawned and we discover evil in what we had formerly accepted as a matter of course, our whole Christian life is at stake. We either move forward or turn in the opposite direction. It is a life-and-death matter for our Christian experience. How great the need of a growing company of the faithful, many of whom have been followers of Jesus Christ for years, but who now see and see with terrible clarity that something is dreadfully out of joint in human society, and who realize that they must give themselves to Christ in a new way. They may be compelled to pass through struggles as convulsive as that when a great sinner turns away from his evil life and starts on the Christian path. Edwin R. Embree issues the solemn warning: "Unless the Christian Church conquers the segregation which it has allowed itself to fall into, it must lose its leadership in the spiritual and social life of America.[15]

The danger of sentimentalism is very real. We may be engulfed in a sea of gushing emotion as we think of suffering humanity and "man's inhumanity to man" and all that; but unless the new experience is grounded in something more stable than fleeting superficial feeling, it will not stand the test of the years. For what lies ahead is a long, long road. The victory for racial understanding and tolerance is not to be won in a day. The malady is too deeply rooted in the texture of men's thinking and in the organization of society to be dislodged and cured by quick-acting nostrums. Bitter disappointment in failure, disappointment both because of the obduracy of the satisfied man at the top and also of the ignorant mistakes and narrow outlook of the man who has not received his due, will test the mettle in the most convinced of men. A deep abiding conviction based on adequate knowledge which always keeps the main issues in sight so that they do not become distorted, together with the unfaltering res-

---

[15] "Color and Christianity," *Religion and Our Racial Tensions*, p. 41.

olution which must accompany it, is the only equipment which will not wear out during the years with their successes and failures.

The Christian church has failed as much at the point of race relations as at any other, if not more; yet it is the only hope of the world today. It is the only organization or movement which has not surrendered to Caesar but lives with renewed vigor in country after country when it has been oppressed by one dictator after another. It may not have been cured of racism in many of its members, but it is the only organization which has taken the gospel to the very people who are suffering the ravages of racism and has made it possible for them to rise and show that they are worthy to take their place as equals of those who consider them inferior. That is, the church is the agency which has lifted the backward races to a new position so that for the first time a question has been raised in the minds of their self-styled superiors whether they have not been mistaken in their estimate of the worth and possibilities of these peoples. This is a great gain and augurs well for the future. In addition, the church is the only body which claims to be universal and to include all men within the scope of its membership. Today it is holding up the torch of light to all peoples and proclaims, in spite of the practice of many in its circle, that they may count on the church of Jesus Christ to stand by and never relinquish its purpose to achieve the equality of all races in every phase of their life. The personality of each man in every race is held sacred and inviolable and must be given the fullest opportunity to develop every capacity it possesses. The church stands for the rule of God on earth, the coming kingdom of love, which is the ultimate reality of an order to which all human beings potentially belong and in which alone they may find their true life and its complete fulfillment.

Because of this attitude of the church there is light ahead. Never again can governments or groups of white men or individual exploiters give themselves to oppression without rebuke from a body which is becoming increasingly unified and which has determined to wage unceasing warfare against every form of racial discrimination. There is also a rising tide of sentiment widely felt in every area of tension against the practices and attitudes which have so long prevailed. The influence of the Christian church is making itself felt. Prominent editors and influential newspapers are sounding a new note, men in public life are becoming convinced that the old attitudes have brought only bitterness and hatred, and the community in general is slowly awaking to the need of doing something to relieve the increasing strain. By education the submerged peoples themselves are coming to a new realization of their possibilities. There is hope and expectancy in the air. No doubt there will be disappointments. These are to be expected in so fundamental and difficult a movement as has now been begun, but there is steady movement in the right direction, and that is the important thing.

In the meantime the Christian ideal must ever be kept before us. It is radical, but only a conviction which reaches to the root of things can keep the zeal of every man and woman of good will at the white heat of earnestness. We are driven to God when we face a condition as serious and as deeply rooted as racism. Only the grace of God can work in the hearts of men the necessary miracle which shall eradicate so deeply lodged a malady. The natural man is proud; he gets satisfaction in feeling that he is better than others and can look for privileges which they cannot enjoy. There are many in our Western world who fortunately may be led to do their part, an important part, in ameliorating the tensions; they may do so on the basis of self-interest or of a desire for a harmonious society; and some may rise to the plane of interest in humanity for its own sake. But more is needed, a growing body of men and women who approach their fellow men through their experience of God as they see him in Jesus Christ. Then something new comes into life, and a widening outlook is opened up before their eyes.

The church is the household of God, a family in which every member has worth and possesses the rights which belong to all the others. Paul in his Ephesian letter tells the Gentiles that, "Ye are no more strangers and sojourners, but ye are fellow-citizens with the saints, and of the household of God." [16] Consider what this means. In a family there are not only the mature and responsible members but the immature, and often the maimed and defective. With all these differences—and they are often serious— no one raises the question of inferiority or superiority. They are all equally members of the same family and belong to each other. A very wonderful thing happens in such a family. With the immature it is only a question of time and nurture, and they too will be able to assume adult responsibilities. For the unfortunate, some of whom may never develop into normal personalities or be able to take their place without assistance because of their handicap, deep solicitude is felt and every effort made to make life as easy as possible and to ease the disability. Their misfortune makes a difference in the lives of all. A wonderful tenderness takes possession of each. He belongs to a family, bound together in indissoluble unity, each feeling the suffering of all the others.

The Christian attitude toward race is rooted in its doctrine of God. There is no clearer statement found in the Bible or in Christian theology than the oneness of the human race as created by God. Paul summarized the undeviating biblical tradition in his declaration in Athens that God "made of one every nation of men to dwell on all the face of the earth." [17] Even more important is the character of God himself. In the Old Testament one of the conceptions of God was that of Father. But it was Jesus' consciousness of God as Father which conditioned his entire gospel. He made it central, so that Father became the distinguishing name of God in the religion which he founded. As Moffatt puts it, "A religion may call God by several names, but there are titles for God without which it would not be itself, and for Christianity the supreme title is that of Father." [18] We need scarcely to be

---

[16] Eph. 2:19 (A.S.V.).

[17] Acts 17:26 (A.S.V.).

[18] As quoted in T. W. Manson, *The Teaching of Jesus*, p. 92.

reminded that the prayer Jesus taught his disciples begins with the words "Our Father," but we do frequently need to realize afresh the breadth of its meaning. The plural "Our Father" is an impressive acknowledgment of the nature of our relationship to God. He is the Father of all. The idea of Christians as members of the family of God, belonging together and thus forming a fellowship, is the deepest meaning of our Christian experience.

There is and can be no Christianity in solitude. Ours is a social religion; we are sons of a common Father and if so then brothers one of another. This thought came as a new revelation to the Apostle Paul. He had been educated at the feet of Gamaliel, a liberal of the School of Hillel, but with all that he had not shed his Jewish narrowness with its belief in special privileges for his people. It took a mighty convulsion for Saul the Jew to become Paul the Christian. Not only did that change involve the new conviction that Jesus Christ was the divine Son of God but, what was equally difficult for the Jew, the acknowledgment that he did not have the slightest advantage over the Gentile before God. "Paul the Jew had to suffer the shattering of his deepest beliefs before he came through to a new conception of a missionary's work. He had to learn that there was no distinction of Jew and Gentile." [19] Not only in the future life in heaven would they gather together about the throne of God, but here and now Jews and Gentiles, as children of one Father and belonging to one family, were to belong to the same fellowship and be one at the sacred meal which came to becalled the Holy Communion.

So we are one by the fact of our common origin and our membership in the family of God, but we are bound together by even stronger bonds. We are one also by redemption. Men are not only sons but sinners before God. In this respect also there is no distinction between men for "all have sinned, and come short of the glory of God." [20] "There is none righteous, no, not one." [21]

[19] C. H. Dodd, *The Meaning of Paul for Today,* p. 45.
[20] Rom. 3:23.
[21] Rom. 3:10; see vss. 9-18.

We all together stand in need of the divine forgiveness, and there can be no forgiveness without repentance. Repentance is an exceedingly leveling process and one which must be repeated over and over again in the experience of every Christian. He cannot but realize through the years that new areas of life are in need of renovation to which he has hitherto been blind. Our salvation is a continuing process beginning with our initial surrender to God's will and the acceptance of his forgiveness and never ending so long as the struggle between the two men within still continues.

Not one of us can afford to miss the import of Jesus' words, "If therefore thou art offering thy gift at the altar, and there rememberest that thy brother hath aught against thee, leave there thy gift before the altar, and go thy way, first to be reconciled to thy brother, and then come and offer thy gift." [22] It would seem that many of us must leave our gift before the altar and first be reconciled to our brothers of other races before we can claim the forgiveness of God. Nothing except confession of sin and an earnest resolve to make restitution will avail if we are to come to God with the humility which is the mark of every effective approach to the throne of Grace.

All races meet as equals about the Cross on Calvary. We look up at our Saviour and come to appreciate the awful havoc sin has wrought, sin against God and sin against our fellow men. We fall on our knees in sorrow and contrition. Our pride is broken, our spirit chastened, our self-confidence dissipated. But that, thank God, is not all. We are also raised up in hope and expectancy. The Cross is also a revelation of the worth of man in God's sight. He must have known that there were undeveloped, even marvellous, possibilities wrapped up in human nature to have formed the purpose of saving us at so high a cost. He must have known that we might become men and women forming a new community of the redeemed of all nations and peoples which should become "a glorious church, not having spot, or wrinkle, or any such thing;

[22] Matt. 5:23-24 (A.S.V.).

but that it should be holy and without blemish."[23] So all of us human beings kneel in gratitude and adoration before him; and, looking far into the future, we may see with John on Patmos a vision of the nations on the stage in the great drama of the final consummation of human history.

After these things I saw, and behold, a great multitude, which no man could number, out of every nation and of all tribes and peoples and tongues, standing before the throne and before the Lamb, arrayed in white robes, and palms in their hands; and they cry with a great voice, saying, Salvation unto our God who sitteth on the throne, and unto the Lamb. . . . Blessing, and glory, and wisdom, and thanksgiving, and honor, and power, and might, be unto our God for ever and ever. Amen.[24]

[23] Eph. 5:27.
[24] Rev. 7:9 10, 12 (A.S.V.).

INDEX

Abraham, 57
Adaptation to environment, 41
Africa
European settlers in, 251
long unknown, 145
Age of discovery and race, 32 f.
Ainu people in Japan, 23, 113 f.
Akbar the Great, 89
Alopen, 108
Amaterasu-Omikami, 115
Ambedkar, 95
American Anthropological Association, 39
American dilemma, 246
American Psychological Association, 39 f.
Anglo-Indians, 102 f.
Angola, 149
Anthropological Association, American, 39
Anti-Semitism
and anti-Judaism, 62
in Argentina, 198 f.
in Germany, 57 ff.
in Russia, 76 ff.
in United States, 218
Anti-Slavery and Aborigines Protection Society, 261
Arabs and Jews in Near East, 249 f.
Areas of characterization, 26
Aristotle on slavery, 32
Armenians, 72
Aryans, 52 f.
in India, 87 f.
Aryo-Dravidians, 90
Asiatic Land Tenure and Indian Representation Act of 1946, 166
Atahualpa, 186 f.
Australians (Australo-Tasmanians), 21
Azerbaijanians, 72
Aztecs, 33, 186

Balfour Agreement, 249
Bandeirantes (Paulistas or Cearenses), 168
Bantu Africa, 146 f.
Barnett, A. E., quoted, 179
Bastards in South Africa, 148

Bathurst, Bishop of, quoted, 142
Belgian Congo, 150
Benedict, Ruth, quoted, 32
Biology and race, 38
Bishop, C. W., quoted, 106
Black Death, 63
Blackfellows in Australia, 129 f., 140
Blood
same in all races, 16
types, 41 f.
Boas, Franz, quoted, 18, 39
Boers (Dutch) in South Africa, 155 ff.
Bolivia, Indians in, 195 ff.
Bolshevik revolution, 75
Brahman priesthood, 92
Brailsford, H. N., quoted, 270, 278
Brain, size of, 45
Brazil
contribution of Indians in, 172
education and race in, 177 f.
freed slaves in, 170
Indians of, 170 ff.
Japanese in, 182 f.
miscegenation in, 171
Protestants and race, 181 f.
racial mixture in, 175
schools and race in, 179 f.
slaves imported into, 173
Brazzaville, conference at, 152, 259 f.
British colonies in Africa, 152 ff.
British Empire, dominions in, 265 f.
Broomfield, G. W., quoted, 161
Brown, I. C., quoted, 226
Bryce, James, quoted, 176
Buchenwald, 65
Buffon, 15
Bushmen in Africa, 148

Cabral, Pedro Alvares, 168
California legislature and Japanese, 120
Cape of Good Hope, 168
Cárdenas, Lázaro, quoted, 193 f.
Carpethaggers, 225

297

Tacitus on ancient Germans, 50
Tadzhiks, 73
Tamerlane, 72
Tatar occupation of Russia, 70
Tatars, 23
Tasmanians, 129
Tel Aviv, 249
Teutons, 56
Thompson, W., quoted, 188
Time element in racial development, 25
Timur (Tamerlane), 72
Tirala, L. G., quoted, 54
Toltecs, 186
Tordesillas, Treaty of, 167 f.
Toynbee, Arnold, quoted, 251
Transval, South Africa Republic, 157
Trustee Council, United Nations, 264
Turkish people, 23
Turkmen, 73

Union of South Africa, 155 ff.
  population of, 157 f.
United Nations
  charter of, 263 f.
  Trusteeship Council, 264
United States
  as melting pot, 200
  races in 24,
Untouchability
  and Christian missions, 95
  and Mahatma Gandhi, 94 f.
Untouchables, 92 ff.
Urals as boundary, 74
Ussher's chronology, 25
Uzbeks, 73

Variags (Varangians), 69
Vasco da Gama, 89, 168
Vernadsky, George, quoted, 70
Victoria, Queen, and India, 97 f.
Vleeschauwer, Albert de, quoted, 150

Wagner, Richard, 56 f.
Waley, Arthur, quoted, 107
Wallace, Graham, quoted, 257
Wanderlust, 26
Warren, Flora, quoted, 206
Washington, Booker, T., 243
Watt, Thomas, quoted, 281
Webb, Sidney and Beatrice, quoted, 79
Wesley, John
  on Indians 34 f.
  on slavery, 221
Westminster, Statute of, 265 f.
White Australia Policy, 141 ff.
White race, 21 f.
White supremacy in United States, 233
Whitney, Eli, and cotton gin, 221
Wilhelm II, Kaiser, 51
Willard, Myra, quoted, 141, 142
Willkie, Wendell, in One World, 112
Wilson, Woodrow, 253
World order, meaning of, 247
Wright, Richard, quoted, 279 f.

Yellow-brown race, 22 f.
Yevsektsia (Yevkom), 78
Yi-Pao Mei, quoted, 108

Zoroaster, 88